Healing through the Centuries

Healing through the Centuries

Models for Understanding

Ronald A. N. Kydd

© 1998 by Hendrickson Publishers, Inc.
P. O. Box 3473
Peabody, Massachusetts 01961–3473
All rights reserved
Printed in the United States of America

ISBN 0–913573–60–4

First Printing — January 1998

Library of Congress Cataloging-in-Publication Data

Kydd, Ronald.
   Healing through the centuries: models for understanding   /
Ronald A. N. Kydd.
   Includes bibliographical references and indexes.
   ISBN 0–913573–60–4 (paper)
   1. Spiritual healing.   2. Miracles.   I. Title
BT732.5.K93   1996
234'.131—dc21   96–44484
                                                              CIP

To
Ian, David, Emilie, Matthew
First Children
Now Friends

Table of Contents

Abbreviations   ix
Preface   xi
Introduction   xv

Chapter 1: Jesus: The Healer   1

Part 1: The Confrontational Model   19

Chapter 2: The Early Years: A Church Triumphant   20
Chapter 3: J. C. Blumhardt: "Jesus Is Victor!"   34
Chapter 4: John Wimber: The Keeper of the Vineyard   46

Part 2: The Intercessory Model   61

Chapter 5: Saints on High: Help from Beyond   63
Chapter 6: Brother André: Miracles on the Mountain   82
Chapter 7: Mary of Medjugorje: Apparitions and Healings   100

Part 3: The Reliquarial Model   115

Chapter 8: Relics and Healing: Bones of Blessing   117
Chapter 9: The Miracles at St. Médard: The Convulsionaries   130

Part 4: The Incubational Model   141

Chapter 10: Männedorf: Place of Mercy   142
Chapter 11: The Message of Morija: Persevering Prayer   154

Part 5: The Revelational Model   167

Chapter 12: William Branham: Prophet of This Age?   168
Chapter 13: Kathryn Kuhlman: A Handmaiden of the Lord   181

Part 6: The Soteriological Model   199

Chapter 14: Oral Roberts: Quintessential Pentecostal   202

Conclusion   213

Select Bibliography   217
Subject Index   233
Scripture Index   237

Abbreviations

AJn	*Acts of John*
ANF	*Ante-Nicene Fathers*
APl	*Acts of Paul*
APt	*Acts of Peter*
ATh	*Acts of Thomas*
CChr	Corpus Christianorum
ChT	*Christianity Today*
CSEL	Corpus scriptorum ecclesiasticorum latinorum
DPCM	*Dictionary of the Pentecostal and Charismatic Movements*, ed. S. M. Burgess and G. B. McGee
ET	English translation
FC	Fathers of the Church
NTAp	*New Testament Apocrypha*, ed. E. Hennecke and W. Schneemelcher, revised edition
IDB	*Interpreter's Dictionary of the Bible*, ed. G. A. Buttrick
LCL	Loeb Classical Library
Lettre	*Lettre hebdomadaire et convocation*
NCE	*New Catholic Encyclopedia*
NPNF	*Nicene and Post-Nicene Fathers*
SW	*Spoken Word*
TDNT	*Theological Dictionary of the New Testament*, ed. G. Kittel and G. Friedrich

Preface

Healing has been a part of my academic agenda since 1974, when I began teaching it as part of a course on Pentecostal distinctives. Nine years earlier it had taken on an intense personal urgency as a result of injuries and illnesses suffered by members of my immediate family. Some of those problems continue today. I have therefore never been able to approach healing from a simply "bookish" perspective. I was happy to undertake this study for two reasons: I had already wrestled with the subject for a long time, and it would give me an additional learning opportunity.

In addition to the extensive work done in Canada, research took me to Bosnia-Herzegovina, France, Germany, Switzerland, and the United States. I worked in libraries and archives, interviewed scholars and participants, and observed contemporary ministries in which healing is important.

There are a large number of people to whom I am deeply indebted. Travel to European locations was done in connection with my participation in the international bilateral dialogue between classical Pentecostals and the Roman Catholic Church. The first trip was underwritten by Calvary Pentecostal Church in Peterborough, Ontario, under the leadership of my friend and pastor, Frank Patrick. These friends also contributed to covering the costs of the second trip along with the Rev. Bert Liira, the Rev. Earl McNutt, the Rev. Bernice Gerard, and the Rev. Jeff Shiplett and his church, Calvary Temple in Brandon, Manitoba. Bernice provided the initiative for both my involvement in the dialogue and the efforts to raise funds. The college at which I currently teach, Eastern Pentecostal Bible College, also gave a study grant that was important in helping with the expenses of the second trip.

In addition to financial assistance, I benefited from the generosity of people in other ways. Jerry Hoorman translated almost illegible handwritten documents that I found in the Kantonal Archiv in Zurich. Terry Kennedy, librarian at Eastern Pentecostal Bible College, went out of her way to help. She gathered relevant doctoral dissertations, pursued articles I requested, and drew my attention to important publications.

Friend and former student Pascal Chapuis gave me a great deal of assistance while I was studying a healing ministry in Yverdon-les-Bains, Switzerland. He conducted preliminary research and then assisted me constantly during my visit to Morija in the summer of 1991. He located archival material, arranged interviews, interpreted for me during conversations in French, and even made it possible for me to stay at Morija, at his expense. He had also laid the groundwork for my visit to a ministry in Männedorf, Switzerland, in 1990. Finally, he critically read the chapter on Morija.

I am deeply indebted to Billy Fraser of Steinenbronn, Germany, for assisting me while I was in the vicinity of Stuttgart during the summer of 1990. Billy and his wife, Sylvie, extended the hospitality of their home to me for several days. Prior to my arriving in Stuttgart, Billy located very important material for me and arranged appointments with key individuals. While I was there, he adjusted his schedule to correspond to mine and served as my interpreter during an important interview. This thoughtfulness was invaluable.

Prof. Hervé Legrand of the Institut Catholique in Paris read parts of chapters 5 and 8 and made helpful comments. Dr. Mark Miravalle of the Franciscan University of Steubenville in Steubenville, Ohio, reviewed chapter 7. Robert Parry of Kanata, Ontario, read the entire manuscript and made invaluable suggestions about style.

Roseanne, my wife, took time away from her doctoral work to read the whole manuscript. Her theological, historical, and stylistic astuteness has improved the work immeasurably. I am very grateful.

Introduction

This study is about "divine healing." In an era of CAT scans and laser surgery, the phrase itself may be puzzling for some people, and their confusion may actually deepen when I clarify what I mean by it. I understand "divine healing" to mean restoration of health through the direct intervention of God. The products of such intervention are miracles. This kind of healing is divine because of God's direct involvement. It occurs because God acts.[1]

This introduction has two parts. First, I will provide an overview of the study. Second, I will deal with the question of how one verifies claims that divine healing has occurred. It is important to grapple with the issue of verification in more general terms before encountering it in relation to specific ministries.

---

[1] This immediately calls to mind a fundamental controversy. Many people, both within the church and especially outside it, think that medical science and prayer for healing are diametrically opposed to each other. On the one hand, some think divine healing as I have defined it is sheer quackery. On the other hand, those who pray for the sick have often scorned the "ordinary" healing that comes about as the natural recuperative powers of the body are assisted by the practice of medicine. This dichotomy is false. I am convinced that there are cases in which people have been truly healed by God's touch. With appropriate care, this study will point to what may be examples. At the same time, remarkable work is being done by medical science. I see both processes of healing, with qualifications in both cases, as manifestations of God's love. Nothing requires us to say that we must assume they are opposed to each other.

Overview

As I began the process of defining, I highlighted the idea
that divine healing is fundamentally the action of God. Insofar
as our thinking about God must be built around Jesus Christ, we
can add precision to the definition by turning attention to him.
The ministry of Jesus as healer must give the primary shape to
this study. His priorities, concerns, and approaches as revealed
in the Scriptures should provide the model to which the ministry of the church ought to be compared. But drawing a standard from Jesus' ministry is more complex than it first appears.

On the one hand, explicit in his ministry are physical,
emotional, and spiritual healings. The paralyzed, the blind,
the demon-possessed received much attention from him. This
could be called Jesus' "narrower" healing focus. Because this
appears to have been his first concern, it will be mine also.

On the other hand, there was also a "wider" healing focus
in Jesus' mind. Implicit in his ministry is the concern to restore
health not just to human bodies and minds but also to human
relationships and to social structures. He did not minister to
isolated individuals. He came to transform the whole of human
experience and human society, challenging everything that was
demeaning and oppressive.[2] Any full and systematic study of
Jesus' work as a healer would have to place significant weight
on these concerns as well as the others. Neither emphasis can
be glossed over.

The church's awareness of just how wide-ranging was the
nature of Jesus' healing ministry has been fleeting at best. The
"strain of the incarnation" has been too much for Christians
to bear. God came to humanity in Christ. Love, compassion,
fairness, and justice were expressed infinitely. Unfathomable
freedom and fulfillment were offered, but the offer pushed humanity outside its comfort zone, demanding Christlike obedi-
ence to God. This intimacy with the divine has proved to be

---

[2] See pp. 3–9 below.

intimidating. Humanity has frequently decided to refashion Christ in its image rather than run the risk of being changed into his. The process has been one of simplifying Jesus, "dedeifying" him, or domesticating him. He had to be brought under control, made safe, predictable.

The way in which this has expressed itself historically with regard to healing means that the church has been much more comfortable with the narrower focus in Jesus' ministry than with the wider. It has directed most of its energies toward the spiritual, emotional, and physical illnesses of individuals, whether through prayer or through the practice of medicine. Those are certainly the kinds of problems its famous "faith healers" have dealt with.

As a primarily historical study, this treatment will be guided by the priorities of the healing ministries it explores. As a result, I will be working with the narrower focus rather than the wider. I am examining what the church has done, not what it should have done or what it should be doing. Furthermore, I am confining myself to healing as it appears in the orthodox Christian church. I accept as "Christian" those individuals and groups that identify themselves by using this term. By "orthodox" I mean people or organizations that believe the main ideas of traditional Christianity as expressed in the historic creeds of the church.

In a work published in 1908 Adolf von Harnack, the famous historian of early Christianity, observes, "Deliberately and consciously it [Christianity] assumed the form of 'the religion of salvation or healing,' or 'the medicine of soul and body,' and at the same time it recognized that one of its chief duties was to care assiduously for the sick in body."[3]

Harnack thought this was one of the church's crucial decisions of strategy. He goes on to say, "Christianity never lost hold of its innate principle; it was, and it remained, a religion

---

[3] Adolf von Harnack, *The Mission and Expansion of Christianity in the First Three Centuries* (2d ed.; Theological Translation Library 19; trans. and ed. James Moffatt; London: Williams & Norgate, 1908) 108.

for the sick."[4] What the church was then, it continues to be now. At the end of the twentieth century divine healing seems to be remarkably widespread.

Raymond Fung, who recently retired as secretary of evangelism at the World Council of Churches after ten years in office, notes, "Quantitatively the number one means of evangelism today, of people coming to faith in Jesus Christ, is probably faith healing."[5] He clarifies this by saying that it does not typically happen through a person's being healed and then coming to faith. Rather, the preaching of healing and deliverance seems to create a climate that awakens faith.[6]

These comments are moderated by genuine concerns Fung has about what he saw. He was troubled by the possibility of the blending of Christian faith with traditional indigenous religions and by the danger of manipulation and corruption. But he underlines the impact of healing ministries in Africa, India, Indonesia, Latin America, China, and Europe. In all of these areas divine healing is ushering people to faith in Christ.

There are so many concrete examples of contemporary healing ministries that one cannot hope to list them all. Francis and Judith MacNutt minister out of Jacksonville, Florida, while Denis Gault focuses primarily on Northern Ireland. Fr. Ralph DeOrio conducts meetings based in Leicester, Massachusetts, and Benjamin Munthe sees miracles in his ministry in Meslan, Indonesia. Reinhard Bonnke preaches to crowds of up to a half million in Africa, with frequent reports of signs and wonders accompanying the ministry of the word. The International Order of St. Luke the Physician, founded in 1930 by John and Ethel Bank and initially within the Anglican communion, is now interdenominational as well as international. Even the National Defence Medical Centre in Ottawa, a branch of the

---

[4] Ibid., 109.

[5] Raymond Fung, "A Monthly Letter on Evangelism" (March/April 1989) 1.

[6] Raymond Fung, interview by author, World Council of Churches, Geneva, Switzerland, July 24, 1991.

Department of National Defence of the government of Canada, has held healing services in which military chaplains prayed for the sick.[7] In addition to these, countless pastors and priests on virtually all continents regularly pray for the sick and see people healed.

Popular interest in healing is running high, too. Not long ago *Time* carried an article by Lance Marrow in which he dealt with the miraculous in a stimulating manner.[8] In *Life* Tom Junod published an extensive piece on Medjugorje, the town in Bosnia-Herzegovina where the Virgin Mary is alleged to be appearing.[9] There is a market for stories of the miraculous.

One of the goals of this study has been comprehensiveness. I have attempted to look at healing throughout the life of the Christian church. The work has two distinct but disproportionate parts. The first, an examination of Jesus' healing ministry, lays the foundation for the rest of the study. The second part, consisting of the remaining chapters, explores how the healing impulse has been expressed during the lifetime of the church. The comprehensiveness I will present, however, is of a somewhat special nature.

As I worked with the material, it became apparent that people who were regarded as having healing ministries developed particular models of healing. They each forged a characteristic practice and a theology, whether explicit or implicit.[10] These models can often be traced to the ministry of Jesus or to New Testament material.

Here is the "strain of the incarnation" again. Jesus' ministry of healing was unbounded in the form it took. Many different ideas and impulses appear in his ministry. Following Jesus'

---

[7] "Faith Surgery," *Sentinel* (June 1990) 41.

[8] Lance Morrow, "How to Believe in Miracles," *Time*, December 30, 1991, 57f.

[9] Tom Junod, "A Miracle of Faith," *Life*, July 1991, 29–36.

[10] Of course, that is not how they would express it. They would all say that their individual methods were simply the ways in which God worked through them, and perhaps their perspective would be more accurate.

ascension, the Holy Spirit, acting through the lives and ministries of Christ's disciples, continues and expands further the healing power of the gospel.

It is as though his infinitude, accommodated as it was to humanity, has been too much for humanity to process. Without conscious effort people cannot avoid reducing and simplifying the Christ. Systems overload when one catches hints of his fullness. Theologians of the early church toiled for centuries to find an acceptable way to say what they believed about him. Those who have performed healings in his name have faced the same problem. Each sensed God at work within him or her in a particular way, and each tended to assume that that was the way in which God always worked. They did not set out to tone down the healing ministry of Christ. Rather, they were understandably preoccupied with their own experiences.

These models of healing appear to be limited in number. I have identified six, which I have called *confrontational, intercessory, reliquarial, incubational, revelational,* and *soteriological.*[11] I approach comprehensiveness in this study not by trying to comment on all instances of healing that have appeared in Christianity but by dealing with all healing models and discussing several illustrations of each. Many more Christian groups would have to be added under each model for the study to be truly exhaustive.

The models I have mentioned are constructs. By this I mean that I have studied the reports of healing among Christians, searching for a way to understand them. I derived the models by grouping accounts on the basis of their fundamental thinking and practice about healing. This is my attempt to impose some sort of order upon highly unstructured human experience. Of course, reality is not nearly as neat as my models might suggest.

Nor are the models completely exclusive of each other. The healing theologies that the various groups developed have

---

[11] Full definitions are provided at appropriate places in the text.

not been simple. In each case there is a dominant idea plus supporting ideas. Some of the supporting concepts turn out to be the dominant ideas of groups belonging to other models. Studying Christian healing by making reference to basic theological and practical considerations is useful, but caution must be exercised to avoid oversimplification.

Having worked through this material with some care, I wish to make a number of preliminary observations. First, it is clear to me that the restoration of health through the direct intervention of God has continued throughout the history of the church, and at no point has it been any more widely seen than it is now. Frequently, the human body handles its own problems, occasionally assisted by medical intervention. But there are times when God simply undertakes. Illness vanishes without explanation—without explanation, that is, until one remembers God. The historical value of the accounts of Jesus' healings and the verification of cures throughout the history of the church are major questions that continue to challenge the Christian community. I will address this issue momentarily. Jesus did heal when he physically walked on earth, and he has continued to do so through the church. Divine healing is an ongoing phenomenon.

Second, the claims of healers and their supporters—usually without any attempt to deceive—are often overstated. In the face of truly extraordinary experiences, people just have difficulty controlling enthusiasm. When healings happen every now and then, it is hard to keep a clear head. Excited claims are made or at least implied.

This seems to have been less of a problem for the Europeans in the study than for the North Americans. People we will meet here, such as Marguerite Chapuis, the de Siebenthals, Blumhardt, Trudel, and those at St. Médard and Medjugorje, have not kept statistics. With the possible exception of Medjugorje, they have not been promoted either. The fervor related to both Medjugorje and St. Médard could lead one to think more was happening than there really was, but I do not believe that the people involved deliberately tried to leave that impression.

On the other hand, North Americans have had to promote and produce. In line with our continental psyche, they have talked numbers. David Harrell cites someone who said that 2 or 3 percent of those for whom Oral Roberts prayed were healed instantly, and then he quotes Oral himself when he said he would be the happiest man on earth if he could bring healing to a quarter of the people who wanted it.[12] Peter Wagner, famous for his involvement in the Church Growth movement, worked out a system of self-reporting that showed that 29 percent of the people he prayed for claimed to have been healed completely.[13] He compared this to the figures compiled by the Small Ministry Teams of John Wimber's Vineyard Christian Fellowship. They registered 26 percent who claimed total healing.

Both numbers may indeed be true. My intuition, however, is that they are "soft." In most of the healing ministries examined here, there is significant uncertainty in diagnoses before prayer and in examination after. There certainly have been healings, but probably not as many as some might like to believe.

Third, the stereotypical healer does not exist. On the one hand, there is the show-time, high-energy Oral Roberts with his white sport coat and his wing-tipped shoes, and on the other, the self-effacing Dorothea Trudel of Männedorf, Switzerland, lying down to sleep beside a psychotic woman. There are the urbane, cultured, Latin-writing Lutheran pastor Johann Christoph Blumhardt of Germany; the former jazz musician and apparently laid-back Californian John Wimber, with his witty stage presence; the culturally deprived populist William Branham; and the would-be socialite Kathryn Kuhlman, with her love for the best in jewels, clothes, hotels, and music. On

---

[12] David E. Harrell, Jr., *Oral Roberts: An American Life* (San Francisco: Harper & Row, 1985) 456.

[13] C. Peter Wagner, *How to Have a Healing Ministry without Making Your Church Sick!* (Ventura, Calif.: Regal, 1988) 243.

the one hand, there is the almost marginally literate Brother André of Montreal, Quebec, and on the other, the well-read Charles de Siebenthal from Switzerland. There is no stereotypical healer.

Fourth, healing flows out of mystery. This should not be surprising. It is God who heals, and our understanding of God is at best partial. Reviewing the ministry of Jesus makes it obvious that he did not follow any patterns or use any formulas. The only feature that appears in all of his healings is Jesus himself. Healing has its source in the grace of God. People were healed, it seems, in the chaos of St. Médard in Paris and in the calmness of Morija's garden in Yverdon-les-Bains, Switzerland. They were healed when someone clamped a hand on their heads and shouted, "Be healed!" and when they knelt on a hill that they reverenced as holy because they thought the Virgin Mary had appeared there. They were healed as they clutched a medal of St. Joseph in Montreal and as they sat in the charged atmosphere of an auditorium in Pittsburgh. Healing flows out of mystery. The claim to have understood healing is evidence that one has not.

Last, healing can never be a proof of doctrinal correctness. Augustine understood this fifteen hundred years ago. In one place he says, "Not only do the good and bad perform [miracles], but sometimes the good perform them not,"[14] and in another,

> For as to the driving out of devils, and as to the working of miracles, seeing that very many do not do such things who yet belong to the Kingdom of God, and very many do them who do not belong to it, neither our party nor your party have any cause for boasting, if any of them chance to have this power, since the Lord did not think it right that even the apostles, who could truly do such things both to profit and salvation, should boast in things like this.[15]

As far as Augustine was concerned, orthodoxy was not proved by the miraculous. This study supports that idea. It is

---

[14] Augustine, *Sermons on New Testament Lessons* 40.5, NPNF[1] 6.394.
[15] Augustine, *The Letters of Petilian* 2.55, NPNF[1] 4.562.

likely that all of the healing ministries we will examine saw miraculous cures at one time or another. Yet there is obvious diversity, even contradiction, among their doctrinal positions on many points. In fact, it is likely that there would be mutual suspicion, not to mention condemnation, among a number of these agents of healing. Healing does not put a seal of approval on doctrine. Doctrinal correctness is one issue; healing is another. Divine healing has little to do with the rightness of all theological propositions any particular healer might believe and everything to do with the endless love of the Divine Person.

Verification

I stated without qualification that divine healings have occurred throughout the history of the church. I am fully aware of the difficulties related to verification that surround that statement. As a matter of principle, I am committed to examining carefully claims to divine healing. Consider the following case.

On Monday, December 9, 1991, Marylyn Peterman was struck with viral encephalitis, an untreatable inflammation of the brain. She was a young mother with three small children, who was supporting her family by operating a day care program out of her home. Her husband, David, was at Bible college preparing for ministry.

When David left early that afternoon to write an exam, Marylyn lay down on the living-room couch, fighting what she thought were flu symptoms. By 8 p.m. she was in the hospital fighting for her life. The attending neurologist told David that her condition could be terminal. Even if Marylyn were to survive, significant brain damage would likely result. During that night she slipped into a coma, and early in the morning she was transferred to the intensive-care unit after going twice into seizure.

By Wednesday morning it had become clear that Marylyn would at least live, but an assessment of any brain damage could only be made when she regained consciousness. That would have to wait. The neurologist expected her to remain in a coma for another five days. The situation was very uncertain.

Behind the Petermans were a great many family members and friends who were praying fervently. Pastors from the Petermans' church and the campus pastor of David's college called at the hospital to pray with them. Several of the medical staff who were attending Marylyn were also Christians, and they were praying, too. Gradually what the Petermans regard as their miracle began to unfold.

On Thursday, many days before expected, Marylyn awakened. Day-by-day improvement continued. She was released from the hospital the day before Christmas, and exactly one month after entering the hospital, her neurologist told her she had made a full recovery. She plunged back into life, caring for her family, operating her day care program, and teaching her Sunday school class. A condition that had threatened everything left no ill effects whatsoever. David's comment: "We praise God together for the miracle of Marylyn's healing."

Was this really a case of divine healing? Reaching a satisfactory answer is not a simple matter. That question is tied to a larger one: do miracles of healing ever occur?

Some say yes. David Lewis cites the case of a nine-year-old girl who was nerve deaf in both ears and whose case was thought to be incurable: "She had attended the audiologist on 8 March 1983, the following night experienced complete healing and on 10 March had further tests showing her audiograms and tympanograms to be normal. The girl's mother remarked that God's timing was remarkable, the fact that Rebecca's aid was damaged the day before her hearing returned emphasized that her healing was instantaneous. The audiologist knew she was deaf the day before."[16]

Physician William Nolen says no, at least as far as the ministry of healing evangelist Kathryn Kuhlman was concerned.

---

[16] David C. Lewis, *Healing: Fiction, Fantasy, or Fact?* (London: Hodder & Stoughton, 1989) 68.

He followed up a meeting she held in Minneapolis and concluded, "None of the patients had, in fact, been miraculously
cured of anything, by either Kathryn Kuhlman or the Holy
Spirit."[17] Later he made that claim even more sweeping, saying
Kuhlman would be wrong to think that anyone had ever been
cured of organic[18] problems in her meetings.[19]

But there is an even more basic question to be raised, and
to raise it is to step into a discussion of the theory of knowledge. This branch of philosophy is known as epistemology. The
question is, How much weight ought one to place on scientific
observation as a means of validating the miraculous?

Two hundred and fifty years ago a similar question was in
the mind of Prospero Cardinal Lambertini (later Pope Benedict
XIV). He listed seven criteria that an event had to meet in
order to be recognized as miraculous. He also drew attention to
essential features that had to be found in the circumstances in
which the event occurred. The context had to be decent, serious, and pious. The list of criteria included such ideas as the
following: the illness had to be extremely serious; the healing
must be instantaneous; the sickness must not return.[20]

Lambertini sounds very much like a man of his time. He
wrote in 1734, in the midst of the Enlightenment. His criteria
illustrate the confidence people felt in the new science that

---

[17] William A. Nolen, *Healing: A Doctor in Search of a Miracle* (Greenwich, Conn.: Fawcett, 1974) 84.

[18] Morton Kelsey (*Psychology, Medicine, and Christian Healing* [San Francisco: Harper & Row, 1988] 58) identifies three categories of human illness.
They are (1) organic—the structure or tissue of the body is damaged; (2) func-
tional—one organ or part of the body is not operating properly; (3) psychic or
mental—personality disorders. The point of Nolen's comment about Kuhlman
is that organic illness is the kind that can be most clearly diagnosed. It is also
the category of illness for which claims of healing can be most readily confirmed or denied.

[19] Nolen, *Healing*, 94.

[20] Prospero Cardinal Lambertini, "Critères canoniques d'une guérison
miraculeuse" [from *De servorum Dei beatificatione et beatorum canonizatione*,
liber 4, pars 1, cap. 8, n. 2], *L'Osservatore romano*, 34 (August 22, 1989) 5.

was being done and in the ability of observation to lead to reality. Assuming one were satisfied with the spiritual atmosphere in which a healing seemed to have occurred, scientific observation could provide all the information required in order to decide whether the event was miraculous. The same kind of assumption would be made now by people who still hold uncritically to the ideals of the Enlightenment. Recently, however, the hold that science has held on Western society has begun to weaken.

The growing sense of the complexity of reality appears in comments made by René Laurentin, an eminent Roman Catholic theologian and expert on the healing phenomena of Lourdes:

> Science has begun to grasp the mysterious complexity of the world. That kind of science is dead which used to think it could say, "Miracles are impossible," "The soul does not exist, I have never found it in any surgical operation," and other similarly naive statements. The very fidelity to experience, so essential to scientific method, has shown that we cannot easily determine a priori what is reasonable and what is not. Science in the 20th century has made progress because it has been open to apparently irrational conclusions: relativity, the relation of uncertainty of Eisenberg, etc. Science, which has become more and more open to experience and more and more aware of its own limits (and of the impossibility of imposing laws on reality in the name of simplistic rationalism), has become an example of humility in the face of reality.[21]

Laurentin is probably attributing more to science than it is prepared to accept, but he seems fairly close to the mark.

Lewis points in a different direction. He implies that we should not be surprised if scientists will not go so far as to endorse the miraculous: "It would be overstepping their professional boundaries if the doctors drew conclusions that certain

---

[21] René Laurentin and Ljudevit Rupcic, *Is the Virgin Mary Appearing at Medjugorje?* (trans. Francis Martin; Washington: The Word Among Us Press, 1984) 11. Gotthard Booth commented on the early stages of this new scientific humility forty years ago ("Science and Spiritual Healing," *Pastoral Psychology* 5 [1954] 21–25).

cures were actually 'miracles,' even if they are unable to explain the cures on medical grounds."[22]

Lewis's comment acknowledges that physicians work under certain limitations. They are competent to comment professionally on the physical but not the metaphysical. Biology falls within their purview; theology extends beyond it. If that is true, it would be unfair to ask a doctor, speaking as a scientist, to say definitively, "That is a miracle."

Theodore Mangiapan, president of the Medical Bureau of Lourdes, underlines the awkwardness physicians face when confronting observations that are difficult to explain. He points out that medical science has made such dramatic strides recently that doctors are very hesitant to say that a particular event was extraordinary. Tomorrow may bring the discovery that will show just how ordinary the event was.[23]

René Latourelle, one of the leading Roman Catholic theologians dealing with the miraculous, comments on how far a scientist might be prepared to go in recognizing the extraordinary. In his opinion, the scientist will admit to facing "something unparalleled, something unexplained and without likely future explanation,"[24] but one should not expect him or her to exclaim, "A miracle!"

The problem before us is how much weight can be legitimately placed on scientific observation as a means of identifying or denying the miraculous. The difficulty concerns what a divine healing is. It is an event that takes place in human experience but that is utterly dependent on a profoundly different being, that is, God. What happens to the human being can be examined effectively, but how does one scrutinize a person who is above all limitations, including those of space and time?

---

[22] Lewis, *Healing*, 45.

[23] Theodore Mangiapan, "Le contrôle médical et la reconnaissance des guérisons de Lourdes," *L'Osservatore romano*, 34 (August 22, 1989) 5. See also the online document at http://abbey.apana.org.au/bvm/Lourdes/allaprov.htm.

[24] René Latourelle, *Miracles of Jesus and the Theology of Miracles* (trans. M. J. O'Connell; New York: Paulist, 1988) 312.

The truth of the matter is that the importance given to observation will be determined by factors unrelated to science or observation. As Latourelle puts it, "The judgment [whether some event is miraculous] is passed at the level of interiority at which the human beings have already decided that they are self-sufficient or, on the contrary, have become aware of their wretchedness and have admitted they are poor, weak, helpless, and 'in need of salvation.' "[25] In other words, long before we have to make a decision on the "facts" of a particular case, we have become inclined to be open to a religious explanation of events, or we have not. Our presuppositions will guide our interpretation of what we observe. People will not be moved to or from the miraculous by "scientific facts."

Fr. Bernard Lafrenière is at St. Joseph's Oratory in Montreal. His opinion is that "miracles are not the proof of faith, but it is faith that makes them possible, and they can be seen only through the eyes of faith."[26] C. Peter Wagner says almost precisely the same thing: "The only ones convinced [to believe in the miraculous through observing miracles], whether doctors or theologians, were those who already believed or those who were disposed to believe."[27]

These comments should serve as a check for the wild enthusiasm that erupts when the inexplicable occurs. Believers may compile lists of miraculous healings; this study will offer some. But those who cannot bring themselves to believe in a God who does this sort of thing will probably not be convinced.

Nonetheless, even if it is futile to point to miracles as grounds for faith, conscience demands that we at least be honest. If no attempt is made to find out whether a claim to a miracle really rests on a miracle, then one has no right to press the claim. Alleged miracles must be exposed to scrutiny. If they are not, the whole concept of the miraculous is sensationalized and trivialized.

---

[25] Ibid., 299.

[26] Bernard Lafrenière, *Brother André: According to Witnesses* (Montreal: St. Joseph's Oratory, 1990) 21.

[27] Wagner, *Healing Ministry*, 240.

The point to which the discussion has come is not particularly comfortable. We have noted the difficulty science has in verifying the miraculous. We have observed that one's presuppositions have a lot to do with what one thinks "the facts" prove. And now I have argued that we cannot simply leave miracle claims alone. We must struggle with verification. How?

One proposal, building on Wagner's work, is that one has to start with the assumption that God performs miracles. Given that assumption, the question becomes "whether this account is backed by the type of evidence that indicates that accepting it as valid would be a reasonable response."[28] Wagner thinks that the kind of evidence he is talking about can be found by taking "the testimonies of sincere, lucid people at face value" unless there is some particular reason why one should not.[29] In other words, the people who are healed, or who witness healings, should customarily be accepted as competent witnesses.

This appears to be a much more casual approach to verification than Cardinal Lambertini would have been prepared to take. It is also too casual for me. It almost looks like a bypassing of the medical establishment.

Some comments by R. C. Finucane are directly relevant here. On the basis of a careful study of medieval material, he demonstrates that diagnostic conclusions reached in a nonscientific,

---

[28] Ibid., 241f.

[29] Ibid., 242. David Lewis recognizes the importance of "patient" reports. Citing David Wilson, dean of postgraduate medical education at the University of Leeds, Lewis says that the information a patient can give about his or her condition, the alleviation of pain, for example, is occasionally more important than the intellectual conclusions that a doctor can reach on the basis of test results and examinations (*Healing,* 44). A comment made by historian Cyril Richardson inclining toward tolerance for testimonies given by people who believe they have been healed might support Wagner and Lewis here. In Richardson's opinion, scientists' presuppositions may make it difficult for them to grasp what the nonscientifically trained might experience ("Spiritual Healing in the Light of History," *Pastoral Psychology* 5 [1954] 17).

nonsophisticated context must be treated with great care.[30] That observation is applicable far beyond the Middle Ages and, in fact, places a question mark over Wagner's proposals.

I find some suggestions Latourelle makes about the verification of claims of the miraculous much more attractive. He draws attention to three criteria that could be applied. First, there must be solid historical proof that the event in question actually occurred. Second, it must be something unusual and difficult to believe. Here competent medical assessment would play an important role. Third, it must have taken place in a setting of prayer and holiness. In addition, Latourelle would reject any event that has the appearance of frivolity, suspect morality, fakery, emotional excitement, greediness, or magic.[31]

These criteria must not be passed off lightly. They give full scope to thorough historical investigation, to personal testimony, to medical examination, and to divine action. They give room to faith, but they control credulity. We can use them as we proceed through this study and far beyond this study. And when we apply the criteria to the Petermans' case, we can conclude that they probably have their miracle.

---

[30] R. C. Finucane, "The Use and Abuse of Medieval Miracles," *History* 60 (1975) 9.

[31] Latourelle, *Miracles,* 310–13.

1

Jesus
THE HEALER

Jesus Christ towers above the Christian church. On the surface
that statement is so self-evident that it sounds trivial. That is not
the way, however, the story of the church unfolded. At countless
points, Christians have allowed other ideas, even other masters,
to overshadow Christ. There are few areas in the experience of
Christians where this is truer than in ministry to the sick.

A review of what Christians have done when they have
encountered human suffering lays bare a bewildering variety of
responses. The need is for a model to which everything can be
compared. That model is Christ.

Latourelle puts it effectively: "A theology of miracles that
follows a sound method cannot begin by studying isolated miracles or miracles that are recent or ambiguous [i.e., question-
able]. It must rather be based on the 'foundational' miracles of
Christianity, namely, those of Jesus. It must begin with the
'explainer,' not with that which is to be 'explained.' "[1]

There is a lot of material to examine. Ministering to the
sick was a major part of what Christ did. Repeatedly he reached
to individuals—a paralyzed servant (Matt 8:5ff.), a woman
with a fever (Mark 1:29–31)—or he responded to groups (Matt
12:1–5). There can be no question about the importance of
healing to Jesus.

---

[1] Latourelle, *Miracles,* 17.

When writers began recording Jesus' life, they acknowledged that emphasis. The proportion of verses in each of the four Gospels dealing with healing ranges from a low of 5 percent in John to 20 percent in Mark.[2] Latourelle brings the picture into even sharper focus by observing that if only that part of Mark which portrays the ministry of Jesus is considered, that is, if the section dealing with the crucifixion and resurrection is excluded, a full 47 percent of that Gospel is taken up with accounts of healing.[3] Ministering to those who were sick and distraught was important to Jesus, and his first interpreters knew that.[4]

A number of questions arise about the connection between Jesus and the miracles he performed. Did he look at them as something trivial compared to providing spiritual salvation for humanity? Were they "bonuses" or "treats" tossed out to people casually?

Precisely the opposite was true. On the one hand, a good case can be made for saying that in the healings we have an invaluable window into the mind of Christ. As he teaches, the curtain is drawn back in one direction; as he heals, it is drawn back in another.[5] These healings are an essential part of who he is. They are unique to him, and they are inseparably connected to him. They are not stock miracle stories floating

---

[2] J. Wilkinson, "Study of Healing in the Gospel according to John," *Scottish Journal of Theology* 20 (1967) 442.

[3] Latourelle, *Miracles,* 54.

[4] The historical value of the healing accounts in the Gospels has always been of interest. Latourelle makes it the subject of a detailed discussion (ibid., 54–69), and Albrecht Oepke offers some particularly useful comments. For example, he states that "it should be accorded that there are several signs that the tradition [the account of Jesus' ministry] received its basic form long before the written records, and that it did so on Palestinian soil (cf. 1 Cor 15:6), so that we are brought back to eye witnesses" ("ἰάομαι," *TDNT,* 3.206). The work of these scholars undergirds confidence in the historical nature of the healing accounts.

[5] See Latourelle, *Miracles,* 15; and Oepke, "ἰάομαι," 212f., on this point.

around in the literature of the time and then plugged into the "Jesus story" in order to make it more gripping. Rather, the miracles are powerful expressions of the dynamic of God in Jesus Christ.

These phenomena certainly helped to make Jesus stand out among his contemporaries. Nobody was making claims that any of the rabbis of Jesus' time could perform healings,[6] and Asclepius, the god who might have rivaled him most closely in the Greek mind, was clearly outclassed. People had been flocking to Asclepius's circular temple at Epidaurus for centuries, but there was a complexity, a fickleness, an egotistical bent to the ministry they thought he had.[7] In marked contrast, and in addition to their solid historical base, Jesus' miracles are characterized by selflessness, simplicity, and love.

These unique characteristics ought not to be surprising, because the healings were only part of a larger program. In Jesus, God was launching a revolution aimed at the total transformation of human experience. It is in this context that the healing ministry of Jesus must be seen if it is to be understood clearly. In this chapter I first sketch the big picture. Then I examine how the concept of the kingdom of God applies in this context. Finally I discuss the role of faith in healing.

The Big Picture

Dealing with almost anything without the benefit of a context makes us vulnerable to distortions, and that is certainly the case with healing. The accounts of individual miracles must be held firmly against the background of Jesus' total

---

[6] See H. W. Beyer, "θεραπεύω," *TDNT*, 3.129; and Oepke, "ἰάομαι," 202. David Flusser ("Healing through the Laying On of Hands in a Dead Sea Scroll, " *Israel Exploration Journal* 7 [1957] 107) presents an interesting argument in support of the idea that a Jewish sect, the Essenes, may have practiced laying on of hands and prayer for the sick in the first century BC.

[7] Beyer, "θεραπεύω," 131; and Oepke, "ἰάομαι," 197–210.

ministry. Ideally, one would come to understand the miracles the way Jesus himself did, but that is not a simple task. Jesus did not commit much time to theorizing about sickness and health. As Harnack commented years ago, "Jesus says very little about sickness; he cures it."[8] For the most part, Jesus' theology of healing must be drawn out of what he did and out of dialogues one is permitted to overhear while he was engaged in healing. Two passages, however, provide some insight into Jesus' thinking about the subject. The first is John 9:1–12.

As the story unfolds, Jesus and his disciples, while traveling, encountered a man who was born blind. With the curiosity of students, the disciples began to look for explanations. Falling back on conventional wisdom, they assumed that if somebody was sick, it was the direct result of sin. Jesus denied this, saying that the disability was not the result of sin committed either by the man or by his parents "but this happened so that the work of God might be displayed in his life" (v. 3). What follows, of course, is a healing (vv. 6, 7). The lesson is that God derives glory from the healing of a protracted handicap.[9]

The second passage is John 11:1–44, which provides the account of the resurrection of Lazarus.[10] Here Jesus volunteered an interpretation of this particular illness: "This sickness will not end in death. No, it is for God's glory so that God's Son may be glorified through it" (v. 4). And he was: Lazarus walked out of the grave (vv. 43, 44).[11] The reality of the power of God that rested upon Jesus was demonstrated as he reassembled the shattered pieces of fragile human life.

---

[8] Harnack, *Mission and Expansion*, 101.

[9] The disturbing part of the account is that the man was an adult who had lived with his handicap for a long time. For God to receive glory out of this, there had been a lifetime of blindness. In this case, illness and suffering came to play an important role in glorifying God.

[10] See also p. 11 below on Matt 11:4 for comments on healings in relation to the kingdom of God.

[11] Although the illness did not end in death, it passed through death, and that death and the sisters' grief were as real as anyone else's. Again, suffering was a means of bringing glory to God.

Using these two passages as a foundation, one can begin to make comments about Jesus' understanding of sickness and healing.

Fundamental is the idea that although illness and death are real, both can be overcome by the power of God, with the result that people will see how great God really is. The thirty or so accounts of healings that the four Gospels give make that point over and over again.

The passages from John also give information about Jesus' thinking on the immediate causes of sickness. Peder Borgen is helpful here. He suggests that illness can be understood in either "naturalistic" or "personalistic" terms.[12] In the first case, sickness comes from natural causes—for example, heat, cold, or germs. The incident in John 9 is a perfect illustration of this. In v. 3 Jesus says, "This happened." There was nothing extraordinary about the blindness. It just happened. Most of the disorders Jesus took care of are to be understood in these terms. Like most sickness today, they occurred for perfectly natural, understandable reasons.

The second perspective, however, called "personalistic," assumes that illness happens as a result of something that somebody does. This "somebody" can be either another human or a spirit being of some sort. We find examples of this in Jesus' ministry, too. Luke 13:10–13 offers a report of an occasion when he healed a woman who had been crippled by a spirit for eighteen years. Here is evidence that occasionally in Jesus' ministry physical problems could be traced to a source that was spiritual. More typically, in the Gospels the influence of unclean spirits, or demons, showed itself in severe personality or behavioral disorders. Mark 1:23–26 illustrates this:

> Just then a man in their synagogue who was possessed by an evil spirit cried out, "What do you want with us, Jesus of Nazareth? Have you come to destroy us? I know who you are—the Holy One of God!" "Be

---

[12] Peder Borgen, "Miracles of Healing in the New Testament: Some Observations," *Studia theologica* 35 (1981) 94.

quiet!" said Jesus sternly. "Come out of him!" The evil spirit shook the
man violently and came out of him with a shriek.

The fact that Jesus saw various kinds of disorders coming
from the presence of evil spirits points to another dimension of
his thinking. He believed there was a connection between sickness and sin. This is evident in an event recorded in Mark 2.
The manner in which Jesus referred to the man's sin and then
his paralysis (vv. 5, 10–12) establishes the fact that they were
part of the same picture. Words of Jesus preserved in John 5:14
make precisely the same connection: "Later Jesus found him
[the man who had been healed] at the temple and said to him,
'See, you are well again. Stop sinning or something worse may
happen to you.'" Sin and the man's sickness had something to
do with each other.

Jesus did not, however, accept the idea that sickness is
always direct punishment for personal sin. This is clear in a passage
that was quoted above in another context, John 9:3—"Neither
this man nor his parents sinned, but this happened so that the
work of God might be displayed in his life"—and many who
have studied Jesus' ministry have picked up on it.[13]

This is where the larger picture emerges. The relationship
between evil and sickness is part of a generalized view of the world.
Morton Kelsey puts his finger on it when he says, "Jesus seemed to
believe that a primary cause of sickness was a force of evil loose
in the world which was hostile to God and the divine way."[14]

Jesus was very conscious of the conflict between himself
and this force of evil. It became strikingly clear to him during
his temptation (Matt 4:1–11 and parallels). He obviously recognized that it was being played out in his ministry:

Jesus was driving out a demon that was mute. When the demon left,
the man who had been mute spoke, and the crowd was amazed. But

---

[13] Oepke, "ἰάομαι," 204; and R. K. Harrison, "Healing, Health," *IDB*,
2.542, 546, for example. See also Gary S. Shogren, "Will God Heal Us?—A
Re-examination of James 5:15–16a," *Evangelical Quarterly* 61 (1989) 106.

[14] Kelsey, *Psychology*, 75.

some of them said, "By Beelzebub, the prince of demons, he is driving out demons." Others tested him by asking for a sign from heaven.

Jesus knew their thoughts and said to them: "Any kingdom divided against itself will be ruined, and a house divided against itself will fall. If Satan is divided against himself, how can his kingdom stand? I say this because you claim that I drive out demons by Beelzebub. Now if I drive out demons by Beelzebub, by whom do your followers drive them out? So then, they will be your judges. But if I drive out demons by the finger of God, then the kingdom of God has come to you." (Luke 11:14–20)

Two other passages are relevant also. In John 12:31 Jesus states, "Now is the time for judgment on this world; now the prince of this world will be driven out," and in the context of his final evening with his disciples, Jesus says, "The prince of this world is coming. He has no hold on me" (14:30). There can be no doubt about Jesus' being keenly aware of the struggle that was swirling around him.

The background to the conflict was the creation of a good world (Gen 1–2) and its subsequent corruption (Gen 3). The world has fallen into a state in which everything stands in need of complete renewal (Rom 8:18–22). This corrupted condition influences human lives in many ways, one of which is disease. Borgen says, "The doctrine of the world as God's creation led to disease being regarded as something abnormal. It belongs to the destructive forces which spoil God's good handiwork."[15] The sickness and disorder to which Jesus ministered were parts of an all-encompassing situation in which everything had gone askew. This is a comprehensive problem with extremely troubling specifics. To this problem, God made a comprehensive response.

It is expressed in capsule form in Matthew 8:16–17: "When evening came, many who were demon-possessed were brought to him, and he drove out the spirits with a word and healed all the sick. This was to fulfill what was spoken through the prophet Isaiah: 'He took up our infirmities and carried our

---

[15] Borgen, "Miracles," 97.

diseases.' " The Old Testament passage quoted is Isaiah 53:4. What Jesus was doing is presented as the fulfillment of that text.[16]

Many see Isaiah 53 as applying to Jesus' "atonement," the act by which he reopened the possibility of a relationship between God and humanity. Old Testament specialists R. K. Harrison[17] and David Boyd[18] make it clear that the language of Isaiah 53:4 includes a provision not only for spiritual needs but also for sickness. Harrison then draws this conclusion: "On this basis . . . it is theoretically justifiable to appeal to the finished work of Jesus for physical healing as well as for spiritual restoration."[19] Many agree. Kelsey writes, "If Jesus had any one mission, it was to bring the power and healing of God's creative, loving spirit to bear upon the moral, mental and physical illnesses of the people around him. It was a matter of rescuing us from a situation in which we could not help ourselves."[20] P. H. Carter comments that "one of the fruits of the atonement is power over sickness. Sickness, because it is rooted in the kingdom of evil, was vanquished by the cross."[21] Borgen states, "The NT view of health embraces the whole person, including both physical health and a religious-ethical life in accordance with God's will. Both forgiveness of sins and the curing of bodily sickness are therefore included in the concept of salvation."[22]

---

[16] Beyer, "θεραπεύω," 130.

[17] Harrison, "Healing," 547.

[18] David P. Boyd, "Mini-Exegesis: Isaiah 53:4–5," *Eastern Journal of Practical Theology* 2 (1988) 24.

[19] Harrison, "Healing," 547.

[20] Kelsey, *Psychology*, 53.

[21] P. H. Carter, "Use of the Bible by Protestant Healing Groups," *Southwestern Journal of Theology* 5 (1963) 51.

[22] Borgen, "Miracles," 101. There is a widely held idea that because healing has a place in the atonement, it is as readily available as salvation. This has created a variety of problems. Carter says this idea "can be convincingly demolished" ("Use of the Bible," 49), but does not show how. Boyd offers some helpful comments. He points out that while spiritual salvation may be experienced now by believers, we are still subject to temptation and sin. The great hope found in the cross is its offer of "assurance of a final separation and removal of sin and its consequences" ("Mini-Exegesis," 26). Similarly, while we

Latourelle makes a very helpful comment: "Miracles can be seen to be the visible traces of the radical change that in Jesus Christ affects human beings and the universe in which they dwell."[23] That is the big picture. Healings point beyond themselves to what was accomplished on the larger scale. A. G. Ikin provides a summary—and an introduction to the next key idea in this chapter, the kingdom of God—when he says, "Sin and disease for Christ were both alien to the kingdom of God, and his ministry was one of redemption, to bring humanity into the sphere within which God's will was fulfilled."[24]

The Kingdom of God

The nature of Jesus' ministry was often raucous. Repeatedly he had to deal with shocking personality disorders coming from demonic activity, and there were no drugs to dampen bizarre behavior, as in Mark 1:23–26, quoted above. Jesus' days were punctuated by that sort of thing. Mark 3:11, 12 says that whenever evil spirits encountered Jesus, they acknowledged his superiority and took orders from him. Luke 8:2 records that while he was traveling from town to town, he met a number of women whom he healed and delivered from demons. One of these was Mary Magdalene, "from whom seven demons had come out." In 6:17–19 Luke speaks of crowds that had listened to Jesus and been healed and freed from evil spirits. That brought the people surging toward him.

---

can look to the cross now for healing, we will have to continue to deal with illness and death because "the provision for wholeness and health will be actualized in the resurrection, the ultimate healing" ("Mini-Exegesis," 26). Surprisingly, Carter ("Use of the Bible," 51) makes some comments that support Boyd. J. Sidlow Baxter would argue that one should talk about healing as occurring *through* the atonement rather than being *in* the atonement (*Divine Healing of the Body* [Grand Rapids: Zondervan, 1979] 133).

[23] Latourelle, *Miracles*, 21.

[24] A. G. Ikin, "New Testament and Healing," *Pastoral Psychology* 7 (1956) 33.

James Dunn provides an important perspective on Jesus' miracles: "The exercise of this power was evidence that the longed-for kingdom of God had already come upon his hearers."[25] The miracles were proof that a profoundly new age had dawned. The concept of the kingdom of God is important. Of course, it does not refer to a place or even a time. It is more of a condition in which people focus on doing what God wants and in which, in turn, they experience his presence. Essential to this notion is the idea of a response to God's call in which people give themselves to him, only to find that he unstintingly gives himself to them. Perhaps one could even say that life in the kingdom of God is life lived in a relationship with God. In Jesus Christ, God was extending his reign to earth. The miracles Jesus performed were an important part of the overall picture. Latourelle sums it all up: "In order that men and women may realize that the race is entering into a new age and a new condition and that this world is already present at the heart of the old, Christ gives visible form to the salvation he proclaims."[26]

The miracles were part of that visible form. Latourelle finds an echo in Oepke:

> The miracles of Jesus are simple and yet powerful signs that the prophecies of the age of salvation are beginning to be fulfilled. The miracles are themselves partial victories of God's rule. The host of demons flees. When Jesus extends help, the kingdom of God is achieved at a specific point, though completely so only when there is comprehension of the miracles in this sense. Each partial victory is a foretaste and guarantee of the final victory.[27]

The Gospel writers were at pains to show that Jesus initiated the reign of God and that the healings were an essential part of it. In Matthew 4:23–24,

---

[25] James D. G. Dunn, *Jesus and the Spirit* (London: SCM, 1975) 47. See also his earlier article, "Spirit and Kingdom," *Expository Times* 82 (1970–71) 36–40.

[26] Latourelle, *Miracles*, 20.

[27] Oepke, "ἰάομαι," 212f.

Jesus went throughout Galilee, teaching in their synagogues, preaching the good news of the kingdom, and healing every disease and sickness among the people. News about him spread all over Syria, and people brought to him all who were ill with various diseases, those suffering severe pain, the demon-possessed, those having seizures, and the paralyzed, and he healed them.

Again in 9:35–36 Matthew links the kingdom and miracles. Mark 1:39 finds Jesus traveling in Galilee, preaching in synagogues, and casting out demons. As far as the Gospel writers were concerned, the kingdom and the miraculous simply went together.

That was the understanding of Jesus himself. In Matthew 11:4 he responded to John the Baptist's query about whether he was the Messiah, the one who would bring the kingdom, by drawing attention to his miraculous ministry and his preaching to the poor. It is clear that Jesus, the kingdom, and the miraculous are tightly bound together. The miracles visibly pinpoint the kingdom at particular moments in space and time, and they are completely dependent upon the person of Jesus. At the same time, they serve him by helping to identify the special role he plays as God's Anointed. He is authenticated by them.[28] Beyer identifies what he thinks is the basic point of the Gospels' accounts of healings: "There is no sickness or weakness that Jesus cannot master."[29]

This is illustrated most graphically in Luke 7:11–17, where Jesus interrupted a funeral. He was wrenched by compassion at a widow's loss. He stopped the coffin and in one swift, magnificent stroke raised the dead. This act demonstrated Jesus' limitless power and authority, and it pointed to the spiritual reality that lay behind the specific moments in which the rule of God was revealed. Jesus could lay waste to death because he was the one who would destroy "him who holds the power of death—that is, the devil" (Heb 2:14). Not only that, he was the one who would,

---

[28] C. E. B. Cranfield, "St. Mark 9:14–29," *Scottish Journal of Theology* 3 (1950) 57–59. See also Latourelle, *Miracles*, 21; and Beyer, "θεραπεύω," 129f. Kelsey takes an opposing position (*Psychology*, 79).

[29] Beyer, "θεραπεύω," 130.

in the words of 1 John 3:8, "destroy the devil's work." Jesus' understanding of the struggle was clear. He announced, "Now is the time for judgment on this world; now the prince of this world will be driven out" (John 12:31), and, "The prince of this world is coming. He has no hold on me" (John 14:30). He was looking through the apparently tragic events that would soon unfold, focusing on the ultimate victory. A coffin was no obstacle to this kind of authority.

The world was being challenged by someone who was brilliantly unique—the someone who said, "I am the bread of life" (John 6:35), "I am the way and the truth and the life" (14:6), and, simply, "I am" (18:5), identifying himself with "I AM WHO I AM"—God (Exod 3:14). Here was God's ultimate response to the chaos caused by disobedience. It was an invitation to a new world, to the "reign of God." Here, in the person of Jesus, was where universal disorder, including disease, would be dealt with. Of course, the reign of God that appeared in Jesus was very much in its early stages. The time of ultimate fulfillment lay far off in the future. But the time when all was just promises was over. The kingdom of God had come.

Faith

Mark 5:21–24, 35–43 gives very important insights into life under God's reign. It is the account of the healing of a young girl, but the feature I want to highlight is the attitude of her father, Jairus. He was convinced that everything would be all right if only Jesus would come and pray for his daughter (v. 23). That conviction is a key element not only of this story but of the whole of Jesus' healing ministry. That conviction is faith, one of the most debated ideas connected with divine healing. Bornkamm says, "In the tradition of Jesus' sayings faith is always linked with power and miracle,"[30] and Oepke adds that

---

[30] Günther Bornkamm, *Jesus of Nazareth* (trans. Irene and Fraser McLuskey with J. M. Robinson; New York: Harper & Row, 1960) 103.

Jesus attaches his greatest promises to faith.[31] Their emphasis is well placed. References to faith come up time and time again in the healing accounts of the Gospels.

In Luke 17:11–19 Jesus healed ten lepers. When one returned to express gratitude, Jesus said, "Your faith has made you well" (v. 19). Mark 10 carries the account of Bartimaeus having his blindness healed. Bartimaeus seized Jesus' attention by crying out. As they talked, the blind man made his wishes as plain as possible: "Rabbi, I want to see" (v. 51). Jesus' response was just as direct: "Go, your faith has healed you" (v. 52), and of course, Bartimaeus could see instantly. Jesus obviously placed great emphasis on the man's faith. In Mark 2:1–12 it was a paralytic who was healed. His friends tore up a roof to get him to Jesus (v. 4), and Jesus acted when he saw their faith (v. 5).

Harnack defined faith as "a conscious intelligent commitment of the person to the will of God in Christ,"[32] and the story told in Mark 9:14–29 serves as an illustration. A father brought a son suffering with something that sounds like epilepsy, caused by the presence of an evil spirit. In desperation he pleaded, "If you can do anything, take pity on us and help us" (v. 22). Jesus' reply sounds harsh: " 'If you can?' Everything is possible for him who believes" (v. 23). Again faith was highlighted. The father's reaction was classic, demonstrating a conscious, intelligent commitment to the will of God in Christ: "Immediately the boy's father exclaimed, 'I do believe; help me overcome my unbelief!' " (v. 24). The child was healed.

It would be wrong, however, to be simplistic about this. Faith appeared repeatedly as Jesus healed people, but it was not always mentioned. Wilkinson points out that in the Gospel of John faith was never asked for as a condition of healing.[33] The record of the healing of an invalid beside the pool called Bethesda (John 5:1–9) makes the point. The man's response to

---

[31] Oepke, "ἰάομαι," 210.

[32] Harnack, *Mission and Expansion*, 547.

[33] Wilkinson, "Study of Healing," 450.

Jesus' question about his wishes (v. 7) makes it clear that he was not even looking to Jesus for help. As far as he was concerned, his hope of healing was in the pool. Verse 9 suggests fairly obviously that the healing took place before any movement by him was necessary. He was not healed because he exercised faith by trying to move when still crippled. It took no faith on his part to stand on legs that had been made well while he was still lying on his mat.

Underlining my word of caution about assumptions regarding the role of faith in healing, I note that there is no mention of faith in the account of Jesus' healing Peter's mother-in-law, either (Matt 8:14). He simply touched her hand and the fever left. Faith may have figured in the event, but if it did, it has dropped out of the record.

This warning about oversimplification notwithstanding, faith does keep coming up in Jesus' ministry. If it was so important to him, we should take the trouble to try to understand what he had in mind.

A lot of people have tried to do this. During his study of Jesus, Bornkamm first talks about faith as counting on the power of Jesus and then as "simply trust in Jesus' power."[34] Dunn underlines the idea of trust, saying, "Faith here must be understood as a trusting in God's power, an openness and receptivity to the power of God to perform a mighty work."[35]

Matthew 9:27–31 certainly provides justification for the position that Bornkamm and Dunn take. In this passage, Jesus was confronted by two blind men pleading for help, and he asked a question that should be looked at carefully: "Do you believe that I am able to do this?" (v. 28). He was attempting to discover what the men thought about him, probing to see if they trusted his ability—Bornkamm and Dunn's point. They answered simply, "Yes, Lord" (v. 28), and that was good enough. Jesus responded by touching their eyes and saying,

---

[34] Bornkamm, *Jesus of Nazareth*, 130.
[35] Dunn, *Jesus*, 74.

"According to your faith will it be done to you," and they were instantly healed. Jesus called their trust in his ability to help them "faith," and he acted on that basis.

The same picture emerges from a number of other passages. Matthew 8:1–4 describes a leper coming to Jesus. He said, "Lord, if you are willing, you can make me clean" (v. 2) The question in the leper's mind had to do with Jesus' willingness, not with his ability. He trusted that completely—and he was healed. The very next story in Matthew 8 (vv. 5–13) tells of the healing of a centurion's servant. Trust in Jesus was again the key. In Mark 5:24–34 a hemorrhaging woman was healed. She was convinced that if she could just touch Jesus' clothes, she would be all right (v. 28), and she was not disappointed. After she had received her miracle, Jesus spoke to her, "Your faith has healed you" (v. 34). The faith Jesus is talking about is a simple trust in his ability to make a profound difference in very distressing situations.

All of these people came to Jesus with certain assumptions about him. The reports they had heard, perhaps what they themselves had seen, led them to believe that Jesus was the answer to their problems. He represented concern, compassion, and power. What they had to do was make contact with him—in other words, establish a relationship with him. C. E. B. Cranfield observes that in the New Testament faith was a relationship with Jesus.[36] That is what these people experienced. Their healings flowed out of their encounters with a person. They saw in him one who could help them, and they opened themselves to whatever he would do in their situations. This relational dimension must be at the heart of any discussion of Jesus' healing. Failure to hold that relationship central in understanding healing could lead to a distorted idea of what Jesus did. One could come to see healing as something achieved almost by magic, through the use of certain formulas and rituals. Healings could become mechanical, ends in

---

[36] Cranfield, "St. Mark 9:14–29," 65.

themselves. In the New Testament they are part of a dynamic relationship between a person and Christ. They are not mere "wonders" performed by a "miracle man." They flow out of a faith relationship, they confirm faith, they lead to faith.

The healings did not rest upon a conviction that at a particular moment a particular person would be healed. Commenting on the healing of the boy with seizures as recorded in Mark 9:14–29, Cranfield notes, "The disciples try to cast out the evil spirit, and fail. It was not that they did not expect to succeed—they did. Their lack of faith did not consist in any failure to expect great things. On the contrary, they tried, because they thought they would succeed."[37]

They found out that expectation, however deeply held, could not trigger a miracle. In fact, demanding that one expect a miracle to happen has more to do with paganism than with Christ. Oepke comments, "Aesculapius [the Greek god with the healing ministry] demands strict belief in the miracle. Jesus does not."[38] When the objective becomes manufacturing enough faith to earn a healing, then one's faith is in faith, not in God. Cranfield calls this idolatry.[39] The healings Jesus performed were parts of a living relationship that Jesus shared with individuals. They arose out of a faith relationship, and they either led to or strengthened that relationship.[40]

Conclusion

This chapter has tried to show that the divine response to illness, as we see it in Jesus, is an important part of something even larger. It is a feature of a total revolution aimed at the transformation of the life experiences of those who become followers of Christ.

---

[37] Ibid., 61.
[38] Oepke, "ἰάομαι," 211.
[39] Cranfield, "St. Mark 9:14–29," 66.
[40] Wilkinson, "Study of Healing," 457ff.

Jesus did not think that either the revolution or the healings would end when he withdrew physically from this planet. In Matthew 10:1 he gave his twelve closest disciples the power to cast out evil spirits and to cure illness. In Luke 10:9 he commissioned the seventy-two to go into towns and "heal the sick who are there and tell them, 'The kingdom of God is near you.'" In John 14:12 he said, "I tell you the truth, anyone who has faith in me will do what I have been doing. He will do even greater things than these [in quantity, not quality], because I am going to the Father."

This is precisely what happened. In the midst of the flooding in of the reign of God, we hear of a lame beggar being healed (Acts 3:1–11), of masses being delivered from evil spirits and restored to health (Acts 5:16), and of a Pauline exorcism (Acts 16:16–18). Jesus was continuing to work through the church. Paul talked about events that happened in his ministry (Rom 15:19; 2 Cor 12:12) and referred to "the message of knowledge" and "gifts of healing" among what we call the gifts of the Spirit (1 Cor 12:8, 9). Hebrews 2:4 and James 5:13–16 make it clear that God was powerfully at work among other Christians also. The rest of this study will focus upon how the ministry of healing continued to unfold throughout the history of the church.

Part 1

The Confrontational Model

THE EARLY YEARS
J.C. BLUMHARDT
JOHN WIMBER

The first healing model I call *confrontational*. This approach corresponds closely to the biblical picture of the ministry of Christ. Healing is seen as part of God's overarching program, in which he has become active not only in human affairs but in the destiny of the entire universe by sending his son to earth to establish the reign of God. By this action, God issued a direct challenge to Evil. Those who argue for this view insist that God's challenge has been successful. The emphasis is upon confrontation, victory, and liberty through Christ. Divine healing is one aspect of this planting of the kingdom of God.

The representatives of this model differ widely. The first is the mainstream of ante-Nicene Christianity, including such people as Irenaeus, Tertullian, Cyprian, Origen, and Lactantius. No one person exercised an extraordinary healing ministry before AD 325, so I have focused on the period in general. Other representatives are J. C. Blumhardt and John Wimber. The exorcism of demons is a significant feature in all three representatives.

It is worth noting that Blumhardt was and Wimber is comparatively well informed theologically. It appears that theological sophistication may be more important to this point of view than other models we will consider.

2

The Early Years
A CHURCH TRIUMPHANT

The challenges the first generations of Christians faced were basic, reducing ultimately to the question of survival in a hostile world. Fundamental to their success was their bedrock certainty about Jesus. He had lived on earth; his resurrection had left them awestruck, and the Holy Spirit saw to it that they were energized by his words and his deeds. One of them, Quadratus, living in the early second century, could testify,

> But the works of our Saviour were always present, for they were true, those who were cured, those who rose from the dead, who not merely appeared as cured and risen, but were constantly present, not only while the Saviour was living, but even for some time after he had gone, so that some of them survived even to our own time.[1]

That is, Quadratus's life overlapped with the lives of some whom Jesus had healed or resurrected.

The story of the early church is spellbinding. The period under consideration extends from about AD 100 to around 325. The sources for a history of what is known as the ante-Nicene church do not yield a complete picture. For example, the spread of Christianity into Egypt or along the southern coast of the Mediterranean Sea cannot be easily traced. It appears full-blown in those places toward the end of the second

---

[1] Eusebius, *Ecclesiastical History* 3, LCL 1.309.

century. The historian can only take the material that scat-tered libraries and the sandstorms of Egypt have given and re-construct the best picture possible.

Jesus had come bringing the kingdom of God. Throughout the period in focus here, that kingdom continued to thrive. One thinks of Tertullian, the brilliant North African defender of Christianity. Early in the third century, he hurled scorn at the entertainment world of his time. As far as he was concerned, it was rotten to the core, and he attacked it vigorously.

By contrast, he described the joys of being a Christian, asking rhetorically what greater pleasure there could be "than to find yourself trampling underfoot the gods of the Gentiles, expelling demons, effecting cures, seeking revelations, living to God? These are the pleasures, the spectacles of Christians, holy, eternal, and free."[2] Here is a confident man. For Tertul-lian, the superiority of Christ over all rivals was beyond ques-tion, and it extended to both exorcism and healing.

Origen, a somewhat younger contemporary of Tertullian, presented the same general picture. Widely regarded as one of the most brilliant people of his time, Origen lived first in Alex-andria, then in Syria. In one of his works defending Christian-ity, he said, "By these [the names of God and Jesus] we also have seen many delivered from serious ailments, and from mental distraction and madness, and countless other diseases, which neither men nor daemons had cured."[3]

Similar information came from Rome in the middle of the third century. One of the ecclesiastical luminaries, Novatian (who later led a schism), commented about the Holy Spirit:

> Indeed this is he who appoints prophets in the church, instructs teachers, directs tongues, brings into being powers and conditions of health, carries on extraordinary works, furnishes discernment of spirits, incorporates administrations in the church, establishes plans, brings

---

[2] Tertullian, *De spectaculis* [*The Shows*] 29, LCL 295, 297.

[3] Origen, *Contra Celsum* 3.24 (trans. Henry Chadwick; Cambridge: Cambridge University Press, 1953) 142.

together and arranges all other gifts there are of the charismata and by reason of this makes the church of God everywhere perfect in everything and complete.[4]

These three prominent figures in the third-century church talked about healings and miracles with which they were familiar. They were convinced that the healing power that was so obvious in Jesus' ministry had flowed over into the life of their church.

Of course there are questions to be raised about how reliable Origen and the others were as witnesses to what was happening among the Christians with whom they were familiar. Elsewhere, I have argued at length that the general level of historical trustworthiness of early Christian leaders is quite high.[5] Victor Dawe takes a similar position: "Allowing for exaggeration and redactions we should be as willing to accept their statements about the reality of spiritual healing as readily as we do their information about the teachings and customs in the early church."[6]

The available sources provide an adequate picture of the ante-Nicene church. Along with other features, Christianity appears familiar with the power of God. This chapter will develop this statement by making several specific observations.

Victory in the Spirit World

First, demonic activity seems to have continued to be an issue throughout the period in question, but again and again

---

[4] Novatian, *The Treatise of Novatian on the Trinity* 29 (trans. H. Moore; London: S.P.C.K., 1919) 70. See my discussion of this passage in "Novatian's *De Trinitate* 29: Evidence of the Charismatic?" *Scottish Journal of Theology* 30 (1977) 313–18.

[5] See my *Charismatic Gifts in the Early Church* (Peabody, Mass.: Hendrickson, 1984) passim.

[6] Victor Dawe, "The Attitude of the Ancient Church toward Sickness and Healing" (Th.D. diss., Boston University, 1955) 94.

Christians claimed to have dealt with it victoriously. Here is naked spiritual confrontation.

Demons were often associated with pagan gods, and they were invariably enemies. The experience of Jesus must never have been far from the mind of the church. He began the shattering attack on the kingdom of Evil, and the church carried it on. Some comments of early Christian authors are little more than shouts of triumph. Justin wrote in the mid–second century, "We believers in Jesus our Lord, who was crucified under Pontius Pilate, cast out all devils and other evil spirits and thus have them in our power."[7]

Minucius Felix, who wrote about fifty years later, sounded much the same. Referring to information demons gave about themselves "when they are driven out of men's bodies by words of exorcism and the fire of prayer," he offered a graphic description of their departure: as they left their victims, "reluctantly, in misery, they quail and quake."[8]

The sense of confidence noted earlier in Tertullian appeared again in one of his most famous works, the *Apology*. In this book, he was trying to defend Christians against persecution by the Roman state. Tertullian fully understood the idea that "the best defense is a good offense," and in chapter 37, he was on the offensive. Attempting to underline the foolishness of alienating Christians, he said,

> But who would rescue you [if Christians were to withdraw] from those secret enemies that everywhere lay waste your minds and your bodily health? I mean, from the assaults of demons, whom we drive out of you, without reward, without pay. Why, this alone would have sufficed to avenge us—to leave you open and exposed to unclean spirits with immediate possession.[9]

This idea of the indebtedness of Roman society to Christians for their spiritual protection also appears in Tertullian's

---

[7] Justin Martyr, *Dialogue with Trypho* 76, FC 6.269.

[8] Minucius Felix, *Octavius* 27.5, LCL 399.

[9] Tertullian, *Apology* 37, LCL 173. See also *Apology* 43, LCL 193, 195.

letter to an official named Scapula, while he was talking about well-placed imperial citizens:

> For, the secretary of a certain gentleman, when he was suffering from falling sickness caused by a demon, was freed from it; so also were the relatives of some of the others and a certain little boy. And heaven knows how many distinguished men, to say nothing of common people, have been cured either of devils or of their sickness.[10]

Christians not only did not create difficulty in society; they fulfilled a positive role. They protected innocent citizenry from assault by demons. Through Christians blessings were distributed indiscriminately, and in the process demons were conquered.

An historical aside is appropriate. Tertullian was writing these works to living Roman officials. He based his appeal for clemency on benefits that were coming through Christians to many people in society. If this were not happening, Tertullian would have simply looked like a fool claiming that it was, making the Christian faith he was trying to defend into a laughingstock. The strength of his argument lay precisely in the fact that anyone could check to see whether there was evidence to support it. If there were no evidence, he would not have dared make these claims.

Another North African churchman, Cyprian, who wrote about a generation later than Tertullian, also addressed the question of demons. The same sense of victory appears in his words: "Yet these [spirits] when adjured by us through the true God, immediately withdraw and confess and are forced to go out of the bodies which they have possessed."[11] Elsewhere, he discussed the impact that the Holy Spirit had on demons, stating that they could not remain in a person in whom the Holy Spirit was beginning to dwell.[12] He assumed that the Holy Spirit

---

[10] Tertullian, *To Scapula* 4, FC 10.173.

[11] Cyprian, *That Idols Are Not Gods* 7, FC 36.355.

[12] Cyprian, *Letter* 69, 15, FC 51.256. There has been disagreement over how the fifteenth paragraph of *Letter* 69 should be translated. (There is also confusion about the correct numbering of the letters. The *ANF* edition identi-

entered a person at the time of baptism. Not all Christians would accept that thesis, although it became part of Roman Catholic doctrine. But at any rate it is clear that for Cyprian demons were helpless in the presence of the Holy Spirit.

The last person from this period to deal with the question of demons is Lactantius. Like Tertullian and Cyprian, he was born in North Africa. Unlike them, however, he spent most of his active life as a Christian in what is now France. One brief passage from his *Divine Institutes* echoes the confident expectation of victory over demons seen in the other two. Lactantius quoted a person named Hermes to the effect that through

---

fies this letter as number 75.) The older English translation by Ernest Wallis handles the passage in such a way as to make the point that if demons had not already left a person, they certainly would at the time of baptism, and they would do so because the Holy Spirit was taking up residence in the person through baptism (*Epistle 75*, ANF 5.402). By contrast, Rose B. Donna's more recent translation reads precisely opposite. In her translation, the text says that demons are capable of staying in a person while and after she or he is baptized (*Letter 69*, 15, FC 51.256). The text itself is ambiguous (Cyprian, *Epistula 69*, CSEL, vol. 3, part 2, pp. 764, 765). I favor the older translation over Donna's for two reasons. First, there appears to be contradiction within Donna's rendering, which reads,

> Yet when it comes to the water of salvation and to the sanctification of baptism, we ought to know and to trust that the devil is oppressed there and that the man dedicated to God is freed by divine mercy. For if scorpions and serpents which prevail on dry land, when hurled into the water can prevail or retain their poison, evil spirits, also, which are called scorpions and serpents, and yet are trodden under foot by the power given through us by the Lord, can remain in the body of man, in whom, baptized and after that sanctified, the Holy Spirit begins to dwell.

The first sentence acknowledges the power of baptism while the second denies it.

The second argument against Donna's reading is that the text behind the second sentence is equally open to a translation that recognizes the power of baptism and thus remains consistent with the first sentence. Along with Wallis, Bayard opts for such a translation and supports it with a comment in a note (Cyprian, *Correspondance* [trans. Louis Bayard; Paris: Les Belles Lettres, 1925] 251 n. 1).

"piety" (the knowledge of God) people were delivered from both demons and fate by God's power.[13]

From Justin to Lactantius the picture remains the same. These Christians believed that there was power that could overcome demons. They were equally aware that this power was derived. That is, it did not belong to themselves. It flowed from the risen Christ. Justin was able to say, "We call Him our Helper and Redeemer, by the power of whose name even the demons shudder,"[14] and Origen commented, "It is not by incantations that Christians seem to prevail (over evil spirits), but by the name of Jesus."[15] Lactantius linked the ministry of Christians with Jesus': "So now his followers, in the name of their Master, and by the sign of his passion, banish the same polluted spirits from men."[16] They were convinced that it was Jesus Christ who overcame evil spirits, and they wanted to testify to the power of his name.

In the midst of all the confidence and rejoicing, there was more than a hint that confrontations with the demonic were not always simple. Bishop Cyprian sounded a cautionary note. Certainly ultimate victory was assured; he did not back away from the confidence observed earlier. But sometimes dealing with demons was a struggle. In one place, he talked about their deceptiveness.[17] In another, he commented that when they were exorcised, they might leave either rapidly or slowly. Cyprian thought this would depend on the faith of the sufferer "or the grace of the healer."[18] Minucius Felix made exactly the

---

[13] Lactantius, *Divine Institutes* 2.15, FC 49.155.

[14] Justin Martyr, *Dialogue with Trypho* 30, FC 6.192.

[15] Origen, *Contra Celsum* 1.6, p. 9f.

[16] Lactantius, *Divine Institutes* 4.27, FC 49.314. Lactantius inserts the words "the sign of his passion" in his statement. The phrase refers to making the sign of the cross. A symbolic act is placed alongside a verbal command. This is a step away from the simplicity of New Testament exorcism and from the directness seen up to this point. Lactantius was a fourth-century person, and practices were undergoing modification by then.

[17] Cyprian, *Letter 69*, 15, FC 51.256.

[18] Cyprian, *Idols* 7, FC 36.355.

same observation and offered the same explanation.[19] These Christians were very conscious of the spiritual battle into which their faith in Christ had propelled them. To them the world of spiritual beings was no quaint abstract idea. They had to face its reality daily. Their experience of the power of Christ was a major source of confidence.

Physical Healing

My second observation relates to physical healing. Ante-Nicene Christians expected that the power of Christ would be sufficient for their health needs as well as their spiritual warfare—they knew the Gospel accounts—and apparently it often was. Along with the general comments from Tertullian, Origen, and Novatian cited earlier, Christian literature from this period yields a number of passages about healing.

The earliest clear passages come from Irenaeus. He was a leading personality in the church in Lyons, in south-central France, then the Roman province of Gaul. He provided leadership there as bishop during the second half of the second century. It was a time when life in the church was far from settled. The organization of Christian communities was developing slowly, and the idea of a true doctrine universally held was only gradually emerging. Indeed, there were many heatedly debated opinions about what acceptable Christian thinking was. Irenaeus entered those debates with a strong sense of pastoral responsibility. His primary concern was to save his congregation from the confusion of what is now called Gnosticism.[20]

In his most famous work, *Against Heresies*, Irenaeus confronted the followers of two teachers, Simon and Carpocrates, charging them with being unable to heal the blind, the lame,

---

[19] Minucius Felix, *Octavius* 27.2, LCL 399.

[20] This was a loosely connected collection of groups that formed around claims to secret knowledge and that imported ideas from Babylonian and Egyptian religions and Greek philosophy, to name only a few sources. These they added to a Christian substructure.

the deaf, the paralyzed, or the injured[21] or to do anything about the demon-possessed. The intent of the argument was to demonstrate the inadequacy of their beliefs. The implication was that Irenaeus's group was performing these kinds of healing fairly frequently, proving its superiority.

In a later passage from the same work, the implication became explicit: "Wherefore, also, those who are in truth His disciples, receiving grace from Him, do in His name perform [miracles], so as to promote the welfare of other men, according to the gift which each one has received from Him. . . . [Some] heal the sick by laying their hands upon them, and they are made whole."[22] If Irenaeus can be trusted, it appears that late-second-century Christians in Lyons were no strangers to miraculous healing.

The next relevant information was written about a generation later than Irenaeus's work. It is found in a document called *The Apostolic Tradition*, written in Rome, probably by Hippolytus, who, like Novatian later, got into trouble with the bishop of his church. In this work Hippolytus outlined procedures to be followed in the ordination of various levels of clergy. The passage that is of interest here is, "If anyone among the laity appears to have received a gift of healing by a revelation, hands shall not be laid on him, because the matter is manifested."[23] The issue Hippolytus focused on was the recognition of ministries. His discussion ranges over the various categories of leadership, outlining the action to be taken in each case. Some think that his comments reflect practices that were followed by the Roman church from the second half of the second century onward.[24] The point here is that if one thinks someone is going to be used as an agent

---

[21] Irenaeus, *Against Heresies* 2.31.2, ANF 5.407.

[22] Ibid., 2.32.4, ANF 5.409.

[23] Hippolytus, *The Treatise on the Apostolic Tradition of St. Hippolytus of Rome* 15.1 (trans. Gregory Dix; London: S.P.C.K., 1937) 22.

[24] For example, see Gregory Dix, introduction to Hippolytus, *The Apostolic Tradition*, xliv.

of healing, an ordination would not add anything. Just wait and see what happens.

This passage is important because it implies that healings were continuing. Hippolytus thought it likely enough that someone would be used to perform healings that he laid down some guidelines in advance. In other words, the occurrence of healing would not be surprising. Hippolytus did not explicitly say there were healings, but he certainly recognized the possibility.

Last, we return to Origen. His observation was that Christians "perform many cures."[25] The statement is blunt, and it shows this churchman calling upon his detailed knowledge of the church in the Middle East. He would not discount physical healing as a real feature of Christian experience.

Witnesses to Resurrections

The following account of resurrections from the dead is much more problematic to modern readers. I share this discomfort; cadavers do not usually come back to life. Nonetheless, the record must not be dismissed out of hand.

Irenaeus is the witness to these resurrections in *Against Heresies*: "Moreover as I have said, the dead even have been raised up, and remained among us for many years."[26] Although specific details are lacking—names, dates, places—there is no question but that he meant to be taken seriously. Indeed, the earlier passage to which he alluded painted the picture even more boldly. There he reported that raising the dead "has been frequently done in the brotherhood on account of some necessity."[27] Irenaeus commented that the resurrections happened as a result of fasting and prayer.

---

[25] Origen, *Contra Celsum* 1.46 (Chadwick, p. 42).
[26] Irenaeus, *Against Heresies* 2.32.4, ANF 5.409.
[27] Ibid., 2.31.2, ANF 5.407.

These comments about people coming back from the dead find some support in Tertullian. In a poetic passage in his essay entitled *Prayer*, Tertullian discussed the same issue:

> Prayer alone overcomes God, but Christ has willed that it work no evil, upon it He has conferred all powers for good. Therefore, it has no power except to recall the souls of the dead from the very path of death, to make the weak recover, to heal the sick, to exorcise demons, to open prison doors, to loosen the chains of the innocent.[28]

The most striking phrase refers to people who had died. "Recall souls" could be another way of saying "raise them from the dead." The passage, however, says that these souls were on the "very path of death." Perhaps Tertullian meant his reader to understand that the people were not quite dead. On the other hand, it may all be just poetry. Tertullian was certainly capable of getting carried away with words. Exaggeration and flights of fancy were not beyond him, even if he was well educated philosophically and legally and capable of the finest in logical discourse.

Irenaeus is different. He emerges from his writing as a down-to-earth, sober person. Wherever his information about the theological systems he criticized can be checked, it turns out to be accurate. Even when he was discussing avowed enemies, he kept the facts straight. This makes it hard to dismiss too quickly what he said about the dead being raised.

Two mitigating observations must be made. First, there are currently frequent references to "near-death" experiences in which people who are judged to be clinically dead in fact retain consciousness and subsequently "come back to life." Second, Finucane demonstrates that people living in antiquity and in the Middle Ages often had difficulty determining who was truly dead.[29] Perhaps at least some of the alleged resurrections can be accounted for in these terms.

---

[28] Tertullian, *Prayer* 29, FC 4.187.
[29] Finucane, "Use and Abuse of Medieval Miracles," 7.

Pastoral Reflections

My last observation will move us in a different direction. Up to this point exorcisms, healings, and even resurrections have been under review. But the story does not end there.

In the middle of the third century, a plague swept North Africa. Along with many others, large numbers of Christians became sick and died. Falling victim to this plague violated their understanding of God's protection. After all, were they not the children of God? How could they fall prey to the same afflictions as the wicked? Like so many others through the generations, these people in crisis turned to their pastor to help them make sense of the situation. Cyprian, bishop of Carthage, theologian, and eventually martyr, reached out as a shepherd of souls in his essay entitled *Mortality*.

Some of his early comments are more heavy-handed than those I would be inclined to make. For example, he said, "You, who cannot endure to lose your son by the law and lot of mortality, what would you do if you were bidden to slay your son?" [30] This allusion to Abraham and Isaac is nonetheless not very comforting. This kind of counsel would not give much solace to someone who was terrified that a child would be carried off by the plague or to someone whose child had already died. Maybe his words reflect a particular cultural and historical setting, but this is not the sort of approach most twentieth-century pastors would take.

As he continued, he became more helpful. He urged his flock not to be offended with God as a result of personal illness or the loss of loved ones. Rather, they should see tragedies as battles in which they could give proof of their faith.[31] Cyprian entered the thinking of Hebrews 11 here, with its account of the heroes of faith, many of whom suffered intensely.

---

[30] Cyprian, *Mortality* 12, ANF 5.472.
[31] Ibid.

He went so far as to argue that the sickness could be seen in a positive light: "All this contributes to the proof of faith."[32] In other words, "If you handle this problem properly, it can demonstrate the reality of your faith." Another passage gives a graphic description of the disease. The symptoms included diarrhea, vomiting, fever, gangrene, and the loss of sight, hearing, and the use of one's limbs. It would be hard to see any of that as positive. Clearly, faith would be necessary, and if these Christians were able to remain positive in the face of all that, they surely would be people of faith.

Further, Cyprian suggested that death through disease should be redefined. Anything so powerful as to take them out of a corrupt and collapsing world and into heaven, where family, friends, and apostles awaited, should not be seen as a complete tragedy.[33]

Certainly, healing was integral to early Christian experience, but it could not be taken for granted. The circumstances Cyprian faced in Carthage revealed an agonizing struggle with unanswered prayer and disappointment. As Christians in every generation, he and his flock had to come to grips with the full reality of their lives.

Conclusion

In chapter 1 I drew attention to the revolution that Jesus set in motion. There were the exorcisms, the healings, the transformation of human experience. There was a directness and a simplicity about it all. This was the power of God erupting among human beings—divine dynamism.

Much of that appears to have continued as the church moved beyond the first century and beyond the immediate area of Palestine. Of course, there were changes. Believers began to struggle with the challenge of figuring out what their faith

---

[32] Ibid., 14, FC 36.210.
[33] Ibid., 26, FC 36.220.

really was. Much of that task stemmed from the need to explain the good news to people from new cultures while wrestling with strange languages and unaccustomed ways of looking at the world. Amazingly, it was done with a New Testament that was just in the process of being formed, and without the benefit of the theological textbooks and manuals that we take for granted. It should be no surprise that there were some dramatic mistakes. In fact, it took them centuries to get sorted out.

Organization was a major concern as well. Ever so slowly they worked out patterns of leadership that would help them to live together and reach out to others. And a constant backdrop to it all was the very real possibility of getting into trouble with the government. The 225 years between the end of the first century and the Council of Nicaea were challenging indeed for Christians.

In the midst of the turmoil, however, there was life. They were sure that the Jesus they were reading about in the Gospels still lived among them, confronting evil in all of its manifestations. The healings, the exorcisms, and the resurrections told them that he was still there.

3

J. C. Blumhardt

"JESUS IS VICTOR!"

Events that he was convinced were miracles led Johann Christoph Blumhardt to precisely the same conclusion that ante-Nicene Christians had reached: Jesus is present in the church to remedy human need. Blumhardt died in 1880 after operating a *Kurhaus* (healing center) in Bad Boll, east of Stuttgart, Germany, for almost thirty years.[1] Blumhardt's place in history was secured by the healing ministry that I will discuss, but he was also one of only three men whom the famous Swiss theologian Karl Barth called "my mentors."[2]

Born in Stuttgart on July 16, 1805, Blumhardt's student career took him to Tübingen for five years. E. G. Rüsch points out that while there he became thoroughly familiar with all

---

[1] See Paul Ernst, ed., *Johann Christoph Blumhardt*, in *Johann Christoph Blumhardt, Gesammelte Werke: Schriften, Verkündigung, Briefe* (Blätter aus Bad Boll, series 2, 9 vols.; ed. G. Schäfer; Göttingen: Vandenhoeck & Ruprecht, 1968–1979) vol. 1, v; and Gerhard Schäfer, "Johann Christoph Blumhardt: Bausteine zu einer Biographie," in *Johann Christoph Blumhardt: Leuchtende Liebe zu den Menschen: Beiträge zu Leben und Werk* (Stuttgart: J. F. Steinkopf, 1981) 37. Blumhardt had been able to purchase the *Kurhaus* from King Wilhelm I of Württemburg at a favorable price. It is still a very impressive building. See Blumhardt to Luise von Scheibler, Möttlingen, Nov. 24, 1851, in *Johann Christoph Blumhardt: Ein Brevier* (ed. Dieter Ising; Göttingen: Vandenhoeck & Ruprecht, 1991) 46; and Blumhardt to Christian Gottlob Barth, Möttlingen, April 15, 1852, ibid., 47.

[2] Barth to Rector Eberhard Bethge, Basel, 22 May 1967, in *Letters, 1961–1968* (ed. Jürgen Fangmeier and Hinrich Stoevesandt; trans. and ed. G. W. Bromiley; Grand Rapids: Eerdmans, 1981) 251. The others were H. Kutter and L. Ragaz.

parts of the theological spectrum, including the works of his older contemporary F. D. E. Schleiermacher.[3] His library, preserved at the European headquarters of the Brüder-Unität, suggests that his theological interests continued to be wide throughout the later part of his life as well.[4]

This breadth of study and reading showed itself in Blumhardt's theological reflections, but it was revealed in other ways also. For instance, some of the answers on exams he took to qualify for the ministry are in Latin.[5] In addition, Paul Ernst notes that there is sophistication in the way he discussed Scripture.[6]

His ministerial career, which extended from 1829 to 1880,[7] included stops at Durrmenz (1829–30), Basel (1830–37), and Iptingen (1837).[8] He was installed at Möttlingen on September 23, 1838, in a parish with 874 members.[9] Although Blumhardt did not identify closely with the state church, while at Bad Boll he was elected twice to attend the national synod. His sincere love for worship is reflected in a proposal of his that led to the publication of a new hymnbook.[10]

---

[3] E. G. Rüsch, "Bemerkungen zum theologischen Studiengang J. C. Blumhardts," *Theologische Zeitschrift* 13 (1957) 108.

[4] Siegfried Bayer at that library cautions, however, that not all of the books may be Blumhardt's (interview by author, Bad Boll, Germany, August 1, 1990). Some were so expensive that they may have been purchased by the King of Württemburg and then left behind when Blumhardt bought the *Kurhaus*.

[5] Johann Christoph Blumhardt, Archiv, A27, 267, Überkirchenrat, Württemburgischen Landeskirche, Stuttgart.

[6] Ernst, *Blumhardt*, in Schäfer, ed., *Gesammelte Werke*, series 2, 1970, vol. 4, 257. For example, Blumhardt compares the parallel readings Matt 20:29, Mark 10:46, and Luke 18:35, noting differences.

[7] Blumhardt, Archiv, A27, 267.

[8] Schäfer, "Bausteine," 25; Wayne Detzler, "Blumhardt, Johann Christoph (1805–1880)," in *The New International Dictionary of the Christian Church* (ed. J. D. Douglas, E. E. Cairns, and J. E. Ruark; Grand Rapids: Zondervan, 1974) 138; G. Schäfer, ed., *Johann Christoph Blumhardt: Der Kampf im Möttlingen*, in Schäfer, ed., *Gesammelte Werke*, series 1, 1979, vol. 1, ix.

[9] Blumhardt, Archiv, A27, 267. See also E. L. Blumhofer, "Jesus Is Victor: A Study in the Life of Johann Christoph Blumhardt," *Paraclete* 19 (2, 1985) 1.

[10] Schäfer, "Bausteine," 23.

Unlike his son, Christoph,[11] who led the ministry at Bad Boll for a time but later wed his doctrine of the end times to the Social Democratic Party in a political career, Johann Christoph Blumhardt has attracted attention almost exclusively because of his reputation as a healer and an exorcist. His background helped create a unique place for him among those who have carried out this kind of ministry.

Only two other modern figures in this study had thorough theological educations: John Wimber[12] and Charles de Siebenthal.[13] When Blumhardt launched into his healing ministry, he did it with a detailed understanding of the theological currents of his day, from pietism to rationalism, and of the emerging critical scientific tradition.[14] This background must have contributed significantly to the stability many have noted in Blumhardt's healing ministry.[15]

---

[11] Upon his father's death in 1880, leadership at Bad Boll passed to Christoph. Like his father, he had been used as an agent of healing, but he soon came to the conviction that the societal healing that he saw as necessary required a political approach. He held elected office from 1900 until 1906 (Gerhard Schäfer, interview by author, Stuttgart, Germany, August 2, 1990), having stopped praying for the sick about the time he was first elected (Christian Tröbst, interview by author, Bad Boll, Germany, August 1, 1990). He took up a number of causes that were politically unpopular but religiously understandable—the difficulties of the poor laboring class, for example, which cost him the support of the aristocracy for the ministry he continued to lead. In 1920, after Christoph's death, the Blumhardt family gave the *Kurhaus* to the Evangelische Akademie Bad Boll and the Hernhutter Brüder-Unität, a religious denomination that grew out of the work of Count Nikolaus Ludwig von Zinzendorf (1700–1760) (Gerhard Sauter, "Zur Blumhardt-Forschung," *Evangelische Theologie* 43 [1983] 380). It was reopened as a *Kurhaus* after World War II, and it currently is served by five medical doctors and has daily evening services (Tröbst, interview, August 1, 1990).

[12] See below, pp. 46–59.

[13] See below, pp. 154–66.

[14] Rüsch, "Bemerkungen," 108.

[15] See Walter Nigg, "Johann Christoph Blumhardt: Ein Heiliger der Neuzeit," in *Wie heilig ist der Mensch?* (ed. Wolfgang Böhme; Herrenalber Texte 69; Baden: Evangelische Akademie, 1986) 38; Rüsch, "Bemerkungen," 108;

On the surface, it is surprising that a person coming from this intellectual environment found his way into a healing ministry. Karl Barth suggests that Blumhardt came to understand the loathing Jesus felt toward the destructiveness of evil as he stood at Lazarus's grave (John 11) and that he took up the struggle against its forces "because he was bound and liberated by the royal repugnance of Jesus."[16] For Barth, Blumhardt did not choose a healing ministry; he was called to it. That is probably how Blumhardt saw it, too.

In light of Blumhardt's intellectual interests, it is important to examine the theological framework of his healing ministry.

The Theological Framework

Several theological topics were particularly important to Blumhardt. The first is eschatology, the doctrine of the end times. Blumhardt placed healing firmly in the context of God's self-disclosure. He argued that the course of history would include three "epochs of revelation."[17] During these periods God would show himself not only through words but also through action—specifically, through miracles. The miracles would gain authority for the message God was sharing about himself. The first two epochs were initiated by Moses and Jesus, respectively. The last would be the period when God's power would extend throughout the whole of creation.[18]

---

and Schäfer, *Kampf,* xi. When I was interviewing Siegfried Bayer, he seemed particularly concerned that I understand this.

[16] Karl Barth, *The Doctrine of Creation* (trans. A. T. MacKay et al.), vol. 3, part 4, of *Church Dogmatics* (ed. G. W. Bromiley and T. F. Torrance; Edinburgh: T. & T. Clark, 1961) 371.

[17] Johann Christoph Blumhardt, "Besprechung Wichtiger Glaubensfragen," in *Gesammelte Werke von Joh. Christoph Blumhardt* (part 3; ed. C. Blumhardt; Karlsruhe: Evangelischen Schriftenverein für Baden, 1888) 76, 77, 107.

[18] Ibid., 105. There are striking parallels between Blumhardt's thinking and my observations on Jesus' ministry. See above, pp. 3–12.

Christian Tröbst, who recently retired as pastor at the *Kurhaus* at Bad Bol, insists that Blumhardt awaited with keen anticipation the final manifestation of God's power and the end it would bring.[19] Barth credits Blumhardt with playing a major role in reminding the church of the orientation it should have toward the future.[20]

The second theological topic of great concern to Blumhardt was Christology. Like Martin Luther, Blumhardt built his theological system around Jesus. The slogan that best sums up Blumhardt's understanding of the Christian faith is *Jesus ist Sieger* (Jesus is victor).[21] The key Scripture passage is Matt 12:28: "If I drive out demons by the Spirit of God, then the kingdom of God has come upon you." Since Jesus was driving out demons by the Spirit of God, the kingdom of God had come. Jesus, who brought the kingdom, was the critical anchor for Blumhardt's call and preaching.

For Blumhardt, Christology was most important in healing. Jesus had access to irresistible power, providing healing not only for physical bodies, not only for whole persons,[22] but for the whole of creation.[23] He came carrying out a thoroughgoing revolution. The exorcisms and healings were to be seen as proof that the world had come under a new spiritual order.[24] Blumhardt

---

[19] Tröbst, interview, August 1, 1990.

[20] Karl Barth, *The Doctrine of God* (trans. T. H. L. Parker et al.), vol. 2, part 1 of *Church Dogmatics* (ed. G. W. Bromiley and T. F. Torrance; Edinburgh: T. & T. Clark, 1957) 633. Prominent Blumhardt scholar Gerhard Schäfer traces Blumhardt's interest in the end times to Johann Albrecht Bengel ("Bausteine," 24f.). Bengel (1687–1752), who spent the whole of his life in and around Stuttgart, has been identified as the originator of the modern discipline of New Testament text criticism. In the 1740s he wrote on eschatology (A. Hauck, "Bengel, Johann Albrecht," in *New Schaff-Herzog Encyclopedia of Religious Knowledge* [ed. S. M. Jackson; New York: Funk and Wagnalls, 1908] 2.52f.).

[21] Gerhard Schäfer, interview by author, Stuttgart, Germany, July 31, 1990.

[22] Blumhardt, "Besprechung," 77.

[23] Ibid., 80; and Schäfer, "Bausteine," 39.

[24] P. Ernst, *Blumhardt*, in Schäfer, ed. *Gesammelte Werke*, series 2, 1968, vol. 1, 347. With a spirit akin to Blumhardt's, Barth alludes to Christ and his

thought that the overcoming of demons and the healing should be seen as a reversal of *creatio ex nihilo* (creation out of nothing). If God could speak something into existence out of nothingness, then he could just as easily speak something out of existence into nothingness.[25] Evil was ontologically impotent.

Blumhardt also pointed to the end of time, when Jesus' superiority would be acknowledged by all.[26] Barth points out that Blumhardt's emphasis upon the absolute victoriousness of Jesus called attention to a concept that was unrecognized by his contemporaries inside or outside the church. It was "merely the content of his own particular perception and confession."[27]

Integrally related to Blumhardt's Christology is another important topic: the ministry of the Holy Spirit. Blumhardt made use of Matthew 12:28 in this context as well. He pointed out that the passage not only makes clear that the kingdom of God has come but also presents the Holy Spirit as the source of the power by which Jesus casts out demons.[28] Blumhardt also saw as particularly significant the exorcisms and healings that the church had continued to perform through the centuries. They were proof that supernatural gifts made available by the Holy Spirit were still present.[29] The Holy Spirit was inseparably involved in the ministry of Christ, whether in the incarnation or during the ongoing life of the church.

---

sacrificial death as the means by which God "marched against that realm on the left," overcame and bound its forces, including sickness, and brought the destroyer himself to destruction (*Doctrine of Creation*, 368).

[25] See M. T. Schulz, *Johann Christoph Blumhardt: Leben—Theologie—Verkündigung* (Arbeiten zur Pastoraltheologie 19, ed. Martin Fischer and Robert Frick; Göttingen: Vandenhoeck & Ruprecht, 1984) 69.

[26] Blumhardt, "Besprechung," 104.

[27] Karl Barth, *The Doctrine of Reconciliation* (trans. G. W. Bromiley), vol. 4, part 3, no. 1 of *Church Dogmatics* (ed. G. W. Bromiley and T. F. Torrance; Edinburgh: T. & T. Clark, 1961) 171.

[28] Blumhardt, "Besprechung," 80.

[29] Ibid., 92. See also Schäfer, "Bausteine," 39.

Blumhardt's five years in one of the world's leading theological institutions had a clear influence on his ideas. But some of what he met there probably clashed with assumptions he carried to the school out of his south German pietism, and it is unlikely that the rationalistic Tübingen taught him much about divine healing. Its professors probably regarded the very idea as more than mildly bizarre. When his healing ministry broke upon him, however, he had the tools for maintaining a perspective.

This, then, is the theological framework of Blumhardt's ministry of healing. But what moved him through the highly intellectual education that he had received to the powerfully dramatic ministry that ultimately evolved? What are the roots of his *Jesus ist Sieger?*

Background

Although the general contours of Blumhardt's theology are clear, the forces that gave it shape are not obvious. The importance of the formal studies at Tübingen and the significance of the Scriptures and pietism have been noted.[30] After tracing these influences on Blumhardt's theology up to 1837,[31] however, Gerhard Schäfer argues that the key formative influence lay elsewhere, in an exorcism.[32]

In her youth, Gottliebin Dittus had come into contact with witchcraft through an aunt.[33] The demonic played a growing

---

[30] See Schäfer, *Kampf,* x; Blumhofer, "Jesus Is Victor," 1; and Nigg, "Ein Heiliger," 35.

[31] Schäfer, "Bausteine," 22, 27, 28. Schäfer (p. 28) describes Blumhardt's view of reality as having four main components: (1) a God who was nearby and who repeatedly touched the hearts of people; (2) a Bible that was very important; (3) a view of repentance that saw it as leading to certainty regarding salvation and as providing a defense against the destruction caused by demons; (4) a conviction that one should pray for a new outpouring of the gifts of the Spirit.

[32] Ibid., 29; and Schäfer, interview, July 31, 1990.

[33] Schäfer, "Bausteine," 30.

role in her life until in desperation she turned to Blumhardt for help. For two years, beginning in December 1841, they struggled with her problem.[34] During this difficult period, Blumhardt developed the practice of praying for Gottliebin repeatedly.[35]

Trying to cope with the angst of not being able to achieve complete victory, he sought the counsel of Professor Wilhelm Stern, who reminded him of Mark 9:29. Some of the manuscript evidence for this passage contains a reference to fasting as well as prayer, and that prompted Blumhardt to give more attention to fasting.[36] The climax was reached about 2 a.m. on December 28, 1843. Blumhardt was praying for Gottliebin when he perceived that her sister Katharina had also come under demonic influence. He had turned to pray for her when suddenly she shrieked, "Jesus is victor! Jesus is victor!" and fell silent.[37] Blumhardt recorded that her screams were so loud that half the village was able to hear them. At that instant both women experienced complete freedom.

Blumhardt immediately sensed the importance of these events, and they became definitive for his theology of healing. As Schäfer puts it, this exorcism had significance for not only one sickroom but the whole cosmos.[38] Gottliebin's liberation was a microcosmic representation of the all-encompassing work of Christ. The lesson Blumhardt drew from this Möttlingen confrontation was clear and simple: Jesus was indeed victor

---

[34] The most interesting source for the incident is a report Blumhardt submitted to the Konsistorium (Presbytery) in Württemburg in August 1844. Blumhardt had already been the agent of deliverance for Gottliebin's brother and sister (Blumhofer, "Jesus is Victor," 2).

[35] But he was careful to point out that he never prayed with her without witnesses (Blumhardt, "Krankheitsgeschichte der G D in Möttlingen," in *Der Kampf im Möttlingen*, in Schäfer, ed. *Gesammelte Werke*, series 1, 1979, vol. 1, 41).

[36] "Krankheitsgeschichte," 49. Tröbst (interview, August 1, 1990) says it was a member of the Brüder-Unität, Johann Conrad Weiz, with whom Blumhardt consulted, and Schäfer agrees ("Bausteine," 24). Over that long a period of time, he could easily have talked with both.

[37] "Krankheitsgeschichte," 76.

[38] Schäfer, "Bausteine," 38.

over all manifestations of evil. The rest of his life and most of his son's were spent exploring the implications of this lesson.

While differing with Blumhardt over significant features of the exorcism, Barth accepts the fundamental lesson: "Blumhardt realized, in contrast to all older Protestantism and basically to the whole of Western Christendom, that in this name [Jesus] not just a psychic but a historical and even cosmic decision is made, and a question not only of disposition but of power is raised, which all those who confess it must face."[39] Barth himself seems to have been prepared to face that power. He acknowledges what Blumhardt affirmed in the experiences of Gottliebin Dittus—Jesus has the capability of dealing conclusively with sin and its consequences.[40]

Blumhardt became famous instantly, with people flocking to him from all parts of society in hopes of healing.[41] He tried very hard to control this surge of interest, hoping to prevent the healing from becoming too important. He wanted healings kept firmly in the context of the church's full message.[42]

The Work of Healing

There are marked contrasts between Blumhardt's healing ministry and the stereotype of the modern faith healer. Schäfer mentioned the superficial difference that contemporary healing ministries tend to be very noisy, whereas Blumhardt believed that God comes in silence.[43] But as Schäfer clearly saw,

---

[39] Barth, *Doctrine of Creation,* 371.

[40] Ibid. By contrast, for Rudolph Bultmann the events under discussion are an embarrassment: "The Blumhardt legends are to my mind preposterous" (*Kerygma and Myth: A Theological Debate* [ed. H. W. Bartsch; ed. and revised trans. R. H. Fuller; New York: Harper & Row, 1961] 120). As a man of the Enlightenment, committed to demythologizing the New Testament in order to render it inoffensive to modernity, he could not imagine learning anything from Blumhardt.

[41] Tröbst, interview, August 1, 1990.

[42] Blumhofer, "Jesus Is Victor," 3.

[43] Schäfer, interview, July 31, 1990. See also Ising, *Ein Brevier,* 14.

the differences are much greater than that, and they have to do with both practice and theology. No lines of people were filing past to be prayed for in Blumhardt's services. There were no healing services.[44] Blumhardt did not look for instantaneous healing,[45] and he referred people to doctors without hesitation.[46] He does not seem to have felt that he had to prove anything about himself or his ministry.

The verification of miracles was as much an issue with Blumhardt's ministry as it has been in connection with anyone else. M. T. Schulz draws attention to this. He also, however, acknowledges that there were many reports of physical and psychological healing associated with Blumhardt.[47] W. Guest, using eyewitness accounts of life at Bad Bol, refers to a professor of medicine from Tübingen who reviewed letters sent to Blumhardt by people who testified to having received healing. Apparently the professor was impressed by the accounts.[48]

One of the most striking features of the earlier healings that were associated with J. C. Blumhardt was that they occurred with very little attention being given to them. Once the flurry over the Dittus case had passed, people were often healed spontaneously, while listening to sermons, with no special acts or instructions on Blumhardt's part at all.[49] Sometimes people experienced healing while Blumhardt was praying for them privately after they had come to confess sin and seek

---

[44] See W. Guest, *Pastor Blumhardt and His Work*, with introduction by Rev. C. H. Blumhardt (London: Morgan and Scott, [1881]) 52; and Pierre Scherding, *Christoph Blumhardt et son père: Essai sur un mouvement de réalisme chrétien* (Etudes d'histoire et de philosophie religieuses 34; Paris: F. Alcan, 1937) 29.

[45] Tröbst, interview, August 1, 1990.

[46] Schäfer, interview, July 31, 1990. See also Frank D. Macchia, *Spirituality and Social Liberation: The Message of the Blumhardts in the Light of Wuerttemberg Pietism* (Pietist and Wesleyan Studies 4; ed. David Bundy and J. Steven O'Malley; Metuchen, N.J.: Scarecrow Press, 1993) 75.

[47] Schultz, *Leben-Theologie-Verkündigung*, 68.

[48] Guest, *Pastor Blumhardt*, 60.

[49] Schultz, *Leben-Theologie-Verkündigung*, 69.

God for forgiveness.[50] Blumhardt usually found out about the healings well after they had happened, and most of the time, he was taken by surprise. The point is that the healings took place coincidentally. People were healed when they were not being prayed for.

The situation changed once Blumhardt moved to Bad Boll. In that setting healing was very close to being the primary concern. But even there the approach can be characterized as understated. Blumhardt thought it was very important that people who were experiencing stress from illness of whatever kind should have access to an environment promoting rest and calmness.[51] They were invited to come to the *Kurhaus* and stay for as long as necessary. Although they were encouraged to participate in the devotional life of the house, the primary concern was to relieve stress.

The initiative in praying for the sick was left with those who needed prayer. All the residents of the *Kurhaus* dined together. After meals Blumhardt remained seated at the table, and people who wished prayer came and made appointments to see him. Later he met privately in his rooms with small groups or individuals in order to counsel them or pray with them.[52] The procedure was designed to revitalize people physically, emotionally, and spiritually. In this context many were prayed for, and many claimed healing.

Conclusion

There was a peacefulness about Blumhardt's approach to the problem of illness, whether physical, emotional, interpersonal, or global. He could say to the sick, "If you're healed, it's from God. If you're not, God will give you strength to bear it."[53]

---

[50] Blumhofer, "Jesus Is Victor," 3.
[51] Schäfer, interview, July 31, 1990.
[52] Ibid.
[53] Ibid.

There was patience, too. Perhaps this unflappable attitude was more than Blumhardt's son could put up with, and perhaps it partly explains his turning from his father's methods of responding to illness in favor of a more direct, political stance.

The elder Blumhardt's practice was rooted in his experience and his theology. He had been with Gottliebin Dittus when the demon had shrieked, "Jesus is victor!" The belief that Jesus had overcome evil became the dominant fact of his ministry. Jesus truly was irresistible. He had ushered in a kingdom destined to revolutionize not only human experience but the whole of creation. Now it was just a matter of exercising faith and waiting on God. Healing was just a small part of a much larger picture. One could be calm because "Jesus is victor!"

4

John Wimber
THE KEEPER OF THE VINEYARD

Within the Evangelical[1] branch of Christianity during recent years, few names have captured more interest or stimulated more controversy than that of John Wimber. The basic facts regarding him and the Vineyard movement can be reviewed quickly. Born in 1933, Wimber was converted to Christ when twenty-nine, and among other things, he has pastored and served as a church consultant.[2] In 1977 he and his congregation established ties with Chuck Smith's Calvary Chapel, but in 1982 he took his church, which had grown to a membership of two thousand, to Vineyard Christian Fellowship, led by

---

[1] It is important to define this term. George M. Marsden thinks Evangelicals are "people professing complete confidence in the Bible and preoccupied with the message of God's salvation of sinners through the death of Jesus Christ" (*Fundamentalism and American Culture: The Shaping of Twentieth-Century Evangelicalism, 1870–1925* [New York: Oxford University Press, 1980] 3). David Bebbington's understanding of the word is similar. He suggests that Evangelicals share four primary features: an emphasis upon conversion to Christ; a commitment to trying to bring people to Christ (evangelism); a deep reverence for the Bible, and a profound belief in the importance of Jesus' death as the means of providing salvation for human beings (*Evangelicalism in Modern Britain: A History from the 1730s to the 1980s* [London: Unwin Hyman, 1989] 1–19).

[2] John Wimber with Kevin Springer, *Power Evangelism* (San Francisco: Harper & Row, 1986) xv.

Kenn Gullikson.[3] Gullikson asked him to take over the organization. Wimber accepted, and under his leadership it has mushroomed.

In February 1991, Wimber and Vineyard—already using a 5,000-seat complex in Anaheim—bought property, including buildings, in Orange County, California, for about $20 million.[4] They began moving into the renovated facility, which contains space both for the congregation and for the headquarters of Vineyard Ministries International, in August 1991 and were completely settled by December of that year.[5] In November 1991 it was reported that a Mennonite missionary to Brazil, Luke Huber, had brought under the Vineyard umbrella 190 churches he had planted in the Amazon River Basin. This lifted the Vineyard Christian Fellowship to a total of five hundred churches internationally.[6] One of the most controversial of these is Metro Vineyard, formerly Kansas City Fellowship, pastored by Mike Bickle and featuring the prophetic ministries of Paul Cain and others. It joined the Vineyard in 1990 during a storm over its prophetic ministry, asking Wimber to assume oversight and direction.[7]

Wimber's critics have lodged many charges against him and the Vineyard movement. Wayne Grudem, who is a member of a Vineyard congregation, listed eight criticisms, including a failure to understand the gospel, negligence in preaching the cross, and the teaching of unorthodox doctrine, and then

---

[3] Les Parrott, III, and R. D. Perrin, "The New Denominations," *ChT*, March 11, 1991, 30.

[4] "The Vineyard Organization . . . ," *National and International Review of Religion*, February 25, 1991, 5.

[5] John Wimber, telephone interview by author, January 6, 1994.

[6] "John Wimber's Vineyard Movement . . . ," *National and International Review of Religion*, November 4, 1991, 4

[7] See John Wimber, "A Response to Pastor Ernie Gruen's Controversy with Kansas City Fellowship," *Equipping the Saints* 4 (4, 1990) 4–7, 14; Kevin Springer, "KCF Renamed the Metro Vineyard," *Equipping the Saints* 4 (4, 1990) 14; and Michael G. Maudlin, "Seers in the Heartland: Hot on the Trail of the Kansas City Prophets," *ChT*, January 14, 1991, 18.

attempted to counter each of them in turn.[8] Abandoning a policy of not being drawn into controversy with those opposing him, Wimber himself attempted a response to some of the criticism,[9] as did associate Jack Deere.[10] In their contributions to the discussions, Grudem and Deere also make reference to correspondence and conversations with leading antagonists.

All of this effort has fallen short of silencing the critics. For example, in 1992 Michael S. Horton edited *Power Religion: The Selling Out of the Evangelical Church*, which, among other things, again raised several of the earlier charges laid against the Vineyard.[11] Wimber continues to try to maintain identity

---

[8] Wayne Grudem, *The Vineyard's Response to "The Standard"* (Vineyard Position Paper 3; Anaheim: Association of Vineyard Churches, 1992) 2–23. Independently, James A. Beverley focuses on the same points of criticism and says, "Such charges are simply false" ("John Wimber, the Vineyard, and the Prophets: Listening for a Word from God," *Canadian Baptist*, March/April 1992, 35).

[9] John Wimber, *Why I Respond to Criticism* (Vineyard Position Paper 1; Anaheim: Association of Vineyard Churches, 1992).

[10] Jack Deere, *The Vineyard's Response to "The Briefing"* (Vineyard Position Paper 2; Anaheim: Association of Vineyard Churches, 1992).

[11] Michael S. Horton, ed., *Power Religion: The Selling Out of the Evangelical Church* (Chicago: Moody, 1992). The papers are of uneven quality. D. A. Carson's ("The Purpose of Signs and Wonders in the New Testament") is a carefully and reasonably argued discussion, while James Boice's ("A Better Way: The Power of the Word and Spirit") has a much harder edge. It is more of an attack than an examination of Wimber's ideas.

A curious feature of John Armstrong's contribution to the book is his suggestion that "the Vineyard movement urges a major paradigm shift from rationalism to a more Eastern worldview" ("In Search of Spiritual Power," 70). As an Evangelical, Armstrong could be expected to be uncomfortable with any weakening of the intellect in theology (see George M. Marsden, *Reforming Fundamentalism: Fuller Seminary and the New Evangelicalism* [Grand Rapids: Eerdmans, 1987] 6, 8), but in his characterization of Wimber's apparently less rationalistic position as "Eastern," Armstrong may be giving evidence of how deeply acculturated he himself is. It has been argued that Western culture tends to see itself as rational, virtuous, and mature, while viewing the East as irrational, depraved, and childlike (see Edward Said, *Orientalism* [New York: Vintage Books, 1978] 40, 108; and Thierry Hentsch, *Imagining the Middle East* [trans. Fred A. Reed; Montreal: Black Rose Books, 1992] 142, 147). Said and

with Evangelicalism, but not everyone within that community is pleased with his efforts.

Wimber first became well known in charismatic circles in the early 1980s as an agent of healing. This is ironic because, according to his report, initially he was shocked by the "healers," thinking their approach was "foolish, weird, or bizarre."[12] I include him in this study because of his healing ministry. Three aspects of Wimber's work provide the framework for the investigation.

The Kingdom of God

Central to Wimber's healing ministry has been the notion of the "already not yet" character of the kingdom of God. He met this concept in the work of George Eldon Ladd, then a professor at Fuller Theological Seminary.[13] His supporter Don Williams draws the concept from Oscar Cullmann,[14] it is found in some of the early work of Dunn,[15] and it is discussed magnificently by Günther Bornkamm.[16] From this understanding of the kingdom, recognized by a variety of scholars, Wimber extrapolated his notion that manifestations of healing will in fact herald the advent of the "not yet."

For Wimber, the kingdom of God is not a place. It is the rule and reign of God in the hearts of women and men.[17] Jesus brought the kingdom when he came into the world in his incarnation. He challenged the devil's mastery over people, and

---

Hentsch represent those who say that in the West "oriental" and "Eastern" have become epithets that are employed to signify inferiority. The tenor of Armstrong's paper suggests that he views Wimber's work as inferior.

[12] John Wimber with Kevin Springer, *Power Healing* (San Francisco: Harper & Row, 1987) 21.

[13] Wimber, *Power Evangelism*, xx.

[14] Don Williams, *Signs, Wonders, and the Kingdom of God* (Ann Arbor: Vine Books, 1989) 107.

[15] Dunn, "Spirit and Kingdom," 37, 39.

[16] Bornkamm, *Jesus of Nazareth*, 65–95.

[17] Wimber, *Power Evangelism*, 6ff.

he defeated him. Nonetheless, the battle continues, the ultimate prize being the lives of human beings.[18] The final outcome is not in doubt. The purpose of the miracles, the "signs and wonders" to which Wimber makes frequent reference, is to demonstrate the superiority of God's power.[19]

This thinking gave birth to Wimber and Kevin Springer's "Power Trilogy"—*Power Evangelism* (1986), *Power Healing* (1987), and *Power Encounters* (1988)—to which *Power Points* was added in 1991. I classify Wimber's approach to healing as confrontational. Tim Stafford describes the power encounters about which Wimber speaks as events "where the kingdom of God confronts the kingdom of this world."[20] Healings are occasions when the overwhelming power of the kingdom of God is demonstrated. There can be no question about the importance of this idea for Wimber's ministry.[21]

Wimber's application of the concept has been a lightning rod for criticism. He has been charged with a kind of dualism in which two gods are locked in a struggle for mastery in the world.[22] He has also run afoul of old-style dispensationalism for not recognizing that the ministry of the gifts of the Spirit, among which are the gifts of healing, ended with the era of the apostles.[23] The document produced by Fuller Theological Seminary to explain the cancellation of a course that Wimber had team-taught, "Signs, Wonders, and Church Growth," slides toward the same dispensationalism, a fact pointed out by

---

[18] Ibid., 14.

[19] Ibid., 89.

[20] Tim Stafford, "Testing the Wine from John Wimber's Vineyard," *ChT*, November 17, 1989, 35.

[21] Robert R. Recker, review of *Power Evangelism*, by John Wimber with Kevin Springer, *Urban Mission* 5 (1988) 43.

[22] Wallace Benn and Mark Burkill, "A Theological and Pastoral Critique of the Teachings of John Wimber," *Churchman: Journal of Anglican Theology* 101 (1987) 102.

[23] Ken Sarles, "An Appraisal of the Signs and Wonders Movement," *Bibliotheca Sacra* 145 (1988) 75.

Grant Wacker.[24] Criticized or not, the concept of the kingdom of God is central to John Wimber's thought about divine healing. It does not, however, stand alone.

The Teaching

Another prominent aspect of Wimber's program is that he teaches about the healing ministry. In this respect he is unique among those whom I have studied. Teaching is the primary thrust of many of the Vineyard's conferences, but it is also offered in other ways, including books, booklets, audiotapes, videotapes, and the monthly periodical *Equipping the Saints.* The Vineyard shows a high level of skill in the use of media.

The primary teacher is John Wimber. In this cursory review of some of his main ideas, I turn first to his definition of healing. He draws this from Linda Coleman, who says, "We prefer to restrict the term 'divine healing' to cases in which God intervenes directly, bypassing the natural processes of the body and the skills of doctors and nurses."[25]

Second, he discusses at some length the principles, values, and practices of healing.[26] The principles he mentions are:

1. God wants to heal the sick today.
2. Corporate ministry is important.
3. Trust in God is demonstrated in action.
4. All Christians are empowered by the Holy Spirit.
5. Loving relationships with brothers and sisters are important.
6. God wants to heal the whole person, not just specific conditions.

---

[24] Grant Wacker, "Wimber and Wonders—What about Miracles Today?" *Reformed Journal* 37 (1987) 18. See Lewis B. Smedes, ed., *Ministry and the Miraculous: A Case Study at Fuller Theological Seminary* (Pasadena: Fuller, 1987) 33.

[25] Linda Coleman, "Christian Healing: Is It Real?" *SCP [Spiritual Counterfeits Project] Journal* (August 1978) 42, quoted by Wimber, *Power Healing,* 7.

[26] Wimber, *Power Healing,* 170–86.

Third, Wimber deals with the question of whether healing is in the atonement. He cites J. Sidlow Baxter, who argues that healing is not *in* the atonement but occurs *through* the atonement. Wimber sees this as an effective way of avoiding the idea that all can and should expect and experience physical healing.[27]

Fourth, Wimber's ministry grants considerable attention to the question of demons; this has raised much concern.[28]

Part of the problem felt by people is that Wimber apparently introduces some new and awkward terms. He wants to lay aside the traditional expression "demon possession" as nonbiblical,[29] replacing it with "demonized" and "severe demonization." These are transliterations of one of the ways in which the Greek New Testament talks about the interactions between human beings and evil spirits. In fact, they had come into use in charismatic circles at least as early as the mid-1970s, partly in response to the space that Christian Growth Ministries (CGM), an independent charismatic ministry, and *New Wine*, its periodical, gave to the issue of demons.[30] Perhaps some of the difficulties Wimber has encountered by association arise from excesses in CGM's teaching.[31]

---

[27] Ibid., 154; and John Wimber, "Were We Healed at the Cross?" *Charisma*, May 1991, 80. I am not convinced that the change of prepositions achieves what Wimber and Baxter want it to.

[28] See Smedes, *Ministry and the Miraculous*, 72–74; and Donald M. Lewis, "An Historian's Assessment," in *Wonders and the Word: An Examination of the Issues Raised by John Wimber and the Vineyard Movement* (ed. J. R. Coggins and P. G. Hiebert; Winnipeg: Kindred Press, 1989) 58f.

[29] Wimber, *Power Healing*, 109.

[30] In 1972 *New Wine* carried at least five articles on the subject: two by Don Basham ("The Censored Message," June, 22, 23, 28–30; and "Right Now, in Your Own Room," August, 14–16); two by Derek Prince ("Can You Keep It?" September, 17–19; and "Exorcism," November, 12–17); and one by Hobart Freeman ("Rulers of Darkness," October, 10–14, 31).

[31] CGM taught that while Christians could not be possessed, they could be "afflicted" by demons, even to the extent of having a demon within their bodies or some parts of their personalities. In addition, CGM was one of the first Christian groups to make effective use of audio and video technology for

Wimber attempts to make a distinction between these two terms. He uses "demonized" to refer to various levels of "demonic bondage" showing itself in habitual patterns of temptation and moral weakness.[32] On the other hand, "severe demonization" means a state in which a person has fallen under at least occasional control of a demon or demons, leading to severely disturbed behavior, violence, and possibly illness.[33]

The greatest controversy surrounding his position on demons relates to their influence in the lives of Christians. He says,

> I am frequently asked if a Christian can be demon possessed. If the question means, "Can a demon own and have the absolute control of a Christian?" the answer is no. But, as I have already noted, the concept of possession is not biblical. A more biblical and significant question is: "Can a believer be demonized?" I believe that believers and nonbelievers alike can be demonized.[34] The solution for both the demonized and those suffering from severe demonization is deliverance through Christ.[35]

---

mass instruction; Vineyard may have learned something from it in this area, too, if only indirectly.

[32] Wimber, *Power Healing,* 110.

[33] Ibid., 110–13.

[34] Ibid., 114.

[35] Ibid., 123–25, 209f., 230–35. The words and actions of Wimber and others—both those influenced by him and those who are not—regarding those who are "demonized" (those suffering from the less severe condition) may be replays of teaching found in part of the Holiness movement in the late nineteenth century.

Some of the Holiness preachers offered complete liberty from sin through a specific experience of sanctification. By means of the experience one could gain complete victory over sin. Some taught that the experience not only freed from sin but also removed the sinful nature, that tendency in a person which leads him or her into sin. This was the doctrine of "eradication."

Wimber and others offer something very similar through the deliverance of those who are demonized. Deliverance breaks habitual patterns of temptation and removes moral weakness. In a moment one can be made holy and victorious. The similarity between this and the older idea of sanctification is striking. The parallel is made even closer by Wimber's own emphasis on holiness. John White observes, "So far as John Wimber is concerned, holiness is

Wimber's demonology also gives a place to what are called "territorial spirits." These are demons of great power who exert influence over wide geographical areas. There is some confusion in the Vineyard teaching about them. Jack Deere states that Wimber rejects the idea,[36] while in *Power Points* Wimber says he believes in them.[37] In conversation, Wimber clarified this by saying that he believes that a particular spirit, violence, for example, may dominate a specific area but that his approach would not be to engage in "strategic-level warfare" attempting to exorcise or bind that spirit. Rather, he would proceed by preaching, basing his talks on biblical passages dealing with the problem in question.[38]

Other aspects of Wimber's teaching have also drawn criticism. First, he has been charged with not giving any teaching to those who are not healed in his meetings.[39] But *Power Healing*, published in 1987, the same year as the article in which the charge was made, devotes twenty pages to doing exactly that.[40] Unfortunately, those who laid the charge, Wallace Benn and Mark Burkill, did not have the benefit of the book.

Second, Wacker faults Wimber for a complete absence of ethical and social concern in his teaching.[41] In fact, in *Power*

a major personal preoccupation and a constant theme of his domestic preaching" (*When the Spirit Comes with Power, Signs, and Wonders among God's People* [Downers Grove, Ill.: IVP, 1988] 179).

Both the Holiness and the Wimberian manifestations of this thinking may be a reflection of New World impatience. The desire for immediate gratification has long been a North American characteristic. It could be argued that it can be found in both the Holiness and the Wimberian approaches to dealing with sin. A process of gradual, incremental sanctification is not fully acceptable to people who are conditioned to expect everything else to happen instantly.

[36] Deere, *The Vineyard's Response*, 7.

[37] John Wimber with Kevin Springer, *Power Points* (San Francisco: Harper, 1991) 182f.

[38] Wimber, telephone interview, January 6, 1994.

[39] Benn and Burkill, "Critique," 106.

[40] Wimber, *Power Healing*, 147–66.

[41] Wacker, "Wimber and Wonders," 18.

Healing, again published the same year as Wacker's article, Wimber states that healing includes "breaking the hold of poverty and oppressive social structures."[42] A talk I heard Wimber give to his congregation in 1989 underlines this genuine social concern. For example, Wimber said that in the previous year the Vineyard had given $100,000–150,000 to caring for the poor and had distributed approximately 175,000 meals to those who needed them. Literature available to the congregation invited junior-high-aged young people to get involved in a program to help take food to the poor. In addition, at least one entire issue of *Equipping the Saints,* that of spring 1989, was devoted to articles dealing with social justice and poverty.

Teaching clearly plays a major role in Wimber's thinking, and the most important part of his educational program is what could be called the "democratization" of healing.

The ministries of many of the outstanding healing figures have been tied to them personally, for example, Brother André, Oral Roberts, and Kathryn Kuhlman. From another point of view, Pentecostals generally have always believed that any Christian can pray for the sick. What makes Wimber different is a conscious, sustained effort to help as many believers as possible to pray for the sick effectively. He devotes almost forty pages of *Power Healing* to careful, detailed instruction,[43] and he uses tapes to do the same thing. So, at the one and the same time, Wimber is trying not only to keep the Vineyard's ministry from being bound too closely to himself but also to coach people in healing to a degree rarely, if ever, done before. Whatever one thinks of the content of his teaching, one certainly must admit that Wimber is doing everything possible to share the ministry of healing with as many people as possible.

---

[42] Wimber, *Power Healing,* 38. This would correspond to what I have called the " 'wider' healing focus." See pp. xvi and 3–9 above.

[43] Ibid., 198–235.

The Impact

The last aspect of Wimber's work considered here is its impact. People have come to very different conclusions about the Vineyard and its keeper. Some—Don Lewis, for example—have attempted to acknowledge both the positive and the negative.[44] Others have judged it more harshly.

In an early review, Stafford charges Wimber with putting healing on the same level as preaching the gospel,[45] while Benn and Burkill think his ministry is distracting attention from that gospel.[46] Ken Sarles faults Wimber with exegeting his own experience rather than Scripture,[47] and Abraham Friesen finds the same spirit about him as animated the sixteenth-century fanatic Thomas Muentzer.[48] The final word goes to Roy Zuck, who dismisses Wimber and the Vineyard as unbiblical in approach and Pentecostal in practice![49] A veritable kiss of death.

Others are much more favorably inclined. John Vooys takes a basically positive stance;[50] John White, not surprisingly, sees Wimber and the Vineyard as a challenge to Evangelical Christianity to live by the Spirit rather than by programs;[51] and Stafford, in a later review article, suggests that Wimber is part of a movement that is a response, a correction, or perhaps a revolution in a society that has banished God to the margins of life.[52]

---

[44] Lewis, "An Historian's Assessment," 54–62.

[45] Stafford, "Testing the Wine," 21.

[46] Benn and Burkill, "Critique," 105.

[47] Sarles, "An Appraisal," 70.

[48] Abraham Friesen, "Wimber, Word and Spirit," in Coggins and Hiebert, *Wonders and the Word,* 36. This is one of the more bizarre comments made about Wimber.

[49] Roy Zuck, review of *Power Healing,* by John Wimber with Kevin Springer, *Bibliotheca Sacra* 145 (1988) 104.

[50] John Vooys, "Church Renewal for the 1980s?" in Coggins and Hiebert, *Wonders and the Word,* 65–68.

[51] White, *When the Spirit Comes,* 189.

[52] Tim Stafford, "The Fruit of the Vineyard," *ChT,* November 17, 1989, 36.

Last, Robert Recker sees the possibility of Wimber making a real contribution to the North American church as demonic activity becomes more a part of the culture.[53]

The jury is still out on Wimber and the Vineyard; it is much too early to make a valid assessment. There is no denying that disruptions have followed Wimber. Lives of congregations have been seriously affected as opinion regarding him has polarized. On the other hand, he seems to be theologically aware, and he and the other leaders of the Vineyard are interested in getting an adequate historical perspective on what they are doing.

The most immediate and direct impact of Wimber's ministry has been on those who have been involved in his conferences and seminars and in the Anaheim Vineyard. Perhaps it has also been the most dramatic. Many have testified to various kinds of healing. In order to get a picture of some participants' experience in these functions, we can turn to a remarkable study by British social anthropologist David Lewis of a conference held in Harrogate, England, November 3–6, 1986.

Lewis participated in the conference himself and distributed a questionnaire to all 2,470 registrants. He received back 1,890 usable questionnaires, 76.5 percent of those distributed. He analyzed the questionnaires, then followed up one hundred randomly selected respondents with personal visits. Where appropriate, he contacted medical doctors, requesting documentary evidence of the claimed physical healings. To my knowledge, there never has been a comparable study. His most pertinent results follow.[54]

First, there were 867 cases of prayer for physical healing. From the reports of the people prayed for, it was determined that 42 percent received little or no healing, 26 percent testified to a moderate amount of healing, and 32 percent claimed high or total healing. [55] Second, of the thirty-five cases of

---

[53] Recker, review of *Power Evangelism*, 45.

[54] Lewis, *Healing*. He also offers a most useful discussion of problems related to the verification of physical healings (pp. 44f.).

[55] Ibid., 22.

physical healing in the randomly selected group, twenty were still healed six to ten months after the conference when Lewis was able to interview them.[56] In other words, while many who were prayed for were not helped, the majority claimed to have benefited, and almost one-third said the improvement was dramatic or complete. Fifty-seven percent of those who had testified to a physical healing were still healed an extended time after the conference. It is clear that a significant number of people were healed as a result of the Harrogate conference, and Lewis found them rejoicing.

While 32 percent of those prayed for regarding physical healing claimed high or complete healing, the figure jumped to 50.5 percent of those who had been prayed for regarding inner healing (healing of various emotional problems) and to 68 percent of those who had been prayed for regarding deliverance.[57]

What about those who were prayed for and not healed or who thought they had been healed but then saw their improvement disappear? The question is important because one of the concerns frequently mentioned about ministries such as Wimber's is that they raise people's hopes only to dash them. Much speculation has centered on the damage that may be done by this kind of disappointment.

Lewis's study gives us information about some of these people, too, through statements given by them during his interviews with them. In no case is there any detectable bitterness toward God or John Wimber. Nor is there any evidence of doubt or spiritual damage of any sort. Mild disappointment appears, but nothing more.[58] The number interviewed is much too small to permit generalization about the whole group. The sparse evidence available, however, suggests that perhaps one does not need to worry as much about those not healed as some have.

---

[56] Ibid., 30f.
[57] Ibid., 125.
[58] Ibid., 32–43.

Conclusion

John Wimber and Vineyard Christian Fellowship have created a major stir within charismatic and Evangelical circles. As White pointed out several years ago,[59] the wider society still has not become aware of Wimber, although the circle of awareness is widening. If growth within the Vineyard continues at its present rate, many more will hear over the next few years.

The Vineyard experience has been dynamic in the richest sense of the word. It has moved through periods characterized by various emphases: healing and the gifts of the Spirit; demons and exorcism; prophecy. In each phase, the primary emphases of previous times have been carried over. As a movement, the Vineyard is showing a noteworthy theological flexibility. It may be that its exuberant worship is its constant, providing a framework for theological growth and discovery.

It is important to reiterate that the kingdom of God plays a key role in Wimber's thinking about healing. I have characterized his approach as confrontational. In his ministry, as in Blumhardt's and that of a large part of the early church, there is the assumption that victory over all forms of evil was won by Jesus Christ. This is the foundation of a confident proclamation of healing.

---

[59] White, *When the Spirit Comes*, 174.

Part 2

The Intercessory Model

SAINTS ON HIGH
BROTHER ANDRÉ
MARY OF MEDJUGORJE

The second model of healing I call *intercessory*. In this approach to finding cures, people look to God for help, but they tend to fix their hopes on special people who are commonly called "saints." Insofar as these men and women were recognized as saints by living lives of exemplary service and devotion, it is assumed that in death they were welcomed by God with particular favor. As special friends of God, it is believed that they have unusual influence with God. Those who have adopted an intercessory approach to healing believe that health can be restored by God through the intervention of one or other of the saints. I will examine the theory behind this model more fully in the chapters that follow.

Within Christianity, the intercessory model of healing has been most characteristic of the Orthodox and Roman Catholic Churches. Taking the history of the Christian church as a whole, it is also the approach that has been by far the most common. It is obviously tied very closely to the veneration of the saints. Although this intimate connection causes great difficulty for most Protestants, any study of divine healing that attempts to be comprehensive must take the intercessory model seriously.

As in the case of the first model, here attention will be focused on three different examples. Starting again with the early
church, the discussion will be launched in the second century
and carried through to the eighth, with a picture emerging that
is significantly different from the one already seen. The second
site is Montreal, Quebec, and the twentieth century. The center of attention will be the man known as Brother André and
St. Joseph's Oratory, an institution that grew up around him.
Last, I will consider a movement that sprang from Medjugorje,
a cluster of villages in Bosnia-Herzegovina. It is believed that
the Virgin Mary has been appearing there to a handful of
people almost daily since June 1981. These three examples of
the intercessory approach to healing differ from each other in
many ways, but together they illustrate very clearly its basic
thinking.

5

Saints on High
HELP FROM BEYOND

The practice of calling on someone else for help when one needs God's favor is firmly established in the life of the Christian church. It probably started naturally enough with people asking friends, or a person with an outstanding reputation for spirituality, to come and pray for them when they were sick, but it did not stop there. People went on to assume that deeply spiritual people could pray even more effectively once they died and entered the immediate presence of God.

This chapter will provide a historical context for the practice, demonstrating that these assumptions about healing achieved their popularity very early. It will also become clear that they are tied to stratification within the Christian community.

The Apocryphal Acts of the Apostles

Up to this point, when we have been looking at material from the early church, I have confined the discussion to official circles—Justin, the philosopher turned interpreter of Christianity; Cyprian, who stated, "One cannot have God as Father who does not have the Church as Mother"; and the brilliant Origen. These persons are known because they wrote and because the church passed their work on. They led the church, promoted it, defended it, suffered for it, and shaped it. But they were far from being the whole church.

Behind them were hosts of ordinary Christians. They left no particular distinguishing marks. They struggled with poverty, were uneducated, and led shockingly insecure lives socially. But they were the backbone of the church, and as at all points in history, they made up its bulk. Yet almost nothing is known of them. The apocryphal acts of the apostles open an avenue to them.

Along with the apocryphal gospels, the apocryphal acts of the apostles form a distinct category of early Christian literature. Those gospels, of course, were modeled after the four Gospels, but the apocryphal acts of the apostles bear little resemblance to the New Testament Acts of the Apostles. The word "apocryphal" comes from the Greek word ἀπόκρυφον, *apocryphon*, meaning "hidden."

I focus on four of the earliest apocryphal acts of the apostles, those carrying the names of Peter, Paul, Thomas, and John. They were written between AD 150 and 230,[1] possibly by women,[2] but there is no consensus on where. They seem to

---

[1] See Dennis R. MacDonald, "Introduction: The Forgotten Novels of the Early Church," *Semeia* 38 (1986) 4; E. Junod, "Créations romanesques et traditions ecclésiastiques dans les actes apocryphes des apôtres—l'alternative fiction romanesque–vérité historique: Une impasse," *Augustinianum* 23 (1983) 271; and Stevan L. Davies, *The Revolt of the Widows: The Social World of the Apocryphal Acts* (New York: Winston/Seabury, 1980) 8.

[2] Even a casual reading shows how important women are in the apocryphal acts of the apostles. They are typically beautiful and often socially well placed. The usual pattern is that they accept an apostle's teaching and then get into trouble by breaking engagements with fiancés or terminating sexual relations with everyone, including their husbands.

Davies (*Revolt of the Widows*, 89–109) constructs a strong case in favor of female authorship of the apocryphal acts of the apostles. His opinion has gained support from both Dennis R. MacDonald (*Legend and Apostle: The Battle for Paul in Story and Canon* [Philadelphia: Westminster, 1983] 36) and Willy Rordorf ("Tradition and Composition in the *Acts of Thecla*: The State of the Question," *Semeia* 38 [1986] 52).

On the other hand, see two works by Jean-Daniel Kaestli: "Les actes apocryphes et la reconstitution de l'histoire des femmes dans le christianisme ancien," *Foi et vie* 88 (1989) 71–79; idem, "Fiction littéraire et réalité sociale:

have been a kind of novel, written to convey a spiritual message, perhaps even to evangelize.[3]

Questions must be raised about how this apocryphal material is to be used historically. It never made it into the mainstream of the official life of the church, and it is neither inspired nor authoritative. The stories encountered are often wild or silly—bedbugs that take orders, smoked fish that comes back to life—and not infrequently offensive.[4] Why spend any time with this material at all?

A comment made by M. R. James points toward an answer:

> If they [the apocryphal documents] are not good sources of history in one sense, they are in another. They record the imaginations, hopes, and fears of the men who wrote them; they show what was acceptable to the unlearned Christians of the first ages, what interested them, what they admired, what ideals of conduct they cherished for this life, what they thought they would find in the next."[5]

Que peut-on savoir de la place des femmes dans le milieu de production des actes apocryphes des apôtres?" *La fable apocryphe*, vol. 1 of *Apocrypha: Le champ des apocryphes, 1990* (ed. Pierre Geoltrain et al.; Turnhout: Brepols, 1990) 294; Kate Cooper, "Apostles, Ascetic Women, and Questions of Audience: New Reflections on the Rhetoric of Gender in the Apocryphal New Testament," *SBL Seminar Papers, 1992* (Atlanta: Scholars, 1992) 147–53.

[3] See W. Schneemelcher, *NTAp* 2.82; MacDonald, "Introduction," 1; Jean-Daniel Kaestli, "Les principales orientations de la recherche sur les actes apocryphes des apôtres," in *Les actes apocryphes des apôtres: Christianisme et monde païen* (Publications de la Faculté de Théologie de l'Université de Genève 4; Geneva: Labor et Fides, 1981) 67; François Bovon and Eric Junod, "Reading the Apocryphal Acts of the Apostles," *Semeia* 38 (1986) 168; Gérard Poupon, "L'accusation de magie dans les actes apocryphes," in *Les actes apocryphes des apôtres: Christianisme et monde païen*, 85; and Eric Junod and Jean-Daniel Kaestli, *Acta Iohannis*, CChr, Series Apocryphorum 1, 685.

[4] One woman is twice humiliated by being dragged naked into a stadium to face execution (*APl* 22, *NTAp* 2.243; *APl* 33–36, *NTAp* 2.245), and there is an instance of necrophilia (*AJn* 70–77, *NTAp* 2.196–99).

[5] Montague R. James, *The Apocryphal New Testament* (Oxford: Clarendon, 1924) xiii. These ideas are echoed by Bruce Metzger (*An Introduction to the Apocrypha* [New York: Oxford University Press, 1957] 263) and by Bovon and Junod ("Reading the Apocryphal Acts," 163).

More recently, R. McL. Wilson supported this opinion, saying that the significance of the whole New Testament apocrypha lies "in the glimpses it affords of trends and tendencies in popular Christianity of the early centuries."[6]

The historical value of the apocryphal acts of the apostles does not lie in what they say about the apostles but in what the authors unconsciously reveal about themselves and their readers. The apocryphal acts of the apostles flesh out the traditional picture of early Christianity, which comes to us through the "big men"—Irenaeus and the others. They let us into the lives of unempowered "little people," both women and men.

The apocryphal acts of the apostles contain a great deal of evidence demonstrating that their authors and readers were very interested in the miraculous. They also show that the miraculous was almost invariably linked to apostles. In spite of what seems to have been the reality among Christians,[7] in the popular mind by the mid–second century extraordinary acts had come to be seen as the work of extraordinary people. The apostles were the "stars" or heroes of ordinary Christians. Their ability to perform miracles surfaces in many contexts.

In the apocryphal acts of the apostles, frequently the apostles provide miracles in order to bring people to faith.[8] For example, in Ephesus John met great unbelief. To counter it, he ordered that all elderly women in the city should be taken to the theater. When this had been done, John arose to address the crowd, saying,

---

[6] R. McL. Wilson, "New Testament Apocrypha," *The New Testament and Its Modern Interpreters* (ed. E. J. Epp and G. W. MacRae; Philadelphia: Fortress, 1989) 429. See also Schneemelcher, *NTAp* 2.85.

[7] See above, pp. 26–28.

[8] Paul Achtemeier, "Jesus and the Disciples as Miracle Workers in the Apocryphal New Testament," in *Aspects of Religious Propaganda in Judaism and Early Christianity* (ed. Elisabeth Schüssler Fiorenza; South Bend: Notre Dame University Press, 1976) 171. Bovon and Junod make a similar observation ("Reading the Apocryphal Acts," 168).

Jesus Christ, whom I preach, in his mercy and goodness is converting you all, you who are held fast in unbelief and enslaved by shameful desires; and through me he wills to deliver you from your error; and by his power I will convict even your praetor's disbelief, by raising up these women who are lying before you—you see what a state, and what sicknesses they are in. And this is not possible for me now <. . .> if they *perish*(?) <. . .> , and will not be removed by healings(?).[9]

The author presents the healings that followed as a means of igniting faith.

The miraculous also appears in the apostolic arsenal in contests in which the prize is the acknowledged superiority of their or their opponent's doctrine. One of the most dramatic accounts is set in Rome and involves the apostle Peter and the magician Simon.[10]

The account says that Simon, defeated in Judaea, journeyed to Rome, where he charmed local Christians by performing various kinds of miracles. In response, the Lord summoned Peter to go to Rome, and the apostle obeyed immediately. A Roman official, the prefect Agrippa, put forward one of his young men, with instructions to Simon to kill the man and with instructions to Peter to bring him back to life.

Simon carried out his part of the test, killing the boy by simply speaking into his ear. The challenge was then Peter's. The apostle rose to the occasion, saying,

"Now that God and my Lord Jesus Christ is tested among you, he is doing such signs and wonders through me for the conversion of his sinners. And now in the sight of them all, O Lord, in thy power raise up through my voice the man whom Simon killed with his touch!" And Peter said to the boy's master, "Come, take his right hand, and you shall have him alive and (able to) walk with you." And Agrippa the prefect ran and came to the boy and taking his hand restored him to life.[11]

The crowd's response: "There is but one God, the one God of Peter!" What else could they say? Not only did miracles

---

[9] AJn 33, NTAp 2.177.
[10] See Acts 8:14–24.
[11] APt 26, NTAp 2.308.

open the way for the gospel; they also demonstrated the superiority of the apostles' message.

Miracles were also associated in a variety of ways with sexual purity, one of the apocryphal acts of the apostles' central themes, and as usual the apostles perform them. For instance, on one occasion the apostle Thomas is said to have exorcised a demon who had troubled a woman sexually at night for five years,[12] and on another he was called upon to participate in a resurrection and a healing when a young man killed his girlfriend, who had refused to enter into a pact of chastity with him.[13]

There can be no question about the apostles' superior positions in the apocryphal acts of the apostles nor about the authors' consistency in presenting them as agents of the miraculous. The authors, however, located the source of the apostles' miraculous powers outside them, in Jesus Christ. In this, these authors were clearly in step with their better-known contemporaries whom we have already examined and who represented the official church. Achtemeier summarizes the apocryphal acts of the apostles' assumption about the source of healing power: "In the great majority of cases . . . it is clearly by the power of Jesus that the disciples are able to perform their miracles."[14] Paul healed Hermocrates of dropsy "through the name of Jesus Christ,"[15] and John healed Cleopatra "in the name of Jesus Christ."[16] For the authors of these stories, power lay in the person of Jesus Christ.

While there certainly are places where they went beyond the credible—Peter and the talking dog,[17] for example—these

---

[12] ATh 42–46, NTAp 2.357f.

[13] ATh 51–58, NTAp 2.360–63. Here it is a young man who accepts Thomas's message and desires sexual purity. This is unusual in the apocryphal acts of the apostles; typically, those struggling to remain pure are female.

[14] Achtemeier, "Jesus and the Disciples," 170.

[15] APl 4, NTAp 2.247.

[16] AJn 22, NTAp 2.174.

[17] APt 9, NTAp 2.296.

authors typically presented the apostles' miracles with a direct-ness that is reminiscent of the New Testament. Poupon sug-gests that the way in which the New Testament talks about the miraculous may have been a controlling factor in the way in which the miraculous appeared in at least the earlier apocry-phal acts of the apostles.[18]

These authors also apparently wanted to distance them-selves from anything that would give grounds to charges of magic and sorcery.[19] The author of the *Acts of John* went so far as to have John appear naked so that everyone would know that he had nothing "up his sleeve" when he performed mir-acles.[20] For these early Christian writers, the power to perform the supernatural resided in God.

The apocryphal acts of the apostles are certainly uncon-ventional. In the fifth century, Pope Leo the Great took a very clear position toward them: "The apocryphal scriptures, which, under the names of the Apostles, form a nursery-ground for many falsehoods, are not only to be proscribed, but also taken away altogether and burnt to ashes in the fire."[21] These are strong words, but the danger is gone for the modern reader. The apocryphal material is considered strange and presents no per-sonal threat. The apocryphal acts of the apostles are not to be regarded as sources of instruction about Christian living, nor as an infallible deposit of otherwise unknown information about the apostles. They are, however, invaluable windows into the

---

[18] Poupon, "L'accusation," 84.

[19] See Achtemeier, "Jesus and the Disciples," 169.

[20] *AJn* 31, *NTAp* 2.177.

[21] Leo the Great, *Letter* 15; *NPNF*[2] 12.26. Whether Leo wrote this letter has been a matter of dispute. Hunt did not translate this letter, as K. Künstle had denied Leo's authorship (*Antipriscilliana: Dogmengeschichtliche Untersuchungen und Texte aus dem Streite gegen Priscillians Irrlehre* [Freiburg; Herder, 1905] 117–26, as cited by Edmund Hunt in Leo the Great, *Letters*, FC 34.67). Sixty years later, however, P. B. Vollmann responded effectively to Künstle, arguing persuasively for his authorship (*Studien zum Priszillianismus* [Kirchengeschichtliche Quellen und Studien 7, ed. H. S. Brechter; St. Ottil-ien: Eos, 1965] 140f.).

souls and lives of ordinary Christians. In the New Testament, the apostles already appeared as special people through their relationship with Jesus. By the second half of the second century, their status had grown dramatically in the minds of most Christians. They had come to be seen as people who had lived truly exceptional spiritual lives, and many had become accustomed to associating the marvelous and the miraculous with them. This laid the foundation for the intercessory approach to healing.

An Era of Wonder-Workers

I have drawn attention to differences with regard to healing between the institutional life of the church, represented by Cyprian and the others, and that part of the church we see in the apocryphal acts of the apostles—between "official" Christianity and "popular." In the former, healing was relatively simple and direct. It was also widely distributed; that is, it could come through almost anyone, clerical or lay.[22] By contrast, in the latter, healing came to be associated with leading personalities. In the second part of this discussion, the period c. AD 320 to c. AD 750, it will become clear that the general approach Christians took to healing is much more like that of the popular strata of the church than the official.

This could be understood as a demonstration of the power of the people. The leaders of a group—in the church, the bishops (or their equivalents) and theologians—can never function without reference to those whom they lead. Their policies and plans must eventually find acceptance with these people. It may be easy or it may be difficult for "the followers" to make their voices heard, but in time they usually do. Leaders may be innovative and clear-sighted or irresponsible, but short of calling upon armed force, they will only be able to go as far as the people will permit them to go. In this instance, those whom people were prepared to support were powerful individuals

[22] See above, pp. 26–28.

through whom God appeared to be working. They became the heroes as the church moved into the Middle Ages.[23]

There is no question about the importance of the miraculous in the minds of Christians living before AD 750. Augustine (354–430) could say, "So . . . sacraments of initiation and great works of miracles are necessary . . . [in order to bring into the church] ignorant men and infidels."[24] Gorgonia, a sister of Gregory of Nazianzus (329?–389?), was neither an ignorant male nor an unbeliever, but the ideas of sacrament and miracle came together in her thinking. After struggling for a long time with a debilitating illness, she crept into her church at night and dragged herself to the altar. Once there, she took some of the bread and wine that had been left over from the last Lord's Supper and rubbed it over her body. The result to which she testified was almost instant healing.[25]

The connection between the Eucharist and healing notwithstanding, Christians of that era usually looked to special individuals for miracles. The writings of John Cassian (360?–435?) provide an example. Abbot Abraham, a monk who usually lived in the desert near Alexandria, was confronted by a woman whose child was dying. The mother's milk had not come in, so she could not nurse the baby. The holy man responded by giving her a cup of water to drink, over which he had made the sign of the cross. Immediately her breasts filled and she was able to nurse the child. On another occasion, the Abbot Abraham healed a man's withered legs by pulling them.[26]

As dramatic as the acts performed by Abbot Abraham were, the person I am going to focus upon here is Martin of

---

[23] See Jaroslav Pelikan (*Historical Theology: Continuity and Change in Christian Doctrine* [Theological Resources 4; New York: Corpus, 1971] 96–114) for a brilliant discussion of the dynamic interaction between church life and the development of doctrine and practice.

[24] Augustine, *Confessions* 12.27, NPNF[1] 1.204.

[25] Gregory Nazianzus, *On His Sister, St. Gorgonia* 17, 18, FC 22.113f.

[26] John Cassian, *Second Conference of Abbot Nesteros* 4, 5, NPNF[2] 11.447.

Tours (335?–400?), who, as his name implies, carried out most of his ministry in what is now France. He was particularly well served by his devoted follower and biographer, Sulpicius Severus (363?–420?). As a general comment, Sulpicius says, "In the matter of healing, Martin had such a power of grace within him that hardly anyone who was sick approached him without at once recovering health."[27] Elsewhere he refers to the many who were freed from the possession of demons by Martin's word or through the use of threads from his robe.[28]

In most cases there is a marvelous twist to the healing accounts that come from this era. They stand at some distance from the simplicity that characterized the ministry of Jesus and the activity of the official level of the ante-Nicene church. It is in this context that unusual details like those found in the apocryphal acts of the apostles begin to arise.

Martin's healing powers took care of a wide variety of illnesses. He healed a leper[29] and a boy who had been bitten by a snake.[30] Twice he used oil in healings, but he did not anoint the sick with it. Rather, he blessed it and then poured some into people's mouths. Both instances involved young girls. In the first case, the girl was healed of paralysis,[31] and in the second, a girl who had been unable to speak from birth was given speech.[32]

He also performed exorcisms. In the *Dialogues*, Sulpicius outlined a procedure Martin would occasionally follow. He would lock himself in a church building with those who were demon-possessed, and then he would lie on the floor and pray. The outcome was dramatic in the extreme. The demons in

---

[27] Sulpicius Severus, *Life of Saint Martin, Bishop and Confessor* 16, FC 7.124.

[28] Sulpicius Severus, *First Dialogue* 25, FC 7.195. This comment comes in the context of what can only be regarded as a game of one-upmanship between Sulpicius, who was promoting Martin, and Postumianus, who was supporting an Egyptian saint.

[29] Sulpicius Severus, *Life* 18, FC 7.127.

[30] Sulpicius Severus, *Second Dialogue* 2, FC 7.204.

[31] Sulpicius Severus, *Life* 16, FC 7.124f.

[32] Sulpicius Severus, *Third Dialogue* 2, FC 7.218.

people would begin to shriek and wail, identifying themselves and confessing their sins. While this was going on, some people would find themselves suspended upside down in mid-air.[33]

On one occasion a man who was under the control of a demon lunged at Martin, trying to bite him. Martin challenged the demon by thrusting his fingers into the man's mouth. The contact with the holy man was so unbearable that the demon had to escape. But because its exit through the mouth was shut off, the demon had to leave through the anus in the midst of a "discharge from the bowels."[34]

Such details are not found in the earlier material from the official side of the church, but they give an accurate impression of this genre of literature. One reason for the inclusion of such details in the accounts might have been a desire to elevate the dramatic nature of the hero's work as highly as possible.

Three occasions are also recorded when Martin raised the dead. On two of these, he lay on the bodies of dead men[35] and prayed, while on the third, he simply knelt and prayed beside a dead boy.[36] The recounting of these stories was obviously intended to demonstrate the power that resided in Martin. Nothing was beyond him.

These healings, exorcisms, and resurrections are unusual in themselves, but some passages in Sulpicius's accounts of Martin go even further. A girl was healed when a letter from Martin, totally unrelated to her illness, was laid on her chest;[37] others were healed by tying threads from his robes around their fingers or necks;[38] Paulinus, who had developed a cataract on an eye, was healed when Martin touched the eye with a small

---

[33] Sulpicius adds that while they were hanging in air, "their garments did not fall down over their faces, lest that part of their body which was exposed should give rise to shame" (*Third Dialogue* 6, FC 7.233f.).

[34] Sulpicius Severus, *Life* 17, FC 7.126.

[35] Ibid., 7, 8, FC 7.113, 114.

[36] Sulpicius, *Second Dialogue* 4, FC 7.208.

[37] Sulpicius Severus, *Life* 19, FC 7.128.

[38] Ibid., 18, FC 7.127.

sponge;[39] and Sulpicius was able to silence a barking dog by saying, "I command thee, in the name of Martin, to be silent."[40]

There is no critical analysis in this material. Martin was a hero of the first order, and Sulpicius's enthusiasm knew no bounds.[41] The atmosphere in this material is very similar to that in the apocryphal acts of the apostles. The primary difference is the transfer of devotion and wonder, earlier centered on the apostles, to others who seemed to have extraordinary relationships with God and unusual powers.

Ministry from beyond the Grave

The remarkable character of these individuals, and the responses they evoked, did not disappear in the grave. It was almost universally believed that the ministry of these "super-Christians" continued even after their deaths.[42]

---

[39] Ibid., 19, FC 7.128.

[40] Sulpicius Severus, *Third Dialogue* 3, FC 7.230.

[41] Commenting on Martin's life, Aline Rousselle offers some useful insights. She points out that in the non-Christian world of fourth-century France (Gaul), people who could afford it traveled to well-known healing sanctuaries to get relief from pain. She suggests that Martin's appeal lay in his substituting a man, himself, for a place: since he carried the power to heal with him, it was no longer necessary to visit the sanctuaries, but only to turn to him ("From Sanctuary to Miracle-Worker: Healing in Fourth-Century Gaul," in *Ritual, Religion, and the Sacred: Selections from the "Annales: Economies, sociétés, civilisations,"* Volume 7 [ed. Robert Forster and Orest Ranum; trans. Elborg Forester and P. M. Ranum; Baltimore and London: Johns Hopkins University Press, 1982] 124). On the assumption that "an unexpected and instantaneous cure reveals the psychosomatic aspect of a given illness," an assumption I do not share, Rousselle argues that Martin carried out his healing by removing the effects of a profound and widespread anxiety that had been spreading through the Roman world since the third century: by becoming a father figure for them, he gave people a sense of security (p. 123).

[42] Comments of John Foster on the process by which people came to expect ministry from some of the deceased are useful. He points, first, to the fact that the ending of persecution of Christians in the early fourth century led to an increase in reputations of holiness for those who had died heroically in the

The theological foundation for this thinking was formed fairly early. Ambrose, bishop of Milan (c. 339–397), cited John 14:12 and argued that since Christ had predicted that his followers would do even greater works than he himself had done, it would be failure to "believe in Christ" to deny that martyrs could continue to help people.[43] But almost four hundred years passed before the theory supporting the idea of posthumous ministry was developed to a greater degree.

John of Damascus carried the thinking furthest. He stated that these special people were soldiers for Christ, as demonstrated by their dying for him, and were also friends of Christ and sons and heirs of God. In addition, God himself dwelt in them.[44] Consequently, the martyrs and saints had to be honored. The honor the saints and martyrs received, however, did not rest with them. Rather, it passed over to the God whom they served.[45] Thus, when a saint was honored, it was God who was being elevated and worshipped. John also taught that the saints were not really dead, only sleeping. He thought that this truth was illustrated by the fact that they performed miracles.[46] That comes close to a circular argument: the martyrs and

---

recent past. Second, he suggests that with the new ease of entry to the church, people who had not separated themselves fully from their pagan backgrounds were able to identify themselves with Christianity, pointing to a situation in which theological assumptions were shaped decreasingly by the teaching of the church and increasingly by "pre-Christian" ideas ("Healing in the Early Church," *London and Holborn Review* 182 [1957] 302). For his part, Harnack saw this as a "full-blown imitation of the Aesculapius-cult within the church" (*Mission and Expansion,* 121).

[43] Ambrose, *Letter 61,* FC 26.383.

[44] John of Damascus, *An Exact Exposition of the Orthodox Faith* 4.15, FC 37.369. This may be a case where a person's assumptions governed his interpretation of Scripture, a not-unheard-of occurrence. As a man of his time, John believed martyrs not only lived on but could also influence human affairs. This led him to see John 1:12; 15:14, 15; Rom 8:17; 1 Cor 3:16; 2 Cor 3:17; and Gal 4:7 as applying especially, if not uniquely, to saints and martyrs, whereas they should be understood as applying to all believers.

[45] Ibid., 4.16, FC 37.372.

[46] Ibid., 4.15, FC 37.368f.

saints are alive, so they can perform miracles; the miracles they perform prove they are alive.

The saints, then, are intercessors. John of Damascus points out that in human affairs it is helpful if you can call upon "a patron to introduce you to a mortal king and speak to him on your behalf." In this essentially political framework, he identifies the saints as "patrons of the whole race . . . who make petitions to God in our behalf."[47]

The notion was that saints were especially pleasing to God while on earth, perhaps even giving their lives for him. Now that they are living in his presence, they are perfectly placed, both by their records of devotion and by their present closeness to God, to influence the way God deals with people who are still on earth. With all due respect, John of Damascus's comments present the saints as a group of spiritual lobbyists. They use their influence with God to benefit those whom they represent.

An "Official" View of Illness and Healing

The above viewpoint on sickness, healing, and health was embraced by the majority of people in the church; it attracted the rank and file and bore marked similarities to the atmosphere of the apocryphal acts of the apostles. But it was not the only kind of thinking present. Something quite different came from some leaders of the church.

First, a positive stance toward medicine is seen most clearly in Basil of Caesarea. In a letter to a physician, Eustathius, he stated that medicine should be ranked as first among the professions. After all, it often freed people from pain and made life worth living.[48] Dawe thinks this view toward medicine had been growing among Christians for some time,[49] and Mary Keenan argues that this was "the approach of choice"

---

[47] Ibid., 4.15, FC 37.369.
[48] Basil, *Letter 189*, FC 13.228.
[49] Dawe, "Attitude," 153f.

adopted by Christians in the late fourth century when they were confronted by illness. She comments that while it is widely recognized that Christians of that time believed in the reality of miraculous cures wrought in answer to prayer, what has not been stressed, but seemingly overlooked, is the equally convincing evidence that the miraculous cure was unusual and that recourse to such methods was had, in most instances, only after natural means had proved of no avail.[50] Although Keenan may go too far in saying that the miraculous cure was unusual, she correctly points out the well-established interest in medicine.

Nothing illustrates this interest more clearly than the hospital Basil founded just outside Caesarea, near the beginning of the church's opening of such institutions, called *xenodochia*, "houses or lodgings of strangers." Basil was motivated by the plight of the poor whom he saw around him. His response led to the creation of one facility after another until after his death his friend Gregory of Nazianzus could speak of "the new city" he had created:[51] the most destitute were welcome there, and it was a place "where disease is regarded in a religious light, and disaster is thought a blessing and sympathy is put to the test."[52] By making his hospital a priority, Basil provided a model that encouraged the wealthy of Caesarea to reach out to the destitute and stimulated the founding of other hospitals. Such institutions were established near Rome,[53] Antioch, and Bethlehem.[54]

In a letter to a government official, Basil is seen engaged in fund-raising on behalf of a hospital. There is an amusing contemporary ring to his words. To the official, who was about to receive a visit from a bishop, Basil wrote, "Without doubt, you will also deign to visit the almshouse in the district which

---

[50] Mary Keenan, "St. Gregory of Nazianzus and Early Byzantine Medicine," *Bulletin of the History of Medicine* 9 (1941) 24f.

[51] Gregory of Nazianzus, *Oration 43*, 63; NPNF[2] 7.416.

[52] Ibid., 63; NPNF[2] 7.416.

[53] Gregory the Great, *Epistle 4*, 15, 27, NPNF[2] 12.150, 153.

[54] Dawe, "Attitude," 162f.

is subject to him and to exempt it entirely from the tax. For, it has already pleased your colleague to free from taxation the petty possessions of the poor."[55] Basil made his request clear, let the official know what another official had done, and expressed confidence that action would be taken.

In the fourth century, the church claimed a place for itself in the field of medicine. While the people were focusing on special places commemorating special people in hopes of finding cures, some among the leadership of the church were looking in other directions, too.

As the church moved out of the third century and through the fourth, it broadened its approach to healing. Care for the sick was occupying a growing place alongside prayer for the sick. In addition, serious analysis of the popular approach to healing was under way. It seems that Augustine would have been pleased if he could have moderated popular devotion to the saints. This is the "official" side of the church speaking—a bishop charged with the order and discipline of a region: "We do not construct shrines, consecrate priests and render rites and sacrifices for these martyrs. The simple reason is that it is not they but God who is our God."[56] From his point of view, there is no question of worshipping the martyrs. In another place, he refers to the practice of his mother, Monica, of taking food and wine to memorials built for martyrs,[57] but elsewhere he describes this as "something, by the way, which is not done by more enlightened Christians and in most countries is entirely unknown."[58] The idea behind the practice seems to have been not to offer this food as a sacrifice to the saint but to have the saint bless it. Nevertheless, Augustine seems to have felt a little uneasy, as he saw the potential for abuse.

While Augustine was convinced that miracles were happening and noted that they came through a variety of means

---

[55] Basil, *Letter 142*, FC 13.291.
[56] Augustine, *City of God* 8.27, FC 14.74.
[57] Augustine, *Confessions* 6.2, NPNF[1] 1.90.
[58] Augustine, *City of God* 8.27, FC 14.75.

(he mentions the sacraments and relics),[59] he hesitated over how much should be made of the miraculous. In one passage he said, "Not only do the good and bad perform them [miracles], but sometimes the good perform them not."[60] In another he repeated this in a slightly modified form, commenting that some who were clearly in the kingdom of God did not perform miracles while some who were not in the kingdom of God did; he then concluded that no one ought to glory in the miraculous. To support his comment, he pointed to Luke 10:20, where Jesus told his disciples to rejoice in having their names written in heaven rather than in any power they had over demons.[61]

Augustine thus did not see miracles as badges of spirituality. Insofar as they could be performed by good and bad alike, they were certainly not useful means of proving that anyone in particular was specially close to God. Furthermore, these comments imply that miracles do not demonstrate the correctness of the doctrine of the one who performs them. An extended passage from the *City of God* carries one a long way into Augustine's thinking:

> It makes no difference whether we say that it is God Himself who works these miracles in the marvelous way that the Eternal operates in the temporal order, or whether we say that God works these miracles through His servants. And, in regard to what He does through His servants, it is all one whether He does these things through the spirits of martyrs, as though they were still living in their bodies, or whether He uses angels and effects His purposes by His orders, which are given invisibly, inaudibly, immutably. In that case, miracles which we think are done by martyrs are the result, rather, of their prayers and intercession, and not of their actions. Or God may have varying means to his different ends and these means may be altogether incomprehensible to the minds of men.[62]

---

[59] Ibid., 22.8, FC 24.432.

[60] Augustine, *Sermon 40*, 5, NPNF[1] 6.394.

[61] Augustine, *Answers to Letters of Petilian, Bishop of Cirta* 2.55, 91.

[62] Augustine, *City of God* 22.9, FC 24.451.

Augustine refused to take a rigid position about healing. The passage draws in nearly all of the explanations that Augustine and his contemporaries had for the miraculous. What he seems to be pointing to is the idea that the roots of the miraculous are hidden in God. And that is precisely what he said in another place: "Who can search into His purpose, or the reason why these miracles occur in some places but do not occur in others?"[63] Again, he is a man of his time, connecting places and miracles, but the thinking is clear: miracles are in the hands of God. They always flow from him, and that must never be lost sight of. At a time when some boasted that they quieted barking dogs by using a saint's name, Augustine demonstrated profound insight. It is not a perspective the church has been able to maintain with consistency.

Conclusion

When Jesus healed, there was a simplicity and directness about it, and a similar comment can be made for how the mainstream of the church talked about healing up to about AD 320. Running beside or beneath that stream was another, which surfaced first in the apocryphal acts of the apostles. Ordinary Christians had begun to think about larger-than-life heroes whose miraculous deeds took on the aura of spectacle. When a miracle was required, some apparently gifted person could be expected to provide it. In the apocryphal acts of the apostles, it was the apostles who were the miracle workers, but as this view of healing moved from the margins to the center of the church, the "saints" took their places beside the apostles as those who could intercede effectively with God for other people.

Crosscurrents created eddies in the stream—for example, Augustine with his apprehensions about saints and shrines, and Basil with his hospital. And while there was still another model

---

[63] Augustine, *Letter 78*, FC 12.378.

of healing in the early church, as we shall see later,[64] the vast majority of Christians of the era assumed that miracles would come through the intercession of spiritual giants. Their experiences and thinking provided a foundation for subsequent generations of Christians.

---

[64] See below, pp. 117–29.

6

Brother André
MIRACLES ON THE MOUNTAIN

St. Joseph's Oratory is an extremely imposing structure. Begun in 1924 and completed in 1967, its copper-covered dome rises to a height of 406 feet, making it one of the tallest Christian structures in the world. It is located on the northwest side of Mount Royal, a wooded promontory in the center of Montreal, Quebec, and serves as the destination of more than two million pilgrims and visitors every year. The physical bulk and social significance of the oratory become even more remarkable when its beginnings are recalled.

St. Joseph's Oratory arose out of the life and ministry of Alfred Bessette, more commonly known as Brother André. It would be hard to imagine a greater contrast between the two. It is grand; he was entirely unpretentious. This humble Quebecer is included here because of his reputation as an agent of healing. His ministry is an excellent example of the approach to healing I have called intercessory. We will look first at the man, then the movement that sprang up around him, and finally the miracles associated with him.

The Man

"The crazy old man of the mountain," as his detractors sometimes called him, has been the subject of many biographies and biographical notes.[1] There are particular challenges related to writing a biography of Brother André. First, as Gauthier points out,[2] Brother André was a private person who was not very communicative at the best of times, particularly about his personal life. Second, Brother André was a very ordinary person, and until recently historians have generally overlooked ordinary people. Third, no new information on Brother André has surfaced recently. The biographers have combed the official records scrupulously, and the eyewitnesses have been thoroughly interviewed. During the examination leading up to Brother André's beatification, 4,235 pages of firsthand accounts were gathered. Analysis will continue, but it is unlikely that very much previously unknown biographical data will appear.

Brother André was born in a small French community in Quebec on August 9, 1845. By age twelve he was an orphan. He worked at a number of jobs in Canada and in the New England states, but poor health consistently troubled him. In 1870 he was admitted to the Congregation of the Holy Cross in Montreal, where he became the doorman at Notre Dame College, a residential school for boys located just across the street

---

[1] The most widely read is Henri-Paul Bergeron, C.S.C., *Brother André, C.S.C.: The Wonder Man of Mount Royal* (trans. Réal Boudreau, C.S.C.; Montreal: Saint Joseph's Oratory, 1988). (C.S.C. stands for Congregationis Sanctae Crucis [Congregation of the Holy Cross].) It first appeared in the late 1930s and still sells forty thousand copies a year. The most exhaustive is Etienne Catta, *Le frère André (1845–1937) et l'Oratoire Saint-Joseph du Mont-Royal* (Montreal and Paris: Fides, 1965). It is meticulous in the best scholarly manner. Other works that are particularly helpful are Bernard Lafrenière, C.S.C., *Brother André,* a series of lectures, published in 1990; and some shorter papers written by Roland Gauthier, C.S.C. Fr. Lafrenière, the vice-postulator for the Cause of the Canonization of the Blessed Brother André, has the responsibility of pushing forward the process by which Brother André may be recognized as a saint by the Roman Catholic Church. Both Fr. Lafrenière and Fr. Gauthier, the director of the Center of Documentation and Research at the oratory, were very helpful to me on those occasions when I visited and worked at the oratory.

[2] Roland Gauthier, *La dévotion à S. Joseph chez le frère André avant la fondation de l'Oratoire du Mont-Royal* (Montreal: Oratoire du Saint-Joseph, 1979) 209.

from Mount Royal, at that time a small, undeveloped mountain covered with forest.

By 1878 reports had begun to circulate that Brother André could perform miracles, and people needing help started to come looking for him. With the passing of time and the claims of more cures, what began as a trickle of troubled people became a flood. One decision led to another, and in 1924 work began on the oratory. It was built according to plans known and praised as far away as Paris and cost more than $10 million by the time it was completed in 1967.[3]

Brother André died on January 6, 1937. His body lay in state in an open coffin in the oratory for seven days as more than one million people filed past. The process that his friends hope will lead ultimately to his full recognition as a saint was put in motion shortly afterward. On June 12, 1978, he was proclaimed worthy of the title Venerable, which meant that he was a model of Christian virtue, and on May 23, 1982, he received the title Blessed when he was beatified by Pope John Paul II. There is still one more step to be taken—canonization—before he receives full status as a saint, and those who visit the oratory are encouraged to pray that it will happen soon.

Understanding Brother André is made easier if we place him in historical context. He was born in the Canadian province of Quebec, colonized by France in 1608 under the leadership of Samuel de Champlain. The territory came under the control of Great Britain in 1759–60 through military conquest. From these roots has evolved a strong French community of six to seven million people whose commitment to their distinct cultural identity is signaled by the provincial motto, *Je me souviens* (I remember).

Throughout Quebec's history, the Roman Catholic Church has been a dominant feature of the society. During what is

---

[3] On one occasion I sat in the choir loft behind the high altar when the building was packed with pilgrims and was vibrating with the tones of its German-built organ. The combination of religious devotion, architecture, and music was powerful.

known as the Quiet Revolution, which took place in the 1960s, the state assumed responsibility for education and social services, and the church's place was dramatically redefined and curtailed. But Brother André had died thirty years earlier, and Lafrenière makes it clear that the little man was very much a child of his culture and of an earlier time in Quebec history.[4]

One prominent feature of religious life in Quebec during the mid–nineteenth century, when Alfred Bessette was born, was a deep interest in St. Joseph, the husband of Mary, the mother of Jesus. St. Joseph had been proclaimed the patron saint of Canada in 1624.[5] On December 8, 1870, Rome officially proclaimed St. Joseph patron of the entire Roman Catholic Church.[6] It was thought appropriate that the man who had protected the Christ as a child should be acknowledged as the protector of the church, the body of Christ.[7]

Alfred resonated with this emphasis completely. Through his mother, his father, his parish priest, and then his religious order, he was led to an intense devotion to St. Joseph.[8] One author referred to this devotion as *un instinct spirituel* (a spiritual instinct),[9] and toward the end of his life, Brother André insisted that he desired to be only "Saint Joseph's little dog."[10]

Brother André expressed this love for Joseph concretely rather than abstractly. He had no time for philosophical speculation but placed high value on medals dedicated to St. Joseph and on statues of the saint and the oil burning in lamps before them. He relied upon these physical objects to remind him of

[4] Bernard Lafrenière, "Le frère André," *Cahier de la Société Historique de Montréal* 1 (4, 1982) 68–70.

[5] Bernard Lafrenière, transcript of interview by Claudette Lambert on "Les pèlerinages," Radio-Canada, November 5–9, 1984, 16.

[6] Gauthier, *La dévotion*, 213.

[7] Bernard Lafrenière, interview by author, Montreal, Quebec, March 15, 1990.

[8] Gauthier, *La dévotion*, 209–14.

[9] Maurice Lafond, C.S.C., " 'Je ne suis que le petit chien de saint Joseph' ou la dévotion à saint Joseph chez le frère André," *L'Oratoire* 75 (1980) 13.

[10] Bergeron, *Brother André*, 169.

Joseph and to help him understand the saint better.[11] This intense interest in Joseph, however, was not the only focus of Brother André's religious life.

Bergeron states that the main point of Brother André's spirituality was "the close relation between the devotion to Saint Joseph and that of the Passion."[12] André was profoundly moved by the death of Christ. Gauthier, citing the accounts of people who were Brother André's intimate friends, comments that he was more preoccupied with the death of Christ and the Eucharist than with any other part of his devotional life because they showed most clearly the Savior's love for all human beings.[13] According to Maurice Lafond, this reflected his primary concern, which was "to lead others to God and . . . to heaven."[14]

Brother André led a highly disciplined devotional life. Particularly when he was younger, he practiced various forms of asceticism. To deepen his sense of suffering over his sinfulness, he occasionally wore a barbed leather belt or a chain around his waist under his clothes.[15] Later he frequently slept only one or two hours a night, and occasionally not at all.[16] But he did not stay awake just for the sake of doing it; he was praying.

One of the strongest features of his religious life was his approach to prayer. As a young member of his religious community, he was often found in prayer in the chapel of Notre Dame College during the night.[17] Later, as parts of the oratory were completed, accounts circulated of his praying for hours before dimly lit altars or in the seclusion of the mountain.[18]

---

[11] Gauthier, La dévotion, 222–23.

[12] Bergeron, Brother André, 127.

[13] Gauthier, La dévotion, 231.

[14] Lafond, "Le petit chien," 12.

[15] Bergeron, Brother André, 16f.

[16] Boniface Hanley, O.F.M., Brother André: All He Could Do Was Pray (Montreal: St. Anthony's Guild, 1979; reprint, Montreal: St. Joseph's Oratory, 1981) 49.

[17] Gauthier, La dévotion, 224.

[18] Bergeron, Brother André, 32–35.

Besides the impact of Quebec culture, the very personal reality of André's own poor physical health[19] played a major role in shaping the way in which he looked at the religious life. Suffering loomed large in his thinking. He frequently told his friends that suffering could have many positive results,[20] and his comments during his last illness applied that idea to himself. Asked if he was suffering, he replied, "Yes, I am, but I thank the Lord for giving me this opportunity to suffer. I need it so much! Sickness is a good thing for it helps us reconsider our past life and make up through repentance and suffering."[21] This is not the response one might have expected, given the stereotypical picture of those who are agents of healing.

Brother André accepted suffering as from God and submitted to it. Tom Sinclair-Faulkner argues that as far as Brother André was concerned, suffering was the central factor in the way a human being lives before God.[22] Gauthier disputes this, insisting that suffering was only one facet of Brother André's spirituality, but he does not deny that suffering occupied an important place in his thought.[23]

There is a tendency for some of the more recent biographers to focus more attention on the theology implicit in Brother André's words and actions than it received in the past—or for that matter, than André himself gave to it. It may be true that Brother André did not overemphasize St. Joseph, that he did teach that all healing came from God, and that his use of medals and oil owed nothing to magic. One wonders, however, what message his contemporaries took from his constant referrals to St. Joseph or from his use of medals in connection with the surfacing of a body in the Montreal harbor.

---

[19] Catta, *Le frère André*, 863.

[20] Bergeron, *Brother André*, 108.

[21] Lafrenière, *Brother André*, 180.

[22] Tom Sinclair-Faulkner, "Sacramental Suffering: Brother André's Spirituality," *Canadian Catholic Historical Association*, Study Session 49 (1982) 122.

[23] Roland Gauthier, review of "Sacramental Suffering: Brother André's Spirituality," by Tom Sinclair-Faulkner, *Cahiers de Joséphologie* 33 (2, 1985) 307.

A dear friend of Brother André, Fire Chief Raoul Gauthier, along with three other men, had been killed in an explosion aboard ship, and their bodies had been lost in the St. Lawrence River. Three were found, with only Gauthier's still submerged. On request, Brother André went to the site, prayed, and threw two medals of St. Joseph into the river where the bodies had been lost. Shortly after, Gauthier's body resurfaced exactly where the medals had been thrown.[24]

There is still more theological analysis of Brother André's work to be done. What is perfectly clear, however, is that he wielded truly amazing influence over the religious lives of a great many people.

The Movement

In 1878 Brother Alderic Giraudeau, who was in the same order as Brother André, had a wound on his leg that would not respond to treatment. He testified to being healed by some oil from a lamp burning before a statue of St. Joseph. He also made reference to four other people who were cured of various ailments in 1877 through the same means.[25] This was of great significance for Brother André because it was he who had recommended that the oil be used in all these cases.[26] Apparently, Brother André had begun to pray for sick people whom he had met when he was out of Notre Dame College, where he lived, carrying out his duties as doorman, mailing letters, or delivering laundry,[27]

---

[24] Lafrenière, *Brother André*, 164.

[25] Gauthier, *La dévotion*, 216–18.

[26] Lafrenière, "Le frère André," 69.

[27] Hanley, *Brother André*, 22. On these occasions he used oil he had taken from a lamp burning before a statue of St. Joseph. Gauthier thinks that Brother André may have obtained the idea of using oil from hearing of similar events that had occurred in France (*La dévotion*, 219) or from hearing of a healing that had taken place in Montreal through the use of oil (p. 219 n. 20). Lafrenière points out that Brother André understood clearly that there was nothing special about the oil he used. He employed it as an aid to faith insofar as it turned people's attention to St. Joseph (transcript of interview, 17).

and word began to circulate that the health of some had improved.

Added to these cases was the experience of a boy who was confined to the infirmary of the college, suffering from a severe fever. He was able to get up and go outside to play immediately after Brother André simply announced to him that he was perfectly well.[28] Anxious college authorities were concerned that André had interfered in matters beyond his competence, but examination by a physician showed that the child was well.

The impression began to spread that Brother André was someone special.[29] People were drawn to him because of his reputation for holiness and piety and because of his apparent ability to heal instantly.[30] Gauthier points out that around 1890, people began to seek Brother André at Notre Dame College.[31] Commenting sociologically on what happened in Montreal, Marie-Marthe Brault notes that people came to see André as an intermediary who could bring the natural and supernatural worlds together. They saw themselves as powerless in the face of their difficulties, but here was someone who could both understand them and do something to improve their situations.[32] Almost immediately controversy boiled up among

---

[28] Hanley, *Brother André*, 23f.

[29] Marie-Marthe Brault, calling upon the work of Marcel Mauss and Levi-Strauss to discuss the relationship between a healer and the following she or he acquires, presents a naturalistic interpretation in which it is argued that people are not seen to be extraordinary because they heal, but they become able to heal because, for some reason, people have come to see them as being extraordinary persons (in Jean Simard, *Un patrimoine méprisé: La religion populaire des Québécois* [Montreal: Hurtubise, 1979] 108).

[30] Guy Laperrière argues that the popularity of a pilgrimage site is related to the miracles performed at them, and he applies this to St. Joseph's Oratory (transcript of interview by Claudette Lambert, on "Les pèlerinages," Radio-Canada, November 5–9, 1984, 9). See also Brault, in Simard, *Un patrimoine méprisé*, 94.

[31] Gauthier, *La dévotion*, 221.

[32] Marie-Marthe Brault, "L'Oratoire Saint-Joseph-du-Mont-Royal: Etude d'un sanctuaire de pèlerinage catholique" (M.A. thesis, Université Montréal, 1969) 140–42.

parents of children at the college, medical doctors in Montreal, and even some of the people in his own order.[33]

In spite of the opposition, what emerged was a genuine movement. Lafrenière holds that "right from the beginning, the Oratory was a vast popular movement." He describes it as a "popular movement of prayer based on signs given by the Lord, a movement of prayer for the glory of God. The movement, so to speak, of a whole nation discerning more and more clearly the special protection that came from the saint who, after Mary, was really the closest to the Lord."[34]

Others have spoken of the oratory in similar terms. Henri Bernard underlines the impact the oratory has had on the lives of ordinary people, pointing out that as material was gathered to support the official recognition of Brother André as a saint, fifty-six out of sixty-seven testimonies came from laymen and laywomen.[35]

Benoît Lacroix, O.P., takes a different approach, calling it a "perfect example of popular Christian religion" in that it provided everything that characterizes popular religion: the solemnity of the Mass and of organ recitals, a store in which to buy religious objects, and the unsophisticated, even superstitious devotions of the people. Lacroix finds further features of popular religion when he suggests that the oratory responds to a deep human need to visualize the sacred, to experience the supernatural concretely, by encouraging people to touch

---

[33] Hanley, *Brother André*, 28.

[34] Lafrenière, *Brother André*, 58, 75. It is not clear what Lafrenière means by "nation." It could be either the French-speaking province of Quebec or Canada as a whole. If he means the latter, the statement is somewhat overdrawn. St. Joseph's Oratory has not influenced western Canada with anything like the kind of strength it has had in Quebec. Joseph is the saint referred to as the one closest to the Lord after Mary.

[35] Henri Bernard, "Le problématique de l'Oratoire Saint-Joseph," in *Les pèlerinages au Quebec* (Quebec: Presses de l'Université Laval, 1981) 143. He finds further evidence of the comfort ordinary people feel at the oratory in the huge labor rallies held there in the 1920s and 1930s and in the fact that pilgrimages to the oratory are often organized by laypeople.

Brother André's tomb, to kiss a relic, to say words that are almost magical.[36]

The popular nature of the movement gave it the energy to carry it through the many building programs that led up to the completion of the present oratory. Lafrenière points out that all Brother André ever asked for was permission to build a small wooden shelter over a statue of St. Joseph that had been placed on the hill to help people pray: "But then Brother André's friends wanted a chapel, and then a shelter behind it, and some heating, and a restaurant, and everything followed by itself. It was Brother André's dream, but not his personal project. To him, clearly, IT WAS SAINT JOSEPH'S PROJECT."[37] He points out that throughout the building efforts, André consistently stayed in the background. At times he insisted on what he wanted, and everyone recognized that without him there would have been no project. Nevertheless, when the actual decisions were being made, he was absent. They were in the hands of other people.[38]

While he never asked for much, Brother André had a clear vision of the ultimate goal. He wanted to see a chapel built that would show the whole world the power of St. Joseph's intercession.[39] For his part, the archbishop of Montreal, Cardinal Leger, saw the oratory as an effective tool to remind a forgetful people of the power of God.[40]

How have these visions for the oratory materialized? How has the oratory fared in a society that during the last

---

[36] Benoît Lacroix, O.P., "L'Oratoire Saint-Joseph (1904–1979), fait religieux populaire," *Cahiers de Joséphologie* 27 (1979) 260–62.

[37] Lafrenière, *Brother André*, 73. Henri Bernard calls the oratory "a true creation of the people," pointing to the many groups of laypeople that played key roles at each stage of its development ("Le problématique," 140–41).

[38] Lafrenière, *Brother André*, 71f.

[39] Gauthier, *La dévotion*, 231.

[40] Roland Gauthier, *L'Oratoire Saint-Joseph du Mont-Royal: A l'occasion du 75e anniversaire de sa fondation* (Montreal: Oratoire Saint-Joseph, 1979) 247.

twenty-five years has pulled away from its traditional Roman Catholic roots?[41]

In the mid-1950s, Philip Garigue saw the oratory serving as a bulwark for Quebec society against the secularizing influence of industrialization. He thought it played a vital role, keeping people securely attached to their roots while they were adapting to profound change all around them.[42] As if to illustrate this, Boniface Hanley pointed out that the oratory became a rallying place for Catholic trade unions.[43] These analysts thought that the oratory had helped preserve the integration of religious and economic components of Quebec society. Within a decade things had changed.

In the 1960s both Catta and Brault saw a crevasse opening between Quebec society and the oratory. Catta viewed this as positive. In his opinion, the oratory was challenging the materialism of the culture.[44] On the other hand, the implications of Brault's work were negative. She can be understood as suggesting that the oratory was increasingly out of touch with Quebec's leap into modern technological sophistication, its pilgrims remaining frozen in a preindustrial view of the world.[45]

A new, thorough sociological study of the oratory is needed. By contrast, there is no shortage of theological comment. Lafrenière suggests that the oratory has served as a visible sign for pilgrims, drawing them to the invisible,[46] and he calls it "a witness to the Gospel."[47] Lacroix thinks it fills a prophetic, eschatological position, symbolizing in its crowds the vast human community and offering a foretaste of an ideal society in

---

[41] See Reginald W. Bibby, *Fragmented Gods: The Poverty and Potential of Religion in Canada* (Toronto: Irwin, 1987) 20f.

[42] Philip Garigue, "Saint Joseph Oratory: A New Look at Its Meaning," *Nouvelle revue canadienne* (1956) 242. Henri Bernard echoes these words in an article written two decades later ("Le problématique," 141).

[43] Hanley, *Brother André*, 48.

[44] Catta, *Le frère André*, 1084.

[45] Brault, "L'Oratoire," 151.

[46] Lafrenière, "Le frère André," 70.

[47] Lafrenière, transcript of interview, 24.

which people come together.[48] One wonders, however, what role the oratory is playing in contemporary Quebec society and in the lives of the current generation of pilgrims.[49]

The Miracles

Rudolphe Fournier is a case study. In 1911, while still a young boy, Fournier contracted a disease in his right knee. He does not identify it, but he does report that a physician said it was terminal. On hearing this, Fournier's father went to the oratory to see Brother André, who instructed him to pray and gave him a medal of St. Joseph and some oil. There was no improvement, so Fournier's father went back again. When he walked into Brother André's room, he was met with a smile and the words "Go and have faith." Returning home, the older Fournier discovered that his son had been healed at exactly the time when Brother André spoke to him.[50]

It was the miracles that brought people to the mountain. No complete count is possible for all of the miracles that have been claimed through Brother André's ministry. Lafrenière offers some figures. During the process leading up to Brother André's beatification, testimony was given of 125 healings,[51] but Lafrenière states that 435 cures were reported in 1916 alone.[52]

Garigue examined the letters received at the oratory between 1937 and 1955. He discovered that 190,876 gave thanks for something, with 59,514, or 31.2 percent, reporting cures.[53] Sinclair-Faulkner examined records from the 1920s and 1930s. He concluded that "during the 1920s only 9–11% of the letters

---

[48] Lacroix, "L'Oratoire Saint-Joseph," 265.

[49] Henri Bernard raised similar questions in 1979 ("Le problématique," 142).

[50] Rudolphe Fournier, "Je suis un des 'miraculés' de frère André," *L'Oratoire* (April 1955) 18.

[51] Lafrenière, *Brother André*, 40.

[52] Ibid., 60.

[53] Garigue, "Saint Joseph Oratory," 244.

mentioned a miracle [a healing or some other desirable thing]. Still more surprising is the fact that during the years 1933–1937 only 7% of the letters referred to a healing or some other favor miraculously granted to the writers."[54] The discrepancy between Garigue's figures and Sinclair-Faulkner's is significant, but it can be accounted for by the fact that they studied different periods and worked with different materials.

Moving away from numbers to specific cases gives us another perspective on what happened at the oratory. Lafrenière cites several dramatic healings. A man with an open, rotting wound on one leg was healed as Brother André invoked St. Joseph and prayed "through the precious blood of our Lord"; the paralyzed arm of a woman was healed when it was rubbed with a medal of St. Joseph under André's instructions; the badly crushed feet of another man were healed after Brother André had, on four consecutive days, rubbed boxes that had been placed around them as protection.[55] All of these were remarkable, well-attested cases.

In his book dealing with the oratory, Arthur Saint-Pierre refers to many cases of healings that were claimed to have occurred through Brother André's intercession.[56] He even offers medical certification for some of the cures. I will quote one example:

> I, the undersigned, testify that Mr. J. O. Dufresne, of Nicolet, has been cured of tuberculosis in a very far advanced stage after a pilgrimage to the Oratory of St. Joseph on Mount Royal.
>
> I attended the patient before his pilgrimage, and then believed that his death was imminent. A year has elapsed since his cure took place, and it still persists.

---

[54] Sinclair-Faulkner, "Sacramental Suffering," 113. In conducting the study, he looked at the February and March issues of the *Annals of Saint Joseph* for each year during the two decades ("Sacramental Suffering," 113 n. 9).

[55] Lafrenière, *Brother André*, 31f.

[56] Arthur Saint-Pierre, *St. Joseph's Oratory of Mount Royal* (Montreal: n.p., 1927) 65–81.

(Signed) G. A. Henri Dufresne, M. D.
262, Roy St., Montreal[57]

This certificate was dated December 14, 1911.

The cumulative weight of all this evidence serves to confirm that miraculous events really have taken place at St. Joseph's Oratory.

All the miracles to which I referred took place some time ago, before 1937 at the latest, the year of Brother André's death. As I worked with the material, I began to get the impression that the oratory had, in fact, become somewhat less concerned with recording and verifying miracles than it once had been. Comments by Theodore Mangiapan, president of the Medical Bureau of Lourdes, proved useful.

He states that the astonishing advances in medical technology in this century have had far-reaching implications for the way in which the church views the validation of miracles.[58] What was once seen as incurable or beyond treatment is often thought now to be well within the reach of medical science. In addition, Mangiapan argues that before 1950 a "medically proven" miracle was thought to be one of the prime ways of demonstrating the existence of God and his almighty power. In the latter part of the century, however, many people have come to believe that miracles should be understood as signs of God's compassion and love rather than as weapons to be used in defense of the faith. Furthermore, it has been observed that whether or not a person thinks a particular event is miraculous has more to do with the inclination of her or his own heart than with science.[59] Lafrenière puts it well: "Miracles are not the proof of faith, but it is faith that makes them possible, and they can be seen only through the eyes of faith."[60]

---

[57] Ibid., 66.

[58] Mangiapan, "Le contrôle médical," 4f.

[59] Evangelical church growth specialist C. Peter Wagner came to the same conclusion through his personal experience with healing ministry (*Healing Ministry*, 239–43).

[60] Lafrenière, *Brother André*, 21.

The process by which these healings were believed to occur is of more than passing interest. A common sequence can be extracted from the many reports of healings. The sick person came to Brother André, who went to St. Joseph, who went to Jesus, the source of the healing. Along the way, André often advised the use of medals of St. Joseph, oil, and novenas.[61] He was often charged with practicing magic or promoting superstition because he used medals and oil. He rejected the charges outright, insisting that he used them in order to build confidence in Joseph and in God.[62]

The constant reference to St. Joseph makes it clear that this healing movement grew around the idea of intercession. Those who have come to the oratory have always been convinced of Brother André's effectiveness as an intercessor. On his part, he consistently tried to divert attention to Joseph: "I do not cure; St. Joseph cures."[63] He believed that Joseph had an intimate, daily relationship with God, and he relied on that. He would also bring together Joseph and Mary in his thinking, commenting, "When the Virgin Mary and Saint Joseph intercede together, *that pushes hard!*"[64]

This does not mean that Brother André did not understand that healing, at its source, flowed from God. Lafrenière insists his attitude to miracles was that "they all came from God, and through the personal care and prayer of Saint Joseph."[65] Bergeron comments, "The secret of Brother André must, then, be found only in his unwavering faith in Providence. God alone was the immediate agent of the numerous

---

[61] Novenas are prayers or religious activities repeated daily over a nine-day period. Lafrenière points out that they are neither biblical nor liturgical, but they are very widely used (ibid., 80).

[62] Ibid., 82, 87.

[63] Hanley, *Brother André,* 30.

[64] Lafrenière, *Brother André,* 123. An unfortunate feature of this statement is its implication that God will only respond to human need if a great deal of pressure is applied.

[65] Ibid., 60.

miracles that took place at the Shrine [the oratory] as a means to establish devotion to Saint Joseph."[66] This corresponds to one of the most characteristic ways in which Brother André referred to God: "the good God." André is quoted using the phrase repeatedly in one of the oratory's tracts about him,[67] and Catta notes the frequency of its use as well. He even entitles one of the chapters in his study of Brother André "Comme le bon Dieu est bon!" (How good the good God is!).[68]

Two final features of Brother André's healing ministry need to be noted. First, what I call "revelation" occasionally appeared to be present. Bergeron records this incident:

> There were many eyewitnesses of the following signal wonder. A great contingent of American visitors had thronged round the doors of the office all morning. At dinner-time, the Brother returned to the rectory. He was already mounting the steps under the eyes of hundreds of pilgrims, when a man went up the steps to stop him and to show him, through the open doors of an ambulance that had forced its way amid the tumultuous crowd, a man lying on a stretcher. "Untie him and let him walk," said the Brother simply, and went on into the house without further ado. The sick man got up and walked barefooted through the madly enthusiastic crowd.[69]

The passage is useful for a number of reasons. It certainly provides a sense of what life at the oratory was like—the surging crowds, the joyous response to a healing. We have no information about the condition from which the man suffered, but the fact that he was brought to the oratory strapped to a bed in an ambulance suggests it was serious. It also shows Brother André acting on certain knowledge that the man would be healed. He did not even wait to see what happened.

---

[66] Bergeron, *Brother André*, 86.

[67] *Who Is This Man?* The only other person I know who had a tract written about him with this same title was William Branham (see pp. 168–80 below). It probably points to the similarly intense devotion of the followers of these men.

[68] Catta, *Le frère André*, 863, 864.

[69] Bergeron, *Brother André*, 69.

There were other times, too, when he seemed to know when a healing would occur. Lafrenière discusses this at length, citing a conversation between Brother André and a friend.

> One priest who lived with him at the Oratory for nine years, Father Emile Deguire, asked him "Can you tell me how you know the difference between a person who is going to be healed and one who will not be. To one you say, 'Make a novena, rub yourself with the medal and the oil of Saint Joseph, pray with confidence . . . ' and to someone else you only say, 'Stand up and walk!' How can you tell that one is going to be healed?"
>
> Brother André answered very simply, "Sometimes it is obvious . . ." What more could he say? As it seems, he received directly from the Lord the intuition that a sign was going to occur under the eyes of the witnesses.[70]

This revelational thread running through Brother André's ministry is striking. We will see it again in others.[71]

The second feature is quite different. Frequently people were not healed when they came to Brother André. As Hanley puts it, "Some were cured, many were not."[72] No numbers are available to give any idea of what proportion of those who came to the oratory looking for healing were cured. To their credit, none of the biographers suggests that all, or even most, of those who came were healed.

In this respect, Sinclair-Faulkner renders a service to Brother André and the oratory by drawing attention to the emphasis on suffering. If people were not going to be healed, they should be helped to understand their experience of pain, and Sinclair-Faulkner argues that this is what Brother André did. He notes that while Brother André's work was being investigated, one of those involved made an observation that stands normal assumptions on their heads: "Those who are healed quickly are either those who do not have faith or those who have little faith, so that they might have faith; while those who

---

[70] Lafrenière, *Brother André*, 27f.
[71] See pp. 177–78 and 184–86 below.
[72] Hanley, *Brother André*, 38.

already have a firm faith are not healed quickly, since the good God would rather test them, make them suffer, in order to sanctify them still more."[73]

Garigue adds that the people who came to the oratory were ordinary Roman Catholics, people with no particular desire to escape this world or what it brought to them. He also notes that there was no attempt to whip up emotion or faith. The message imparted to the afflicted was that they should have faith but also patience.[74] That corresponds to what I observed while attending a service for the sick at the oratory. People's attention was turned to God, Brother André, and St. Joseph, in that order, then the matter was simply left alone, or, more accurately, left in God's hands.

Conclusion

Other questions about the oratory and about Brother André await answers. Some have to do with the man. When will he be recognized as a saint? What place does he occupy in the mind of the modern Quebecer? Some are more general. What role does the oratory play in contemporary Quebec?

The oratory is an outstanding feature of Montreal; tourists flock to it. And Brother André still commands the devotion of hundreds of thousands of people. They see him as a special friend of St. Joseph and of "the good God," as one who can intercede effectively for them. In this role, Brother André is a prime example of the intercessory approach to healing.

---

[73] Sinclair-Faulkner, "Sacramental Suffering," 125.
[74] Garigue, "Saint Joseph Oratory," 253.

7

Mary of Medjugorje
APPARITIONS AND HEALINGS

The last example of the intercessory approach to divine healing arises from a relatively isolated Roman Catholic parish of
about three or four thousand people living in four small villages
collectively named Medjugorje ("between the mountains").
It is located in the tragically war-torn republic of Bosnia-
Herzegovina, not many miles inland from the Adriatic Sea.

I will focus on the accounts of healing that come from
there, but they are only part of a much larger and truly intrigu-
ing phenomenon. Alleged appearances of the Virgin Mary in
Medjugorje began to be reported in 1981. Such claims have
continued ever since, making this little parish the center of a
major international movement.[111]

In June 1991 an estimated 100,000 people flocked to
Medjugorje to celebrate the tenth anniversary of the

---

[1] Of course, alleged apparitions of the Virgin Mary are not confined to
Medjugorje. The phenomenon as it occurs globally was discussed at a conference
held in July 1991 in Pittsburgh, Pa., involving five thousand participants (*National and International Religion Report*, Aug. 12, 1991, 6). Earlier famous appearances are those claimed to have occurred at Lourdes, France, in the
mid–nineteenth century and at Fatima, Portugal, in the early twentieth century.
See Mark I. Miravalle, *The Message of Medjugorje: The Marian Message to the
Modern World* (Lanham, Md.: University Press of America, 1986) 104, 110; and
René Laurentin and Ljudevit Rupcic, *Is the Virgin Mary Appearing at Medjugorje?*
(trans. Francis Martin; Washington: The Word Among Us Press, 1984) 9f.

apparitions. This was before the brutal three-sided civil war started in Bosnia-Herzegovina, but vicious fighting had already broken out in nearby Croatia, one of several republics that declared independence from the former Yugoslavia beginning in 1991. This undaunted 100,000 was only a fraction of the approximately 14 million people who have struggled to this sun-baked plateau from everywhere on the globe over the last fourteen years,[2] drawn by reports of the appearances of the Virgin Mary and by hopes of spiritual and physical healing.

The Apparitions

The accounts of the appearances point out that not everyone who is in Medjugorje sees the Virgin Mary. The apparitions have been almost exclusively to six people, most of whom are in their twenties now.[3] They include four young women—Vicka, who was almost seventeen when the visions started, Mirjana, who was sixteen, Marija, sixteen, and Ivanka, fifteen—and two young men, Ivan, sixteen, and Jakov, ten.

By now the appearances number into the thousands. This is entirely unprecedented in the history of the Christian church.[4] They have lasted from less than one minute to forty minutes, and while usually occurring around Medjugorje, they have occasionally happened in countries as far removed as Russia and the United States when the visionaries were traveling.

In the visions, the visionaries claim, the mother of Jesus delivers messages, sometimes for them as individuals and sometimes for the whole Christian church or the whole world. The

---

[2] Pilgrimages have continued, with interruptions, in spite of the civil war ("Medjugorje Has Become Mecca for Catholics," *Buffalo News*, September 5, 1992, A-6). Medjugorje was stabilized by Croatian forces in the summer of 1992 (Henry Kovacic, director, Ave Maria Centre of Peace, Toronto, interview by author, January 24, 1994). For the most up-to-date information on Medjugorje see http://www.medjugorje.org/medpage.htm.

[3] Vicka is in her thirties.

[4] A fact that has drawn both critical comment and attempts at explanation. See Laurentin and Rupcic, *Is the Virgin Mary Appearing?* 104–6.

content of the messages usually concerns the present, but sometimes it applies to the prophetic future. It is upon the content that the priests and theologians who are associated with Medjugorje place their emphasis. When I heard Fr. Svetozar Kraljevic speak in St. James, the parish church, in July 1990, he was attempting to deflate the curiosity about the apparitions and the many signs that have gone along with them. He wanted people to focus on the message of Medjugorje.

According to the young people who claim the visions, Mary is calling the world and the church to repentance and to prayer. Fr. Bob Bedard of St. Mary's Parish in Ottawa, Ontario, sums up Mary's message in the following way:

> It must be carefully noted that she is not promoting additional devotions to her nor suggesting that this is the solution to our problems. Rather, the solution, she says, is repentance and turning to Jesus, her Son. She proclaims him to be the Lord, one Mediator and one Savior of us all. She tells the youngsters she has no plans for the church. This, she says, is the role of the Father. It is his will that must prevail. She has told them she has no power, but that the power we need comes from the Holy Spirit.[5]

Bedard's comments are illustrated by a statement published in 1991 in which Mary is quoted as saying,

> My children, how many times have I invited you here in Medjugorje to prayer and I will invite you again because I desire you to open your hearts to my Son to allow Him to come in and fill you with peace and love. Allow Him, let Him enter! Help Him by your prayers in order that you might be able to spread peace and love to others, because that is now most necessary for you in this time of battle with Satan.[6]

It is surprising to hear Mary quoted so freely. Allegedly, almost every day for the last sixteen years, sometime between 5:30 and 7:00 p.m., Mary has appeared to one or another or all of the visionaries somewhere in the world and given them messages.

---

[5] Bob Bedard, *Medjugorje: Prophecy for Our Time?* (Ottawa: n.p., 1984) 8.
[6] "News Nuggets," *Medjugorje Messenger*, July 1991, 6.

In a doctoral dissertation submitted to the Pontifical University of St. Thomas Aquinas in Rome and later published, Mark Miravalle exposes Mary's message to very careful examination. He identifies main themes and analyzes the message in the light of the historic teaching of the Catholic Church, the discussions of the Vatican II, and official documents issued by the Roman Catholic Church since Vatican II. He finds a high degree of correspondence, indicating that there is nothing novel or bizarre in what is being said at Medjugorje and that therefore Mary's message fits well with universally recognized doctrine of the Roman Catholic Church.[7]

A genuine international movement has grown up around these apparitions, and its development has been nothing short of phenomenal.[8] The lives of the six young people will never be the same again, and the impact on Medjugorje has been dramatic. But controversy has been rife.

First, those gathering around the apparitions met harassment and persecution from the local authorities; this only gradually changed.[9] Second, there was severe tension between the

---

[7] Miravalle, *Message of Medjugorje*, 45–49, 63–79, 121.

[8] See the discussions in "A Medjugorje Diary," *Medjugorje Herald*, July 1990, 6; Mart Bax, "The Madonna of Medjugorje: Religious Rivalry and the Formation of a Devotional Movement in Yugoslavia," *Anthropological Quarterly* 63 (1990) 68–72; and Bedard, *Medjugorje*, 14ff. Fr. John Schneid of Ottawa, who has visited Medjugorje twice (July 1984 for two days and April 25–May 4, 1991) shared observations with me on the development of this movement. He noted that while the apparitions are still of great importance, the Mass and the life of the church had become much more significant at Medjugorje in 1991 than they were in 1984. He also pointed out that whereas the visionaries were the clear center of attention earlier, the clergy were taking a much more prominent role in 1991. He saw these developments as positive. They were raising the level of teaching that pilgrims were receiving. Previously the emphasis was upon the phenomenon of the visions and the events that accompanied them. In 1991 a more concentrated attempt was being made to show how what was happening at Medjugorje was to be integrated with the whole of Christian life (interview by author, Ottawa, August 17, 1991).

[9] See Nicholas Bartulica, *Medjugorje: Are the Seers Telling the Truth? A Psychiatrist's Viewpoint* (Chicago: Nicholas Bartulica, 1991) 90–118. Jozo

people involved at Medjugorje and their bishop, Pavao Zanic of Mostar, who had primary responsibility for dealing with such issues as reports of apparitions. Initially he supported the young people, but he then withdrew that support, apparently in response to comments attributed to Mary that seemed critical of decisions he had made in his diocese.[10] Robert Faricy, a professor of spirituality at the Gregorian University in Rome, believes that the criticism was well placed.[11] When Zanic retired in 1992, he was replaced by Ratko Peric, who subsequently demonstrated the same skepticism toward the apparitions that Zanic had.[12]

The background to the tension is a struggle that has gone on in that region of Bosnia-Herzegovina between the regular Roman Catholic diocesan structure and the Franciscan order for more than a hundred years.[13] Standing behind it is ethnic and religious hatred that has occasionally boiled over into atrocities or war,[14] as happened in 1991 and continued into 1994. Before his retirement, however, Zanic and Medjugorje seemed to move closer together.[15]

Everyone has been concerned to evaluate the apparitions carefully.[16] Bishop Zanic set up a committee (or committees) to

---

Zovko, one of the Franciscan priests who supported the visionaries early in their experience, was imprisoned for eighteen months as a result of his involvement (p. 78f.).

[10] Laurentin and Rupcic, *Is the Virgin Mary Appearing?* 113.

[11] Lucy Rooney, S.N.D., and Robert Faricy, S.J., *Medjugorje Journal: Mary Speaks to the World* (Chicago: Franciscan Herald Press, 1988) 125.

[12] Mark I. Miravalle, director, Marian Office of Contemporary Apparitions, Franciscan University, Steubenville, Ohio, telephone interview by author, March 28, 1994.

[13] Bax, "Madonna of Medjugorje," 63.

[14] F. W. D. Deakin, *The Embattled Mountain* (New York and London: Oxford University Press, 1971) 99; Paul N. Hehn, *The German Struggle against Yugoslav Guerrillas in World War II* (New York: East European Quarterly, Boulder, 1979) 8; and Serbian Eastern Orthodox Diocese for the United States of America and Canada, *Martyrdom of the Serbs: Persecutions of the Serbian Orthodox and Massacre of the Serbian People* (n.p., n.d. [during WW II]).

[15] "News Nuggets," 3.

[16] "A Medjugorje Diary," 6.

study events. Contrary to the statement of Denis Janz that one committee issued a unanimously negative report,[17] no official report has been given.[18] On May 2, 1986, the Vatican took the matter out of Zanic's hands.[19] At a 1991 meeting of the Roman Catholic bishops of Yugoslavia, the Medjugorjean apparitions were granted a *non constat de supernaturalitate* status—that is, their validity was neither affirmed nor denied.[20] The bishops also set up a "supercommission" to supervise the sacramental and pastoral life of Medjugorje. The latest statement by the Vatican was released on Aug. 21, 1996. It affirmed that the status granted in 1991 had not changed.[21]

While official church committees conducted their deliberations, others sought concrete medical information. Teams from several countries traveled to Medjugorje to carry out examinations. With the cooperation of the visionaries, extensive batteries of tests have been run, including electrocardiograms, hypnosis, electroencephalograms, and psychiatric assessments. Laurentin discusses this work at some length, stating clearly that there are limitations to what science can do.[22] He discusses these limitations in terms of "receivers" (the ones seeing the apparitions) and the "transmitter" (the one alleged to be giving the apparitions): "Science can reach the receiver (visionaries) but it cannot read the transmitter who is perceived by the receiver alone. Thus, by identifying the conditions surrounding the visionaries' perceptions, the phenomenon will be more clearly defined and many possible hypotheses eliminated."[23]

---

[17] Denis Janz, "Medjugorje's Miracles: Faith and Profit," *Christian Century* 104 (1987) 725.

[18] Rooney and Faricy, *Medjugorje Journal,* 156.

[19] Bartulica, *Medjugorje,* 147.

[20] Miravalle, interview.

[21] "Vatican Releases Latest Statement on Medjugorje." Online: http://www.medjugorje.org/cns.htm [cited 14 August 1997].

[22] René Laurentin and Henri Joyeux, *Scientific and Medical Studies on the Apparitions at Medjugorje* (trans. Luke Griffin; Dublin: Veritas, 1987) 37.

[23] Ibid., 4.

Henri Joyeux, who led a very impressive medical team, describes their work in the following way:

> The research programme which we put together therefore aimed at a clinical and paraclinical study of the visionaries of Medjugorje before, during and after the apparition, from the point of view of differences in the functioning of their particular receptive organs: brain, vision, hearing, voice and, in particular, the vegetative cardiac functions.[24]

This scientific evaluation concludes, "The ecstasies are not pathological nor is there any element of deceit. No scientific discipline seems able to describe these phenomena. We would be quite willing to define them as a state of active, intense prayer, partially disconnected from the outside world, a state of contemplation with a separate person whom they alone can see, hear and touch."[25]

It is difficult to identify events in the history of the church that have been exposed to as much multidisciplinary examination as those at Medjugorje. The Roman Catholic Church has not taken an official and definitive position. Bedard,[26] Laurentin,[27] and Wayne Weible,[28] a Lutheran who became interested in Medjugorje and has since converted to Roman Catholicism, believe the apparitions are authentic, while others take a negative position.

---

[24] Ibid., 48f. On a much less scientific level, one visionary was physically lifted from the floor by an examiner and another was pricked with a pin to the point of drawing blood (see Laurentin and Rupcic, *Is the Virgin Mary Appearing?* 128–34).

[25] Laurentin and Joyeux, *Scientific and Medical Studies*, 75. Joyeux also says, "The clinical study of the visionaries before, during and after the ecstasy allows us to eliminate formally all clinical signs comparable to those observed during individual or collective hallucination, hysteria, neurosis or pathological ecstasy" (p. 53). Sensitive to the need for documentation, Laurentin and Joyeux provide readings from electroencephalograms (56–61), electrooculograms (62f.), an electrocardiogram (67), and an "evoked auditory potentials" test (56–69).

[26] Bedard, *Medjugorje*, 6.

[27] Laurentin and Rupcic, *Is the Virgin Mary Appearing?* 128.

[28] Wayne Weible, *Medjugorje: The Message* (Orleans, Mass.: Paraclete Press, 1989).

Priests belonging to the Franciscan order have provided the spiritual leadership at Medjugorje. Mart Bax implies that they are responsible for the apparitions, suggesting that they stimulated them to serve their own political ends:

> What began about nine years ago with six young people's supernatural experiences in a small peasant village has now developed into a firmly established Franciscan-run devotional movement with an impressive number of international branches. . . . One can therefore only expect the visionaries and their heavenly messages to disappear from public view when, in the opinion of the Franciscans, some satisfactory solution has been found to the conflict that binds them to the bishop and his priests.[29]

I found much at Medjugorje to admire. While I did not see all of the visionaries, I did see Vicka. She makes herself available to meet with groups so that people can ask questions. Her house is on a very narrow, winding street in the little village that stands at the foot of the hill on which Mary first appeared. It is where she lived before the visions started. Only its coat of white plaster distinguishes her home from the other stone houses to which it is attached.

When Vicka appeared, she was wearing jeans and a black-and-white top. She wore her hair very casually, and she had no makeup on. Over the years hundreds of thousands, perhaps millions, of people have sought her out. They believe that she and the others enjoy an intimate relationship with the "Mother of God." Vicka could have capitalized on this for her own benefit, but she appeared to have resisted that, standing on the old stone steps of her parents' house, chatting with people in a very unassuming, unpretentious manner and radiating sincerity.

Father Philip Pavic also made a strong impression on me. He is a well-educated American Franciscan who has lived and worked in Paris and Jerusalem. The day I visited his cramped, unair-conditioned office outside the church, the temperature hung around 106 degrees Fahrenheit. I was uncomfortable

---

[29] Bax, "Madonna of Medjugorje," 69, 72.

sitting in the coolest summer clothing I had; he was in his long dark brown robes. That day he had already delivered a number of talks and heard confession for several hours in a confessional exposed to the full power of the sun. He had been counseling someone before I arrived, and another person was sitting on the steps waiting for him when I left. His day was not going to end for another eight hours.

He lives in the rectory beside the church. Given the thousands of pilgrims who ebb and flow around the church praying, laughing, weeping, singing choruses to the accompaniment of guitars and tambourines, it must be somewhat like living on the midway at a fair! He slips away for a week's vacation once or twice a year. This is a life of remarkable dedication. There is a lot of reality at Medjugorje.

Healings

Among the realities, I would include at least some of the claims to healings. The claims began very shortly after the young people first reported seeing Mary,[30] and the number mounted rapidly. Sometime before 1985, Fr. Ljudevit Rupcic sent records on fifty-five cases to the head of the medical bureau at Lourdes. Of these, Laurentin thought thirty should not be dismissed as mere superstition, even though they had not been confirmed adequately.[31] When Bax was doing his research at Medjugorje between 1985 and 1988, two hundred to five hundred healings or other answers to prayer were being recorded at the rectory every day.[32] From among these, Laurentin reports, "Dr. Ivan Tole, born at Rodoc near Mostar, who belongs to the International Committee of Lourdes, considers that three or four of the healings are certainly miraculous."[33]

---

[30] Ibid., 66.
[31] Laurentin and Rupcic, *Is the Virgin Mary Appearing?* 150.
[32] Bax, "Madonna of Medjugorje," 70.
[33] Laurentin and Rupcic, *Is the Virgin Mary Appearing?* 134.

The following accounts are representative of a large number that can be found in the literature dealing with Medjugorje. Damir Koric, who was hydrocephalic and hemorrhaging, was healed in 1981 while Vicka prayed, and Iva Tole, who suffered from multiple sclerosis, was healed in the same year when invited by Jakov to pray.[34]

Joyeux and Laurentin present the case of Diana Basile of Milan.[35] She, too, was healed of multiple sclerosis at Medjugorje on May 23, 1984. Joyeux and Laurentin review the evidence of Basile's loss of sight in the right eye, motor difficulties, and incontinence, and they give the names of four physicians at the Specialist Clinical Institute of Milan who attested on July 5, 1984, to her complete healing.

Finally, there is the case of Heather Duncan of Scotland. Paralyzed for five years following a car accident, she traveled to Medjugorje in 1990, and she was healed. When she returned in March 1991 to give thanks, she brought X-rays and a medical diagnosis confirming that she would probably never walk again, or if she did, it would be with great pain. She also now had a medical certificate indicating that she was completely well.[36]

Bridget Green, who was born on December 19, 1973, and was living in Houston, Texas, in 1988, was brought to my attention by Fr. Philip Pavic. He gave me a copy of the file the family had brought back to him after Bridget had been healed. The following material is drawn from that file.[37]

At eight years of age, Bridget was diagnosed as suffering from myasthenia gravis, a neuromuscular disorder related to muscular dystrophy. It is a terminal illness. The attending

---

[34] René Laurentin, *La prolongation des apparitions de Medjugorje: Délai de miséricorde pour un monde en danger?* (Paris: O.E.I.L., 1986) 80f.

[35] Laurentin and Joyeux, *Scientific and Medical Studies*, 100–105.

[36] "News Nuggets," 4.

[37] S. J. Culotta, "A Synopsis of Significant Events Related to the Healing of Bridget Green at Medjugorje," 6 pages (incl. letter) to Philip Pavic, n.d.; Robert S. Zeller, "Case Summary of Bridget Green, Myasthenia gravis," 1988; idem, "Progress Note Bridget Green," Nov. 29, 1988.

physician was Dr. Robert S. Zeller, head of research at the Muscular Dystrophy Foundation in Houston, Texas. He had his diagnosis confirmed by the head of the Department of Neurology at Baylor College of Medicine.

In November 1988, Bridget and her mother went to Medjugorje. On the evening of Monday, November 7, while on the hill where Mary first appeared to the young people, Bridget became convinced she was healed. She discontinued her medication that night. She and her mother completed their pilgrimage and returned to Houston. On November 29 she went to see Dr. Zeller. The following is from a transcript made of the interview:

Z: "I understand you went to Yugoslavia. Where in Yugoslavia?"

B: "Medjugorje."

Z: "What did you do?"

B: "I prayed, I went to church."

— (a period of silence) —

Z: "Are you off your medication?"

B: "Yes."

Z: "For how long?"

B: "For three weeks."

Z: "Wonderful, I never wanted you on that stuff anyway. It's a miracle! What can I say. I'm delighted. It's a miracle. . . . Bridget is cured, it's a miracle."[38]

Later, when Zeller wrote up a report on the interview, he said, "She [Bridget] went to Yugoslavia to a religious retreat and stopped her medication. She was cured of her disease by the Lord. She is no longer on medication and when I saw her most recently on 11/29/88 she had no evidence of myasthenia gravis and indeed is as strong as any normal child her age."

---

[38] Culotta, "Synopsis" (a record of appointment ["Progress Note"] Nov. 29, 1988).

This is a clearly documented healing. It is rare to find a physician ready to attribute a cure to divine intervention, as does Dr. Zeller.[39]

In the early days of Medjugorje, the approach to praying for the sick was more informal than it is now. Then the visionaries were more accessible and more clearly at the center of events. After an apparition, they assisted at Mass, then joined different prayer teams to minister to those who requested prayer for healing. They tried to speak with each sick person in order to understand the nature of her or his illness and to comfort.[40] But the emphasis is shifting to the church, teaching, and the clergy. It is part of that refocusing I referred to before.[41]

The practice of praying for the sick following evening Mass, known as "the healing prayer," has continued and, in fact, has taken on greater importance. The visionaries, however, are rarely present now, if ever. During the healing prayers I observed in July 1990, there was no gathering around anyone and no one touched anyone else. It seemed a conscious attempt was being made to turn attention away from any human agent and to focus it on Jesus.

The prayers were held outside because of the heat in the church. They were parts of very long evenings of religious

---

[39] Another case that has received widespread attention is that of Rita Klaus of Pennsylvania. She appears to have been healed of multiple sclerosis in June 1986. In her case, muscular atrophy from the twenty-year-old disease disappeared immediately, as did the accompanying physical deformity. See Deborah Deasy, "Medical Mystery: Teacher's Recovery Is Investigated as Miracle," *Pittsburgh Press*, January 24, 1988, A11.

[40] Yanko Bubalo, *"Je vois la Vierge": Aînée des voyants de Medjugorje Vicka raconte les apparitions et son extraordinaire expérience* (Paris: O.E.I.L., [1983]) 162.

[41] See p. 103 n. 8 above. Eric Hobsbawm offers valuable insights into the creation of traditions: "It is evident that any social practice that needs to be carried out repeatedly will tend, for convenience and efficiency, to develop a set of such conventions and routines, which may be de facto or de jure formalized for the purposes of imparting the practice to new practitioners" (Eric Hobsbawm and Terence Ranger, eds., *The Invention of Tradition* [Cambridge: Cambridge University Press, 1984] 30).

services. Both evenings I was present, the prayers were led by Father Slavko Barbaric, who stood quietly behind the altar. The devotion was palpable. Some people knelt motionless in front of the low platform while others were on their knees or sitting among wooden benches. Here and there people who had knelt were doubled over so that their faces were pressed into the rough gravel. Dusk had settled in, spreading a deep calm over the scene. Speaking in several languages, Barbaric called us to focus on Jesus. This prayer is not the heart of Medjugorje, but it is highly significant.

At Medjugorje, the dominant theological idea about heal- ing has been Mary's role as intercessor. In 1983 Fr. Yanko Bubalo asked Vicka how she and the others first came to lay hands on the sick and pray for their healing. The answer was, "That is part of Our Lady's message. She has often spoken of it."[42] Fr. Svetozar Kraljevic quotes a message said to have been given by Mary on July 21, 1982: "You should pray and fast on behalf of the sick. It is easy for God to heal them, but it is not easy for man."[43] And he notes, "The evening service ends with a prayer for the sick. Many pilgrims are always on hand—some have come from the most distant places—to ask the Mother of God to intercede for them in their illnesses, asking God to heal or comfort them."[44] These comments highlight the fact that the initiative for praying for the sick is thought to have been taken by Mary.

This thinking appears also in the case of Bridget Green. When Dr. Zeller asked Bridget if she could not have just prayed and gone to church in Houston, her response was, "I went in hopes to see Mary, our Blessed Mother." Clearly, Bridget thought her chances of being healed would be increased if Mary became involved in her case.

---

[42] Bubalo, *"Je vois la Vierge,"* 162.

[43] Svetozar Kraljevic, *The Apparitions of Our Lady at Medjugorje, 1981–1983: An Historical Account with Interviews* (Chicago: Franciscan Herald Press, 1984) 118.

[44] Ibid., 53.

And when an infant showing signs of epilepsy was healed in 1981, his mother commented, "Jakov told us, that the Madonna said that we, the parents, should fervently believe, and if we did, Danijel would be cured," and his father added, "It's the Madonna who helped him."[45]

The importance of Mary is unmistakable. In one of the two questions Laurentin and Rupcic put to the visionaries about healing, they asked, "Does Our Lady perform miracles? Has she healed people?" It is interesting in itself that they should phrase the question in this way, but the answer is of greater importance. Jakov, Vicka, Ivanka, Mirjana, and Ivan all said, "Yes."[46] Marija responded more precisely, "There are many healings through the intercession of Our Lady." She presents Mary as intercessor rather than healer—a point made also by Miravalle on the basis of his analysis of the messages attributed to Mary.[47] I suspect that the other visionaries, Laurentin, and Rupcic would agree.

Mary has been the dominant figure in the Medjugorje approach to healing, but that may be changing. During the healing prayers I attended, there was no reference to her. In fact, there was very little oral instruction. We were reminded that Jesus was present, but there was not much explicit theology beyond that. Fr. Barbaric, however, provided visual instruction. He held up a crucifix throughout the prayer. There was no magic in this, as Protestant prejudice might assume. He was making the statement that everything one receives from God, healing included, flows from the cross. His action was part of a conscious concern to fix Medjugorje firmly on a christological center.[48]

On the other hand, popular thinking has taken some pilgrims in quite a different direction. Laurentin records several instances in which healing has been claimed through the use of

---

[45] Ibid., 181, 184.

[46] Laurentin and Rupcic, *Is the Virgin Mary Appearing?* 60.

[47] Miravalle, *Message of Medjugorje*, 8.

[48] Fr. Philip Pavic confirmed this interpretation of Barbaric's action (interview by author, Medjugorje, July 24, 1990).

dirt, flowers, or herbs taken from the hill on which Mary first appeared.[49]

Conclusion

Events that have occurred in this obscure setting in Bosnia-Herzegovina are among the most interesting in the church of the late twentieth century. The apparitions are supposedly continuing. How long can they go on? What decision will the Roman Catholic Church finally come to about them, and when? There is no way to answer these questions. Neither is there any way to predict how the devotion at Medjugorje will develop or what will become of the original visionaries or the town itself.

It is clear, however, that Medjugorje has been important in the spiritual lives of many people and that there is an ongoing attempt to focus Medjugorje on Christ. And it is virtually certain that there have been authentic healings associated with Medjugorje.

---

[49] Laurentin and Rupcic, *Is the Virgin Mary Appearing?* 152–57.

Part 3

The Reliquarial Model

RELICS AND HEALING
THE MIRACLES AT ST. MEDARD

In addition to the confrontational and the intercessory, there is a third approach to healing, which I call the *reliquarial* model, from the word "relics." Advocates of this approach believe that miracles come through the remains of special people, or "saints." F. P. Chiovaro defines "relics" as "the body or whatever remains of a holy person after death, as well as objects that had actual contact with the saint's body during his lifetime."[1]

This definition should be broadened. P. Séjourné suggests three subcategories: corporeal relics (remains of bodies); real relics (objects that saints used while on earth—for example, clothes, things employed in day-to-day life, instruments of penitence, and material related to their captivity, such as chains); and representative relics (for example, tombs, covers of tombs, objects people placed against saints' remains or their tombs, and even lamps hung in the places where their bodies were buried).[2] The term "relics" includes a wide and diverse range of objects, because it grew out of the piety of the faithful rather than the reflections of scholars.

---

[1] F. P. Chiovaro, "Relics," NCE, 12.234.
[2] P. Séjourné, "Reliques," *Dictionnaire de théologie catholique* (ed. A. Vacant et al.; Paris: Letouzey and Ané, 1939), vol. 52, col. 2313.

Two examples of this approach to healing will be examined. The first arose from the church of late antiquity[3] and the Middle Ages. The second example was a fascinating group of healings from eighteenth-century Paris centered on the tomb of François de Pâris.

---

[3] The reader will note that the first three approaches to healing all appeared in the patristic church.

8

Relics and Healing
BONES OF BLESSING

This territory is foreign to most Protestants. Those who stand in the line of Luther, Calvin, and Zwingli have given very little credence to claims for the healing efficacy of body parts of the saints. By contrast, both the Orthodox and the Roman Catholic Churches have been comfortable with the concepts found here.

The reliquarial approach to the miraculous dominated Christian thought and practice with regard to healing much longer than any of the others. From late antiquity through the Middle Ages, that is, from the mid–fourth century until the late fifteenth, claims to healings associated with relics were common. I will provide an overview of the concepts and then examine the miraculous cures associated with relics.

Overview

Interest in objects associated with special people arose early. Séjourné points to the woman who was healed by touching Jesus' clothes (Matt 9:20–22) and to the handkerchiefs and aprons that touched Paul (Acts 19:11f.),[1] but Chiovaro observes, "It is . . . vain to seek a justification for the cult [formal

---

[1] Séjourné, "Reliques," col. 2316f.

worship] of relics in the Old Testament; nor is much attention paid relics in the New Testament."[2]

The earliest recorded occasions when people showed special concern for the physical remains of outstanding Christians occurred in relation to Ignatius of Antioch, who died in Rome c. 117,[3] and his friend Polycarp of Smyrna, who was martyred forty years later. Polycarp's congregation wanted to save his body because, impressed with his devotion to Christ, they thought it appropriate to love deeply one who was so attached to his King and Master.[4] Still, there was no liturgical celebration devoted to martyrs before the end of the third century.[5] Developed acts of worship centered on the remains of saints are not explicitly mentioned until the fifth and sixth centuries, when they appear in epitaphs from Africa, Spain, and Gaul.[6] So, while interest in physical remains of saints arose within the first century of Christian experience, a considerable time lapsed before formal devotions to them surfaced in the worship life of the church.

There were significant differences in the ways the Latin West and the Greek East approached relics. The West, under Roman influence, was hesitant to open graves and move bodies;[7] the East was much more prepared to do so.[8] The West's attitude was illustrated clearly in the late sixth century, when Gregory the Great, bishop of Rome, denied the empress Constantina's

---

[2] Chiovaro, "Relics," 234.

[3] Ironically, Ignatius had hoped that there would be no remains when the lions were through with him.

[4] See Séjourné, "Reliques," col. 2319; and Chiovaro, "Relics," 234.

[5] Séjourné, "Reliques," col. 2323.

[6] Ibid., col. 2330.

[7] Although it did happen. In AD 386 Ambrose, bishop of Milan, exhumed the bodies of the martyrs Protasius and Gervasius and moved them to a more prestigious location (Ambrose, *Letter 61*, FC 26.376ff.).

[8] See Basil, *Letter 155*, FC 13.210. The earliest translation (ceremonial movement from one place to another) of a relic may have occurred between 351 and 354 when Caesar Gallus moved the body of St. Babylas (Patrice Boussel, *Des reliques et de leur bon usage* [Paris: Balland, 1971] 19).

request for the apostle Paul's head. In explanation, Gregory said, "let my most tranquil lady know that it is not the custom of the Romans, when they give relics of saints, to presume to touch any part of the body."[9] He offered to substitute filings from the chain that had held St. Peter during his captivity in Rome.[10] By contrast, John of Damascus, writing 150 years later, had no such scruples. He argued that the prohibition on touching the dead did not apply to martyrs who were awaiting the resurrection because they were not really dead, just asleep.[11]

While these attitudes were being shaped, relics were enjoying a remarkable rise in popularity because of their apparent ability to produce miracles. Their importance for the consecration of new churches can be seen in the correspondence of Ambrose[12] and, later, of Basil of Caesarea, whose friend Bishop Arcadius had built a new church. Basil implores, "If we are able to find relics of martyrs anywhere, we beg that we may contribute to your undertaking."[13] Much later, canon (regulation) 7 of the Council of Nicaea (AD 787) specified "that relics shall be placed with the accustomed service in as many of the sacred temples as have been consecrated without the relics of the Martyrs. And if any bishop from this time forward is found consecrating a temple without holy relics, he shall be deposed, as a transgressor of the ecclesiastical traditions."[14] And in Charlemagne's empire, altars without relics in them were to be destroyed.[15]

---

[9] Gregory the Great, *Epistle 30*. The Western church, however, had not been entirely consistent in acting on this policy. In one letter, Augustine refers to people carrying relics of St. Stephen (*Letter 212*, FC 32.52).

[10] Gregory the Great, *Epistle 30*, NPNF[2] 12.155.

[11] John of Damascus, *An Exact Exposition*, FC 37.87.

[12] Ambrose, *Letter 61*, FC 26.376.

[13] Basil, *Letter 49*, FC 13.132.

[14] Canon 7, *The Canons of the Holy and Ecumenical Seventh Council*, NPNF[2] 14.560.

[15] Patrick J. Geary, *Furta sacra: Thefts of Relics in the Central Middle Ages* (Princeton: Princeton University Press, 1978) 42.

Relics, and the miracles they produced, were also extremely important to missionary outreach in Europe.[16] Further, in AD 803 Charlemagne made the practice of swearing oaths on relics or in churches normative for his empire.[17] For these reasons, relics came to occupy a growing place in people's minds and their use became customary over a widening area. When the Norman raids began in the tenth century, the influence of relics spread even further when harassed monks carried their precious saints with them as they fled before the marauders.[18]

The institutional emphasis on relics and their growing popular significance created an extraordinary demand for them, which in turn stimulated a large number of specialized entrepreneurs. One of the most famous was the deacon Deusdona, who lived near Saint-Pierre-ès-Liens in France. He acquired bones from a cemetery in Rome and sold them in Germany and France.[19] Indeed, the catacombs and cemeteries in and around Rome began to be mined for human remains. Bodies were broken into many pieces in order to respond to an insatiable hunger for relics in northern Europe.[20] This practice sounds rather cavalier, if not bizarre. Peter Brown, however, sets it in a different light, suggesting that this dispersion of relics prevented "the holy" from being confined to a limited number of sites and kept salvation from being seen as something relevant only to the distant past. The relics, he proposes, brought a sense of "deliverance and pardon into the present."[21]

---

[16] R. C. Finucane, *Miracles and Pilgrims: Popular Belief in Medieval England* (Totowa, N.J.: Rowman & Littlefield, 1977) 20.

[17] Geary, *Furta sacra*, 44.

[18] Boussel, *Reliques*, 42.

[19] Ibid., 35.

[20] Chiovaro, "Relics," 237. Pope Paschal I (817–24) facilitated this trade by ordering the abandonment of the catacombs and the transfer of relics to churches in Rome; this made the "inventory" more readily accessible.

[21] Peter Brown, *The Cult of the Saints: Its Rise and Function in Latin Christianity* (Haskell Lectures on History of Religions, n.s. 2; Chicago: University of Chicago Press, 1981) 90f.

Relics came to occupy a position of importance in medieval European society that is hard for people living at the end of the twentieth century to comprehend. Finucane states, "From Rome to Lindisfarne the powers of holy bones were recognized by the simplest Christians, innocent of theology, and for a thousand years these beliefs, though sometimes challenged, would dominate much of the folk-Christianity of Europe."[22] Commenting on the role of relics in the ninth and tenth centuries, Geary adds, "It was at this period that their importance was at its zenith, not only for the 'people,' but in every segment of Christian society."[23]

This enthusiasm for relics was irrepressible. It prompted thousands of people annually to interrupt their lives and go on pilgrimage. They would travel great distances to the universally recognized shrines at Jerusalem, Rome, or Santiago de Compostela in northwest Spain, where the remains of St. James were to be found. Alternatively, they would visit regional shrines, such as the one at Canterbury, holding the remains of Thomas à Becket, or one of the many local holy places scattered across Europe. For those coming simply as an act of devotion, the stay might be brief, but for others seeking healing, it would be different. They frequently moved into a location as near as possible to the relic and settled down there waiting for a cure.[24] Relics were major features of the European worldview throughout the Middle Ages.[25]

Various explanations have been offered for the place that relics came to occupy. Geary thinks that the way had been prepared for them by the pagan cult of heroes. There was no direct

---

[22] Peter Brown, *The Cult of the Saints: Its Rise and Function in Latin Christianity* (Haskell Lectures on History of Religions, n.s. 2; Chicago: University of Chicago Press, 1981) 90f.

[23] Geary, *Furta sacra*, 30.

[24] See Finucane, *Miracles and Pilgrims*, 48f.

[25] In *Twelfth Night*, act 3, scene 3, Shakespeare has Sebastian and Antonio entering a town in Illyria. Finding himself in a new place and in want of entertainment, Sebastian says, "What's to do? Shall we go see the reliques of this town?" The Bard seems to have been well aware of the popularity of relics.

connection between that cult and the honor granted to the re-mains of the saints, but, he argues, it established in society the habit of venerating the bodies of outstanding people. He adds that the Christian belief in the resurrection was important. The expectation that the saints would be back for their body parts made the remains particularly special.[26]

Both Séjourné and Finucane highlight the importance of the influx of large numbers of relatively uninstructed pagans, es-pecially after Constantine made Christianity legal early in the fourth century and Theodosius made it the only legitimate religion in the empire sixty years later,[27] but Brown points in a different direction. He argues that the growth in importance of relics and shrines had less to do with pagan masses than with "changes in the quality of leadership within the Christian community itself,"[28] and he thinks that Ambrose set the style. In the late fourth century, bishops were coming from empowered families and were called upon to administer vast wealth acquired through endowments. They could not spend it on themselves, but they could lavish it on the promotion and development of buildings, feasts, and chari-ties related to saints and relics. The efforts of these powerful "new men" to find suitable outlets for recently acquired wealth con-tributed to the elevation of holy bones and holy places.[29]

Brown adds that the popularity of relics and shrines was strengthened by the opportunities they afforded women. In the European culture of the time, women's activities were tightly cir-cumscribed. Their context of life was the private home or con-vent, while men moved publicly in the world at large.[30] Shrines offered women public places to which they could go with less

---

[26] Geary, *Furta sacra*, 33.

[27] Séjourné, "Reliques," col. 2332; and Finucane, *Miracles and Pilgrims*, 19.

[28] Brown, *Cult of the Saints*, 36.

[29] Ibid., 38f.

[30] See Carla Casagrande, "The Protected Woman" (trans. Clarissa Bots-ford), in *Silences of the Middle Ages*, vol. 2 of *A History of Women in the West* (ed. Christiane Klapisch-Zuber; Cambridge, Mass.: Belknap Press of Harvard Uni-versity Press, 1992) 70–104.

chance of being molested by either their families or predators. They could also give directly to the charities of shrines, whereas in general charitable giving was seen as a political act and was therefore reserved for men.[31]

The extraordinary popularity of saints, relics, and shrines with thousands of people circulating among them, together with the almost uncontrolled trafficking in body parts, occasioned many abuses,[32] and many voices across the centuries were raised in protest,[33] even before John Calvin's trenchant *Traité des reliques*, published in Geneva in 1536.

Theologians struggled, with little success, to shape the devotion given relics. Finucane says that among the new Christians of Europe, "the powers of holy men both living and dead took the place of abstruse doctrine and theological subtleties," and he sums up the dilemma facing medieval church leadership: "The hierarchy could neither deny the sanctity of relics and the intervention of saints, nor condone the excesses committed not only by the lay public but even by some of its own clergy, in their dealings with these very saints and their relics."[34]

As Séjourné puts it, the theologians were confronted with the task of developing doctrine that would bring together the current practices of the faithful and the facts of the Christian faith.[35] Relics were also a part of the deliberations of the Council of Trent,[36] but in spite of, or because of, the tinkering of churchmen and theologians, the belief of the faithful in relics remained strong up until recently.

---

[31] Brown, *Cult of the Saints*, 44, 46.

[32] See Séjourné, "Reliques," col. 2333; Carl J. Peter, "Relics," in *The New Dictionary of Theology* (ed. J. A. Komonchak, Mary Collins, and D. A. Lane; Wilmington, Del.: Michael Glazier, 1987) 862; and Ernst Nierrmann, "Relics," in *Sacramentum mundi: An Encyclopedia of Theology* (Montreal: Herder & Herder, 1970) 5.245.

[33] See Chiovaro, "Relics," 235; Geary, *Furta sacra*, 36; and Boussel, *Reliques*, 57, 66.

[34] Finucane, *Miracles and Pilgrims*, 23, 38.

[35] Séjourné, "Reliques," col. 2338.

[36] See Nierrmann, "Relics," 245; and Chiovaro, "Relics," 238.

While it has not disappeared,[37] devotion to relics has declined sharply during the last two centuries.[38] Along with the
waning interest among Catholics at large, relics have not figured
prominently in recent official documents of the Roman Catholic
Church. They are given one brief mention in *Sacrosanctum conci-*
lium, Vatican II's document on the liturgy: "The saints have been
traditionally honored in the church and their authentic relics and
images held in veneration."[39] They do not appear in the encyclical
letter published by Pope John Paul II in 1991, *Redemptoris missio*.
This is significant because the encyclical discusses missionary
outreach and evangelism, areas in which relics and the miraculous
were thought to be so important in the Middle Ages.[40] Finally, the
word "relic" does not appear in the index of the 698-page *Cate-*
chism of the Catholic Church published in 1994. Perhaps, just as
popular devotion to relics elevated them in the Roman Catholic Church, a sag in popular interest has led to their decline.

The Miracles

Whatever the current status of relics is and however
theologians have attempted to understand them, "in practice,
among the barbarian peoples recently Christianized, the prin-
cipal interest in relics centered on the miracles and prodigies
associated with their cult," according to Ambrose.[41] Above all
else, it was the miracles that mattered.

---

[37] See Joan C. Cruz, *Relics* (Huntington, Ind.: Our Sunday Visitor, 1984).

[38] Boussel, *Reliques*, 91.

[39] *Sacrosanctum concilium* 111, in *The Documents of Vatican II* (ed. Walter
M. Abbott, S.J.; New York: Guild Press, 1966), 170.

[40] See Finucane, *Miracles and Pilgrims*, 20ff.; Geary, *Furta sacra*, 20; and
Aline Rousselle, *Croire et guérir: La foi en Gaule dans l'antiquité tardive* (Paris:
Fayard, 1990) 198.

[41] Chiovaro, "Relics," 235. When the saint being sought for a miracle
did not deliver on the healing, the atmosphere could become tense. Benedicta
Ward refers to prayer "in an aggressive and demanding tone" as suppliants tried
to "bully" saints into delivering miracles ("Miracles and Miracle Collections,
1015–1215" [D.Phil. diss., Oxford University, 1978] 197ff.).

In AD 386 Ambrose and his congregation had the good fortune to find the physical remains of two men who were identified as the martyrs Gervasius and Protasius. Later Ambrose wrote to his sister describing the events and sharing the sermons that he preached to his congregation on that occasion.

In the first sermon, delivered on the day when the bodies were discovered, he said to the congregation,

> You know, and, in fact, have seen many persons cleansed of the evil spirits. And many who touched the clothing of the saints with their hands were rid of sicknesses which troubled them. Miracles from times past are beginning anew as when at the coming of the Lord Jesus great grace poured itself upon the earth. You have seen how many have been healed by the mere shadow of the bodies of the saints. How many handkerchiefs have been passed about! How many garments which were laid upon the sacred relics are now said to possess healing power in their very touch! Everyone is glad to touch the outer cloth and touching it he will be cured.[42]

Ambrose's plan was to rebury the relics immediately, but the congregation pleaded to delay the ceremony. Ambrose agreed to leave the bodies in the church overnight, presumably so that people would have the opportunity to get as close to them as possible. On the next day, before the burial, Ambrose preached again. He had acknowledged that a man had been healed as the bodies were being moved,[43] and he now provided more details. The man, a butcher named Severus, was able to call on those who had helped him while he was blind to testify to his healing. Ambrose said, "He cries out, saying that when he touched the hem of the martyrs' garment in which the sacred relics were covered light was restored to him."[44] To Ambrose and many others, the direct contact with a representative relic brought about the healing. This pattern appears repeatedly in accounts of healing by means of relics.

---

[42] Ambrose, *Letter 61*, FC 26.376.

[43] Ibid.

[44] Ibid., FC 26.382. Augustine also was familiar with the details of this case (*Confessions* 9.7, NPNF[1] 1.134).

Augustine, bishop of Hippo, was also interested in miraculous cures through relics. He dedicated chapter 8 of book 22 in the *City of God* to a discussion of healings. He countered the suggestion that while miracles were common earlier in the story of the church, they were no longer occurring in the fifth century:

> The truth is that even today miracles are being wrought in the name of Christ, sometimes through His sacraments and sometimes through the intercession of the relics of his saints. Only, such miracles do not strike the imagination with the same flashing brilliance as the earlier miracles, and so they do not get the same flashing publicity as the others did. The fact that the canon of our Scriptures is definitively closed brings it about that the original miracles are everywhere repeated and are fixed in people's memory, whereas contemporary miracles which happen here or there seldom become known even to the whole of the local population in and around the place where they occur.[45]

Many miracles appear to have been occurring. Augustine cited the case of a man named Innocent, who was healed from rectal fistula (hemorrhoids?), and he also gave an account of a miraculous healing of breast cancer experienced by a woman named Innocentia.[46]

Of particular interest for our present purposes are Augustine's comments about healings through the relics of St. Stephen. Augustine suggested that they were many, and expressed his frustration at being caught between having to conclude his book and wanting to recount the miracles:

> If I kept merely to miracles of healing and omitted all others, and if I told only those wrought by this one martyr, the glorious St. Stephen, and if I limited myself to those that happened here at Hippo and Calama, I should have to fill several volumes and, even then, I could do no more than tell those cases that have been officially recorded and attested for public reading in our churches.
>
> This recording and attesting, in fact, is what I took care to have done, once I realized how many miracles were occurring in our own day and which were so like the miracles of old and also how wrong it would be

---

[45] Augustine, *City of God* 22.8, FC 24.432f.
[46] Ibid., FC 24.433–37, 445f.

to allow the memory of these marvels of divine power to perish from among our people. It is only two years ago that the keeping of records was begun here in Hippo, and already, at this writing, we have nearly seventy attested miracles.[47]

We do not know how the claims to miracles were examined, but Augustine clearly thought that many unusual events were occurring. He insisted that "it is a simple fact, then, that there is no lack of miracles even in our day."[48]

John of Damascus wrote about three hundred years later than Augustine. One brief passage in his *Exact Exposition of the Orthodox Faith* is relevant: "In the relics of the saints the Lord Christ has provided us with saving fountains which in many ways pour out benefactions and gush with fragrant ointment."[49] Healings no doubt were included in the "benefactions."

Thus three luminaries, one from the early Middle Ages and, especially, two from the early church, associate healings with the physical remains of saints.

There are many such accounts from throughout the Middle Ages. One of Finucane's studies "is about 3,000 medieval people who claimed that they had experienced a 'miracle,' in most cases a miracle of healing."[50] Boussel cites a study of miracles that were obtained by the relics of St. Gibrien at Reims in the middle of the twelfth century; a record of miracles was kept by monks at Gibrien's tomb. Of 102 miracles, 98 were healings, 50 of them instantaneous, with 7 or 8 occurring each week for the period during which the account was kept.[51]

The medieval person lived in the keen awareness that at any moment something extraordinary could happen through the relics of saints. Brown perceptively comments that the miracles that occurred at shrines were seen not only as responses to the fear of death but also as evidence of God's power and his

---

[47] Ibid., FC 24.445.
[48] Ibid., FC 24.447.
[49] John of Damascus, *An Exact Exposition*, FC 26.368.
[50] Finucane, *Miracles and Pilgrims*, 9.
[51] Boussel, *Reliques*, 45.

concern for the flesh and as proof of a future resurrection. At saints' graves, the eternity of paradise and the first touch of the resurrection came into the present.[52]

Standing behind any discussion of relics and healing is the issue of how much confidence is to be placed in the evidence. In one of his studies, Finucane raises serious doubts. He suggests that "the idea of a 'cure' could only be a social generalization,"[53] that is, a conclusion reached by a society on the basis of knowledge available to it. By this he means that one must have a certain level of medical competency before one can identify a cure. There must be some idea of what health and illness are, what particular symptoms mean, what degree of illness is present, what the prognosis is, and what constitutes recovery. At best, medieval people could make only partial responses to these kinds of concerns, and often they would be completely wrong. Finucane presents evidence showing that people living a thousand years ago frequently had difficulty determining who was alive and who was dead. Certain and accurate diagnosis of much illness was quite beyond them. Finucane concludes that because their understanding of these matters was so rudimentary, "any alleviation, however slight, however incomplete, and however temporary, was a boon, a wonderful thing, a miraculous cure when attributed to a saint."[54]

In a slightly modified position, another "reliquarian," Benedicta Ward, draws a distinction between miracles alleged to have been performed by saints while they were alive and accounts of healings at shrines: "While the records of miracles at shrines for this period were generally speaking a painstaking record of what people believed had happened to them personally by the power of the saint, miracles in saints' lives cannot be taken at their face value in the same way."[55] The latter, she argues, were focused on embellishing the reputation of the saint

---

[52] Brown, *Cult of the Saints*, 77.
[53] Finucane, "Use and Abuse of Medieval Miracles," 7.
[54] Ibid., 9.
[55] Ward, "Miracles," 249.

and typically gave accounts of fabulous deeds, such as finding water. On the other hand, the former were primarily concerned to give accounts of healings that had happened to particular people. But caution must be exercised. As Finucane points out, the people who kept the records may have been eager to scrape together all the miracles they could find in order to build their saint's reputation.[56]

One must avoid rank credulity when faced with these accounts. Nonetheless, I find it difficult to state categorically that nothing extraordinary ever happened. The story of Ambrose's butcher who received his sight back is remarkable by any standard.

Conclusion

The accounts of miracles occurring through various kinds of relics bulk large. Much within them must be classified as sheer magic, superstition, or myth. This body of material cannot, however, simply be dismissed. Augustine and others realized that some effort had to be made to validate claims. How successful they were in distinguishing the truly miraculous from the merely ordinary or the patently false is impossible to say. But even from this distance, struggling with the significant time lapse and the dramatic difference in worldviews, I believe there are grounds for assuming that at least on some occasions something beyond the ordinary occurred. Our view of the role of relics depends on the theology we bring to the question.

---

[56] Finucane, "Use and Abuse of Medieval Miracles," 6

9

The Miracles at St. Médard
THE CONVULSIONARIES

The second example of the reliquarial approach to healing comes from early eighteenth-century Paris. It is found in a truly exotic series of events centered on a small cemetery in the working-class quarter of St. Médard. The remaining space of what was once the cemetery is a walled-in, tranquil flower garden, but as tranquil as it is now, for a six-month period, between July 1731 and January 1732, it became the eye of an intense religious and political storm.

The focus of attention was a grave. It disappeared early in our century, but in 1731 people laid the sick on its horizontal stone, leaped on it themselves, or crawled under it, between it and the ground, and lay there praying. Often, as soon as they touched the grave, they would be seized by violent convulsions, and sometimes, when the convulsions passed, they would find themselves healed of some disease.

The hope of healing gave the tomb its drawing power. Before, but especially after, July 1731 the narrow streets and lanes of the parish of St. James, in which the cemetery lay, were frequently jammed with people, rich and poor, surging toward the burial ground. Individuals' claims of healing are the focus of our attention, but the context should first be understood.

Religious Turmoil

The circumstances in which the healings appeared were anything but tranquil. At their center was François de Pâris, who lived from June 30, 1690, to May 1, 1727. Born into a so-cially well-placed family, de Pâris decided on a life in the church. He was ordained a deacon in 1718 and never rose above that level, believing himself to be spiritually unworthy.[1]

De Pâris was appointed to St. Médard and threw himself into the work of his parish, devoting himself particularly to the poor and helpless. His reputation for piety, however, rested not only on his service to others but also on his life of extreme self-denial, marked by rigid fasts. This rigorous lifestyle probably contributed to, if it did not cause, his early death. B. Robert Kreiser describes the event: "Serene and composed, François de Pâris now received extreme unction. Although he continued for hours to struggle against his impending death and even temporarily regained some strength, the deacon eventually succumbed that evening, a *suicide religieux*, two months before his thirty-seventh birthday."[2]

Nevertheless, de Pâris cannot simply be written off as an overzealous ascetic. There was an active intellectual pulse there, too. Alphonse Adhemar d'Ales discusses a 238-page document on systematic and moral theology, surviving in François de Pâris's own handwriting. It was not an original creation of de Pâris—by examining volume and page references given by de Pâris, d'Ales was able to trace the work to an earlier author, Gaspard Juenin (d. 1707), from whom de Pâris largely copied.[3] Nevertheless, the work gives interesting clues to de Pâris as a person.

First, he knew Latin, although this was not unusual for a clergyman of his time. Second, his interest in theology ran deep enough that he was prepared to devote considerable time and energy to copying out the book. Third, notes that de Pâris

---

[1] B. Robert Kreiser, *Miracles, Convulsions, and Ecclesiastical Politics in Early Eighteenth-Century Paris* (Princeton: Princeton University Press, 1978) 83–90.

[2] Ibid., 90.

[3] Alphonse Adhemar d'Ales, "La théologie du diacre Pâris," *Recherches de science religieuse* 10 (1920) 375–78.

added to Juenin's document make it clear that he understood well at least some of the theological currents that were flowing around him. He was a Jansenist,[4] and this allegiance helped determine the course of events in and around St. Médard.

Jansenism had arisen in the seventeenth century around the teaching of Cornelius Otto Jansen (1585–1638). Jansen tried to reshape Catholicism, appealing to St. Augustine, but to the mind of the church he had gone much too far. In 1653 Pope Innocent X condemned his ideas as heretical,[5] but they did not disappear. Jansenism burst to the surface again in 1699 in a book entitled *The New Testament with Moral Comments on Each Verse*. On September 8, 1713, Pope Clement XI attacked it in the decree *Unigenitus*. Jansenism was again labeled as heresy.

These events served to pull to center stage another person who is of great importance to this study: Cardinal Louis Antoine de Noailles. He had ordered the publication of the book after he had revised and expanded the original version, by Pasquier Quesnel in 1671. In the opinion of the historian Louis Cognet, some of the book's propositions exalted the grace of God to the point that human liberty was destroyed, while others limited the church to only those who were predestined. On the other hand, some propositions were very similar to formulas accepted by orthodox Augustinians.[6]

Noailles had spent most of his life in the service of the church. After a creditable early career that saw him become a bishop at age twenty-eight and the archbishop of Châlons a year later, he was named archbishop of Paris in 1695 and made a cardinal in 1700. He was a scholar with a doctorate from the Sorbonne and was widely known for his exemplary life and piety[7]— not the sort of person one would expect to find stumbling into heresy. He blended his leanings toward Jansenism with very

---

[4] D'Ales, "La théologie," 387.

[5] D. C. Steinmetz, "Jansenism," in *The New International Dictionary of the Christian Church* (ed. J. D. Douglas; Grand Rapids: Zondervan, 1974) 524.

[6] Louis Cognet, "Unigenitus," *NCE*, 14.397f.

[7] D. R. Campbell, "Noailles, Louis Antoine de," *NCE*, 10.476f.

strong feelings in support of the idea that the French Roman Catholic Church had the right to wield major control over most of its affairs, a position known as Gallicanism.

In his opposition to *Unigenitus*, Noailles was a leader among several thousand French clergymen and a very large number of politicians who stood against both pope and king.[8] His position was principled, but it cost him access to the court of Louis XIV. Noailles held out against *Unigenitus* until the last year of his life. He formally accepted it in October 1728.[9] Unfortunately, this last year was the worst. His mental power had declined sharply, and he came under the influence of first one party and then the other, and then back again. Here was a distinguished but aged man being exploited shamelessly.[10]

The situation was very complex. A powerful archbishop leading a faction of French society in a struggle against the throne and the papacy; a set of theological ideas viewed as heresy; a well-loved young deacon dying after extreme self-denial. Then, shortly after de Pâris's death, events took a sudden and dramatic turn. Reports began to circulate of healings associated with the deacon. The first was supposed to have happened when someone touched his feet before his body was buried.[11] Word spread and many flocked to his grave. Soon new healings were claimed.

Daniel Vidal, who has authored a major study on the subject, insists that what happened at de Pâris's grave in the cemetery of St. Médard has to be interpreted against the wider background of Jansenism. He and others argue that, in fact, the St. Médard healings stood in a long line of Jansenist miracles.[12]

---

[8] Louis Cognet, "Jansenism in Eighteenth-Century France," in *The Church in the Age of Absolutism and Enlightenment* (trans. G. J. Holst), vol. 6 of *History of the Church* (ed. Hubert Jedin and John Dolan; New York: Crossroad, 1981) 403f.

[9] Campbell, "Noailles," 476, 477.

[10] Cognet, "Jansenism," 403f. See also Kreiser, *Miracles*, 94.

[11] Kreiser, *Miracles*, 92.

[12] Daniel Vidal, *Miracles et convulsions jansénistes au XVIIIe siècle: Le mal et sa connaissance* (Sociologie d'aujourd'hui, ed. Georges Balandier; Paris: Presses Universitaires de France, 1987) 19. See also Kreiser, *Miracles*, 72.

They note that the Jansenist opponents of *Unigenitus* began to claim that the miracles proved the correctness of their theology.[13] The idea that miracles could put the stamp of truth on doctrine was by no means new, and it has appeared repeatedly since.

Ward identifies three factors that, in her view, had to be in place in order for a shrine to become a popular destination for pilgrimage: a propaganda machine to publicize events; the familiarity of the person in question to the local population; and a political element.[14] All three ingredients are evident in the case of François de Pâris. The Jansenists made sure that news of what was going on in the cemetery was spread as quickly as possible; the people of the parish had loved their deacon; and the Jansenists were locked in a theological-political struggle with the pope. All this conspired to make the tomb of de Pâris a strong attraction for the devout and the curious.

Kreiser, who also wrote an important study of these events, notes that by 1731 it was not only the destitute who were making their way to St. Médard but also the wealthy and well placed.[15] Records kept by police who were posted at the gates of the cemetery to maintain order bear this out. François de Pâris had an appeal that reached across the boundaries of social class. Then another surprise of even greater magnitude occurred.

In July 1731 a young woman, Aimée Pivert, was brought to the cemetery to touch the tomb in search of healing. She suddenly fell into a violent seizure, but to everyone's amazement, when the convulsion ended, she was found to be completely

---

[13] See "Convulsionaries," in Douglas, *The New International Dictionary*, 260; Cognet, "Jansenism," 424; and Kreiser, *Miracles*, 96–98. Blaise Pascal, French mathematician and Jansenist sympathizer, comments in his notes that miracles lent weight to the Jansenist argument (*Pensées* [trans. A. J. Krailsheimer; London: Penguin, 1966]): "It is a fact that doctrine should be supported by miracles" (287); "Miracles exist for the sake of doctrine and not doctrine for the sake of miracles" (289); "Doctrine must be judged by miracles, miracles must be judged by doctrine" (289); "All faith rests on miracles" (291).

[14] Ward, "Miracles," 234.

[15] Kreiser, *Miracles*, 153.

healed.[16] R. A. Knox's picture of what happened next strains credibility. Perhaps he was too ready to accept what was shocking in his sources, which in themselves were questionable.[17] His portrayal, however, which features speaking in tongues, prophesying, healings, and convulsions, finds support in the work of others.

With the convulsions came pain that could only be allayed by methods of *secours* (relief). Some of these were *petits secours* (gentle relief), involving pressure or moderate blows applied to the parts of the body in which there was pain. Others were called *grands secours* (strong relief) or, even more frighteningly, *secours meurtriers* (deadly relief!), in which people clubbed each other or stabbed each other with swords.[18]

The documents suggest that the following kind of scene would not have been unusual. On de Pâris's tomb someone is writhing in a seizure. Under the tombstone another is groaning and desperately praying for healing. Near the grave a man repeatedly hoists a club and crashes it down on another, who is contorted on the ground. Two women appear to be fighting viciously, but one is really providing *secours* to the other. A person dying with a thyroid condition lies mouth agape in the shadow of the wall. Someone who has just been healed sobs hysterically while her friends pummel each other and shake with laughter. And all around them surges a tide of humanity captivated by the hope of health and well-being.

Conditions in the cemetery were chaotic, and they continued day and night. Finally, on January 27, 1732, King Louis XV issued an order closing the cemetery. At 4 a.m. two days later,

---

[16] Cognet, "Jansenism," 422. See also Kreiser, *Miracles*, 173.

[17] R. A. Knox, *Enthusiasm: A Chapter in the History of Religion*. Knox himself says one of his two main sources, P. F. Mathieu (*Histoire des miraculés et des convulsionnaires de Saint-Médard* [Paris, 1864]), approached his work uncritically (373) and the other, Abbé Grégoire (*Histoire des sectes religieuses* [1828]), came to the study with strong emotional distaste for the more extreme behavior of some of de Pâris's followers (374).

[18] Kreiser, *Miracles*, 259–61.

police and troops clattered through the streets and cordoned it off.[19] The immediate effect of this action was to produce a resilient underground movement lasting decades. It centered around what today might be called cell meetings at which almost anyone, regardless of social standing or gender, was welcome. The activity usually included Bible study, prayer for the sick, and convulsions.[20] While this group, frequently referred to as the Convulsionaries, continued to exist for a long time, it rapidly lost the support of mainstream Jansenists. The convulsions had turned the movement into a political liability rather than an asset.

The Miracles of St. Médard

Our primary interest is the miracles associated with François de Pâris. But it would be wrong to try to divorce them from the strange movement that grew up around them, for the strength and long life of the movement were crucial to preserving the memory of the miracles themselves. Nonetheless, the question of what actually happened in the cemetery of St. Médard is still to be resolved.

In his masterful work on the miraculous, Latourelle discusses the procedure by which miracles come to be seen as authentic. He identifies two levels of recognition: the spontaneous, in which a person intuitively sees the hand of God in events, and the theological, which entails painstaking reflection following careful guidelines.[21] Latourelle argues that the process of approving a miracle finds people oscillating from one level of recognition to the other until a final decision is made.

However it is done, in the Roman Catholic Church the Council of Trent in the sixteenth century gave the responsibility to local bishops.[22] In the case of the alleged miracles of de Pâris, the local bishop, Cardinal Noailles, was prepared to

---

[19] Ibid., 214.
[20] Ibid., 255–56.
[21] Latourelle, *Miracles*, 300.
[22] Kreiser, *Miracles*, 142.

perform his duty. He had acted two years earlier in another case,[23] and he set the wheels in motion again. The proceedings can be followed closely.

Noailles commissioned Achilles Thomassin to carry out the preliminary investigation. In the record of work preserved in the Bibliothèque Nationale in Paris, Thomassin identifies himself as a priest and a doctor (professor) at the Sorbonne and states that he had been instructed by Noailles on June 15, 1728, to look into the miracles credited to François de Pâris.[24] Sixty-one pages of testimony remain, written in several different hands, each entry carefully notarized.

Thomassin went to work very quickly. The first entry in the record is dated June 22, 1728. His investigation extended over several months; the last entry is dated October 5, 1728. Noailles discharged him on April 12, 1729. Thomassin experienced the frustration of never seeing his report acted upon. The period of his mandate was the last enfeebled and confused year of Noailles's life. Kreiser thinks that Noailles was on the verge of declaring de Pâris's miracles valid on the basis of Thomassin's investigation.[25] At that critical moment, however, the cardinal fell under the influence of people who wanted to prevent the Jansenist deacon from getting any more honor than absolutely necessary. Along with the record of Thomassin's work is a copy of a letter that he wrote to Noailles's successor, Archbishop Vintimille. Thomassin explains that he took steps to preserve the written records when Noailles decided not to publish them.[26] In fact, he had hidden them. His actions seem justified in view of the fact that a year and a half later Vintimille rejected another miracle that had been attributed to de Pâris.[27] Vintimille might have been tempted to treat Thomassin's records harshly.

---

[23] Ibid., 74.

[24] Achilles Thomassin, Fr. 22, 245, Bibliothèque Nationale, Paris.

[25] Kreiser, *Miracles*, 94.

[26] Thomassin, Fr. 22, 245, pp. 34–36.

[27] Cognet, "Jansenism," 422.

The healings in question varied greatly in nature. Some were claimed to have been instantaneous. Others were more gradual and even involved the use of physical objects. The case of Pierre Lero illustrates the latter. It is given in some detail in a document presented by twenty-three clergymen to the parliament in Paris. They had tried to persuade Archbishop Vintimille to declare that the de Pâris miracles were authentic, but he had refused to respond. In frustration they had turned to the politicians.

One of the cases they presented focused on Lero, who had severe ulcers on his left leg. Treatment had done nothing to cure them, and he had gone to St. Médard in September 1727. A Mass for healing had been said, a woman had prayed over him, and he had received a small piece of wood from de Pâris's bed, which he placed on his leg. He testified to complete healing within a month.[28] The Mass and the prayer were thought to be important in bringing about the cure. But the relic, the wood from the bed, was also seen to be of great importance.

It was common to take dirt from de Pâris's grave, or water from the well in the backyard of the house in which he had lived, to bring about cures.[29] Ward notes the same practice in her study of medieval shrines and comments, "The power of healing the sick obtained by mixing earth from a holy place or using water connected with a saint was close to the ancient use of the four elements for obtaining power."[30] She sees this as a demonstration of a belief in magic that had carried over from pre-Christian times, and refers to many such objects: the hair of a saint, nail parings from his or her body, dust from the tomb, or water in which the saint had been washed.[31]

---

[28] *Requeste présentée au Parlement par vingt-trois curés de la ville, faux-bourgs & banlieue de Paris, contre l'instruction pastorale de M. Languet, archevêque de Sens, imprimée en 1734, au sujet des miracles opérés par l'intercession de M. de Paris* (Paris, 1735) 5f.

[29] Kreiser, *Miracles,* 295.

[30] Ward, "Miracles," 17.

[31] Ibid., 92.

However the practice of using relics should be explained, those who made the presentation to parliament were convinced that the holiness of François de Pâris carried over to the relic and that it brought healing.

Arriving at a precise assessment of the miracles claimed for de Pâris is very difficult. Ward says that in the Middle Ages the reports of miracles served primarily as advertisements for shrines or saints.[32] The accounts of what went on in St. Médard certainly did. Still, the claims of authenticity for at least some of them carry weight. No less a skeptic than David Hume writes of the healings in the cemetery of St. Médard, "Many of the miracles were immediately proved on the spot, before judges of unquestioned integrity, attested by witnesses of credit and distinction, in a learned age and on the most eminent theatre [Paris] that is now in the world."[33] Hume does not identify the sources of his knowledge, but he was in France in the mid-1730s, and he traveled to the Continent from time to time afterward.

Cognet thinks that he can see fraud and hysteria in some of the cases, but admits, "In some cases one seems in fact to be confronted by strange and extraordinary phenomena which are hard to understand."[34] Kreiser, commenting on reactions in the eighteenth century, observes, "Orthodox defenders of the faith had been greatly embarrassed and unsettled by the amazingly strong evidence supporting the miraculous character of many of the Paris cures."[35] That is a vote for the presence of substance in the accounts despite anomalies and enigmas.

---

[32] Ibid., 45.

[33] David Hume, *An Enquiry Concerning Human Understanding* (1748; reprint, Buffalo: Prometheus Books, 1988) 113. Hume rejected all miracles, but on grounds of formal logic. That discussion is beyond the scope of the present study.

[34] Cognet, "Jansenism," 424.

[35] Kreiser, *Miracles*, 399.

Conclusion

The name of François de Pâris continues to excite attention[36]. His original grave has been either moved or built over. The men and women of his parish, and soon many others, were convinced that as he had cared for them in life, so he would care for them in death. They longed for tangible remembrances of him, a vial of water, a splinter of wood, a thimble of dust—relics. Whatever we think, they believed that the holiness of their beloved deacon could flow through those relics and give them medical solutions that they would have great difficulty finding any other way. Their simple faith became wildly entangled with the church politics of the day. Who of them could have guessed that kneeling beside their deacon's grave would lead to armed troops galloping through the streets in the middle of the night? Fanaticism, controversy, and suppression broke over them. And in the midst of it all, it is very likely that some of them were healed.

A major feature of the events at St. Médard was a people's devotion to a man who they thought was especially holy. The benefits of that holiness, they thought, could be mediated through mundane articles associated with him.

---

[36] He and the phenomena of St. Médard have been treated positively by some adherents of New Age religion. As this book nears publication, examples are available on the world wide web at http://www.newgaia.com/tshaman/book/where.html and http://www.nhne.com/wind4.html.

Part 4

The Incubational Model

MÄNNEDORF
THE MESSAGE OF MORIJA

Three different approaches to healing have been discussed. Common to them, however, has been the hope that divine intervention in cases of human suffering would be swift. In the latter part of his career, Johann Christoph Blumhardt provided an exception to this norm, for he was able to pray for the sick without feeling the pressure of time. For the rest, whether it was the early church praying directly for healing or petitioning a saint for intercession, or John Wimber, or Brother André, in most instances they looked for God to manifest divine love and power suddenly. The fourth approach is called *incubational*.

The image of an incubator brings into mind specific associations. One is a nurturing, hospitable environment in which a new baby is cared for. Another is progress and improvement over time. These are what the incubational ministries offer. They have grown out of the conviction that God wishes to heal people, and they have introduced a unique feature: welcoming the sick into residences that they have opened. There, over longer or shorter periods of time, they pray for their recovery. Testimonies abound that the incubational approach to healing has been effective.

The two ministries examined here are located in Switzerland. The first is in Männedorf, south of Zurich, and the second is in Yverdon-les-Bains, near Lausanne.

10

Männedorf
PLACE OF MERCY

The Elim Institution, a Bible and retreat center[1] in Männedorf, states its purpose in a booklet published in 1979: "to serve those who are suffering in body, soul, and spirit."[2] The atmosphere that prevails within the cluster of substantial two- and three-story buildings suggests that it can.

The heart of the center is a truly lovely, light-filled chapel that seats about a thousand people. The grounds and buildings are maintained with legendary Swiss care. At present, one can find families from various parts of Europe on holiday at the center, taking advantage of the well-prepared meals and the nearby lake and countryside and attending services in the chapel. Along with them are a number of older people who are waiting for places in the seniors' home, Emmaus, located nearby. The staff stands ready to pray for those in need upon request.

This substantial, well-run ministry began about 140 years ago under the leadership of Dorothea Trudel. Trudel was born in the canton of Zurich in 1813 and died at Männedorf during an outbreak of typhoid fever in 1862. She rose through a difficult

---

[1] This ministry is identified as the "Elim Anstalt" on the monument in the local cemetery that identifies the plot where Dorothea Trudel, Samuel Zeller, and others are buried.

[2] *Bibel- und Erholungsheim Männedorf: Entstehung-Weg-Auftrag* (Männedorf: Bibel- und Erholungsheim, 1979) 29.

personal life to become a profoundly devout woman who carried on an internationally known ministry of prayer and preaching.[3]

Upon her death, the oversight of her ministry passed to the equally pious Samuel Zeller (1834–1912), a young man whom she had specially chosen to succeed her. His nephew, Alfred Zeller, assumed leadership after Samuel's death and was followed in turn by Johann Käser and Jakob Grossenbacher.[4] Throughout these shifts in leadership, a strong insistence on continuity has been maintained. There has been continuity, but also change.

People now go to Elim for refreshment and renewal. It is primarily a retreat center. In earlier decades, the ministry dealt with highly distressed people in extremely demanding circumstances. At the heart of its work was healing through prayer. The emergence and development of the ministry make a compelling study.

Early Ministry

Information about the beginning of Elim comes from a document Trudel herself wrote.[5] About 1850, while she was living with her nephew, five men who worked in the business he ran became sick. They did not respond to medical treatment, and as their illness worsened, Trudel stayed up to nurse them throughout eight nights. Finally, she began to pray for their healing. Miraculously, they recovered, and a ministry was born. Within a year another healing followed,[6] and in 1852 Trudel moved out of her nephew's house into her own residence, planning to spend her time visiting patients in asylums for the insane.

---

[3] Konrad Zeller, *Dorothea Trudel von Männedorf: Ihr Leben und Wirken* (Lahr-Dinglingen [Baden]: St.-Johannis, 1971) 28, 43.

[4] *Bibel- und Erholungsheim Männedorf*, 18, 22.

[5] It is found in Zeller, *Dorothea Trudel*. Zeller does not indicate the location of this document or others that he quotes at length; I assume they are in the archives at Elim. When I visited the retreat center, I was unable to gain access to the facilities because the archivist was on holiday.

[6] Dorothea Trudel, in Zeller, *Dorothea Trudel*, 34–36.

But events did not unfold as she expected. Rather, her home became a refuge for desperately ill people. One of the first was Regula Walder, who had previously been confined in an asylum. After a period with Trudel, she was able to leave healed,[7] but many others came to fill her place. Trudel dealt with them with what can only be called great love. At personal risk, she would often sleep near seriously ill women. She made it a practice to sit up through the night with those who were critically sick, frequently driving herself to exhaustion.[8] She became known as one through whom the gift of healing worked,[9] and this brought people from many places with many problems to Männedorf. Trudel developed a reputation for being effective at dealing with the mentally and emotionally ill. Restraining devices were used, however, including straitjackets and lightly weighted sacks.[10]

A document Samuel Zeller prepared for the Department of Health in 1869 indicates that some of the patients at Männedorf had been referred by medical doctors.[11] The diagnoses are not precise by current standards—words such as "dejected," "melancholic," and "insane" are used—but the people were from all over Switzerland, from Strassburg, and from Stuttgart. Between seventy-seven and eighty-seven were receiving ministry.[12]

A biblical foundation has been important for the ministry of Trudel and everyone who has followed her at Elim.[13] A

---

[7] Ibid., 37–38.

[8] Arnold Bovet, ibid., 44.

[9] Carl Bachtold, ibid., 47.

[10] Ibid., 56. The latter were attached at night to the hands of some patients to prevent masturbation (Samuel Zeller, *Directory of the Mentally Ill*, February 26, 1869, *Besick Meilen, 1857–1889*, Kantonal Archiv, Zurich; trans. Jerry Hoorman).

[11] Zeller, *Directory*.

[12] The uncertainty about the number was due to the fact that some of the people Elim was caring for were living in houses in town and not at the center.

[13] An interesting example of Samuel Zeller's approach to Scripture is found in "Liebe Gottes in Vergangenheit, Gegenwart, und Zukunft," in *Gerne*

number of texts are cited, such as Matthew 10:8 and Mark 16:18. But the passage that appears most often is James 5:14–15: "Is any one of you sick? He should call the elders of the church to pray over him and anoint him with oil in the name of the Lord. And the prayer offered in faith will make the sick person well; the Lord will raise him up. If he has sinned, he will be forgiven." This passage appears in many contexts. Trudel commented on its importance for her when she first began to pray for the sick.[14] The 1979 booklet presents it as the foundation for the care given at Elim,[15] and Samuel Zeller referred to it in a defense of his ministry made to the Board of Governors of Medical Affairs of the Canton of Zurich.[16] Throughout its history Elim has seen itself as under orders to pray for the sick.

The laying on of hands has also been important to Elim. This practice, common throughout the Christian church, entails placing one's hands on the person for whom one is praying. Dorothea Trudel began this at the outset of her ministry. She would have especially sick people placed on each side of her during prayer times so that she could lay hands on both at once.[17] Samuel Zeller continued the practice in his ministry.[18] The cantonal government commented on it when dealing with Zeller's ministry in 1901.[19]

The most characteristic feature of Elim's ministry to the sick, however, has been the willingness to accept that there

---

will ich Sie lieben (2d ed.; Männedorf: n.p., 1904). There are no signs of technical exegesis, but he handles the texts fairly and draws legitimate lessons from the passages in question.

[14] Trudel, in Zeller, *Dorothea Trudel*, 34, 35.

[15] *Bibel- und Erholungsheim Männedorf*, 9.

[16] Samuel Zeller, *To the Board of Governors of Medical Affairs of the Canton of Zurich*, May 28, 1869, *Besick Meilen, 1857–1889*, Kantonal Archiv, Zurich (trans. Jerry Hoorman).

[17] Bovet, in Zeller, *Dorothea Trudel*, 41.

[18] D. F. Hauss, *Väter der Christenheit* (Wuppertal: R. Brockhaus, n.d.) 478.

[19] *Aus dem Protokoll des Regierungsrates*, 1901, sec. 656, Privatkrankenanstalten, Kantonal Archiv, Zurich.

may be a time lapse before a person who has been prayed for will be healed. This had much more to do with observation than expectation. Trudel and the others did not teach that this was the way in which healing should occur. From the very beginning of their ministry, it simply happened that way. Trudel had to pray several times over the first five who were healed, and Regula Walder was healed over nine weeks.[20] While at Männedorf, Carl Bachtold saw a number of healings, noting that sick people would go through a gradual improvement on their way to full health.[21]

In 1944, when Alfred Zeller was reviewing the story of Elim, he pointed to several important miracles. It is clear that each of these miracles had taken time. Zeller notes that people had been at Elim for from fourteen days to four and a half months before they were healed.[22] The time lapse was common. The job of the staff at Elim was to pray for people and to provide a safe environment for them until they were healed. Describing this ministry as incubational is therefore appropriate.

One question Elim has had to face, along with all other modern healing ministries, is the relationship of its work to standard medical treatment. If the ministry was going to bypass methods that are reasonably effective in restoring health in some cases, then it should have to justify its doing so. Hauss argues that Samuel Zeller never came up with any laws about healing. Rather, he says, Zeller thought that God could heal in many ways, and he did not disapprove of doctors. The only limitation Zeller put on medical treatment came when a person was receiving the laying on of hands and being prayed for: he did not want the individual to receive medical attention at that time.[23]

When interpreting the ministry that he would head during most of the first half of this century, Alfred Zeller took a

---

[20] Trudel, in Zeller, *Dorothea Trudel*, 37, 38.

[21] Bachtold, ibid., 49.

[22] Alfred Zeller, *Zweierlei Wunder* (Basel: Heinrich Maier, 1944) 74–91, 133–39.

[23] Hauss, *Väter der Christenheit*, 477–78.

responsible position. He stated that as a rule, when sick people at Elim were receiving the laying on of hands, they should refrain from medical treatment, the same position as Hauss outlined for Samuel Zeller, but he also acknowledged the legitimate place of the practice of medicine.[24] This is not quite the position that Trudel and Samuel Zeller took. Explaining her practice of healing, Trudel insisted that she never imposed her views on anyone. For herself, however, she solidly trusted the Savior to be her doctor.[25] On one occasion, when Samuel Zeller found himself hard pressed on the matter, he claimed that from the very beginning Elim had operated on the conviction that standard scientific means of healing were not to be used. Rather, one should look to God alone for help.[26] He argued that people knew Elim's position yet they came there willingly, and so the authorities should not try to force medicine or medical supervision on the home. These positions are stronger than Hauss and Alfred Zeller suggested.

There seems to have been some moderation of Elim's position on medicine as it moved into the twentieth century. Alfred Zeller also commented on the general attitude the people at Elim brought to prayer for the sick, and what he said seems to be equally applicable whether early or late in the group's history. He stressed that no one ever presumed to tell God how to heal. On the contrary, they understood that their job was to pray for the sick. What God did after that was up to him completely.[27]

Whatever the theories were, the testimonies about healings are strong, despite problems with inadequate diagnoses, with imprecise observations on recovery, and with the lack of medical certification. Hauss recounts the story of a young man

---

[24] *Was er dir Gutes getan: 28. November 1860–28. November 1910: Rückblicke beim 50jährigen Arbeitsjubiläum unseres lieben Hausvaters Samuel Zeller in Männedorf* (Männedorf: Bibel- und Erholungsheim [1910]) 208–9.

[25] Trudel, in Zeller, *Dorothea Trudel,* 34.

[26] Zeller, *To the Board of Governors.*

[27] Zeller, *Zweierlei,* 127, 128.

with cancer of the lip who stated that he had been healed through prayer.[28] In a list sent to cantonal authorities giving the names of people at Elim who suffered from various mental disorders, Samuel Zeller mentions Eugenie Hoffet from Strassburg, who he says had been delirious and had been the worst case that a Dr. Niehaus in Bern had dealt with in nineteen years—"now healed."[29] We have only his word for it, but he was making the claim before scrupulous government officials and must have been trying to be accurate, since he knew that claims could be investigated.

Last, we have the comments of August Bachtold (1838–1912). He studied theology at Basel and Tübingen, pastored a church, did historical research, and was an archivist when he died. This man was a credible witness. Bachtold apparently spent seven weeks at Elim during the summer of 1860. He himself received a healing (of precisely what we are not told), and he saw others who gradually improved until they were well. He insisted that these were real healings, not just the results of nervous excitement or enthusiasm.[30] It would be difficult, if not impossible, at this point to verify these claims of miraculous healings. What is certain, however, is that they carried weight for many of those who heard about them. Elim stood at the center of a far-reaching movement, and it was the miraculous that gave it its appeal.

Elim's Development

Elim has been a ministry characterized by prayer throughout its history,[31] but its story has not been tranquil. In 1857 Trudel was summoned before state authorities, fined 60 francs, and ordered to close the doors of her ministry,[32] on the grounds that

---

[28] Hauss, *Väter der Christenheit*, 478.
[29] Zeller, *Directory*.
[30] Bachtold, in Zeller, *Dorothea Trudel*, 52.
[31] *Bibel- und Erholungsheim Männedorf*, 30.
[32] Trudel, in Zeller, *Dorothea Trudel*, 38.

she was operating an unlicensed medical-care facility. She insisted that she complied with the order, but no sooner had some people left than others flooded in. Trudel built her ministry on the Bible. She held extended readings after each of the four daily meals served in the house. In the early days she often read sermons after the Bible, but eventually she began to preach. Those who heard her reported that she preached powerfully. People looked forward to the sermons although they were hearing her four times a day.[33] The high level of activity continued at Elim. More and more people received word of the ministry and came to seek help. Trudel was nearly overwhelmed. Carl Bachtold reported that she once went fourteen nights without proper rest.[34]

In 1861 the sudden death of a resident brought Elim under investigation.[35] The result was a decision that Trudel had repeatedly broken health laws in the canton of Zurich. She was fined 150 francs and ordered to dismiss all patients immediately. This time she decided to fight the ruling.

The problem seems to have been the residential nature of Elim. There is nothing in the documents to suggest that authorities were particularly concerned with her praying for the sick. What worried them was her caring for them in something very like a hospital with no medical supervision whatsoever. Some of the patients at Elim were very disturbed people. It was occasionally necessary to use means of restraint in order to manage them, and the government took this very seriously. The case was heard in the Supreme Court of Zurich on November 13, 1861.[36] Trudel was represented by an outstanding lawyer, Heinrich Spondlin. She won complete acquittal and was able to continue with her work.[37]

The pace of ministry at Elim did not slow down when Samuel Zeller succeeded Trudel in 1862. Sick people continued to

---

[33] Bovet, ibid., 39.
[34] Bachtold, ibid., 54.
[35] Zeller, *Dorothea Trudel*, 62, 63.
[36] *Besick Meilen, 1857–1889*, Kantonal Archiv, Zurich.
[37] Zeller, *Dorothea Trudel*, 66.

come. Along with them came offers to relocate in a variety of places, but Zeller decided to remain in Männedorf.[38] He was granted seven years of relative calm before the storm of government concern broke out again.

Exactly what brought about this new crisis is unclear, but the archival records for 1869 show a flurry of activity. On both February 27 and May 25, Zeller was summoned to appear before the Department of Health, but he refused to attend. He knew that he would receive negative orders about Elim. He attempted to shelter behind the Supreme Court ruling of November 13, 1861,[39] and he argued the same position on June 5 in letters to the Office of the Governor and to the Medical Direction of the Canton of Zurich.[40] The case was dealt with at Supreme Court level on November 1, 1869,[41] and like Trudel before him, Zeller won his case and was free to continue dealing with the sick as he chose.[42]

All this difficulty seems to have stimulated caution and an awareness of the need for more careful public relations. In 1882 a document appeared that seems to have been aimed at the residents of Männedorf. It was a very careful attempt to provide a detailed picture of Elim. Included were a floor plan, information on funding, and a discussion of engineering questions such as water supply. It also listed the members of the asylum committee. The authors probably thought it would not hurt if people knew that the committee included a judge, a councilor of the canton, a state councilor, a medical doctor, and an actuary.[43]

---

[38] *Bibel- und Erholungsheim Männedorf,* 13.

[39] Zeller, *To the Board of Governors.*

[40] Samuel Zeller, *To the Office of the Governor,* Meilen, June 5, 1869; and *To the Medical Direction of the Canton of Zurich,* June 5, 1869, *Besick Meilen, 1857–1889,* Kantonal Archiv, Zurich (trans. Jerry Hoorman).

[41] *Besick Meilen, 1857–1889.*

[42] Alfred Zeller, *Samuel Zeller: Züge aus seinem Leben* (Lahr-Dinglingen: St.-Johannis, 1979) 177.

[43] *Erster Bericht über das Krankenasyl Männedorf an die Gemeindseinwohner,* July, 1882, Kantonal Archiv, Zurich.

The next year saw publication of a clear set of regulations governing Elim—"the asylum," as the regulations called it—including a requirement of medical documentation before admittance.[44] The same year a set of Provisional Statutes for Elim was drafted. The document produced is very formal and carefully crafted. It ensures that people of all creeds would be accepted at Elim according to need, and it promises that they will be cared for with Christian love.[45] The statutes make no reference to healing through prayer, and they minimize the work with the mentally ill.[46] They leave the impression of being carefully framed so that they would influence people positively.

With all this effort, it must have been disappointing when difficulty arose again at the end of the century. Government records show that Elim had continued to grow. In 1900 there were 111 patients, and the next year that figure rose to 116. Perhaps the increased numbers prompted the government to look again.

Elim was visited in November 1900. It was observed that the residence served a number of seriously ill mental patients who were controlled by various means of restraint. More important, there was no medical supervision. On November 22, 1900, the decision was taken to forbid Zeller to admit the mentally ill because he could not guarantee they would be cared for under the supervision of a licensed doctor.[47] Zeller fought the decision, but he could not overturn it this time.[48] The restrictions came into effect on July 1, 1901.

The implications for Elim were dramatic. The institution had ministered to the mentally ill from the very beginning. It had laid hands on them and prayed for them, and it claimed to have seen many of them healed. Now that aspect of its work

---

[44] *Hausordnung für die Patienten des Krankenasyls Männedorf*, 1883, Kantonal Archiv, Zurich.

[45] *Provisorische Statuten für das Krankenasyl Männedorf*, July 5, 1883, Kantonal Archiv, Zurich, 1.

[46] Ibid., 2.

[47] *Aus dem Protokoll*.

[48] *Bibel- und Erholungsheim Männedorf*, 16.

was gone. In 1944 Alfred Zeller could claim that people were being prayed for, with many being healed in his day just as they had been under Trudel and Samuel Zeller.[49] Perhaps he was right. But the clientele had changed significantly. Elim was well on its way to becoming primarily a retreat center and a place where the elderly could be cared for.

Conclusion

Today on a warm summer's afternoon, Elim is a very pleasant place nestled on the slope overlooking the town of Männedorf and Lake Zurich. There is a subdued atmosphere as older residents and younger families who are on holiday gather in the dining room for meals. Everyone seems polite and respectful. The gardens are well kept with beautiful flowers. Between 100 and 140 years ago the atmosphere must have been very different. In those days Samuel Zeller was meeting trains at the little station. Raving people in straitjackets were delivered to him, and he wrestled them up the hill to what might be the last place of hope for them. It is hard to imagine what Elim must have been like. Men and women were shrieking and struggling against restraints while others sat rigidly catatonic or muted by depression. There were physical ailments, too, ranging from tuberculosis to epilepsy. In the midst of it Dorothea Trudel, Samuel Zeller, and other staff members moved from patient to patient, praying for them and doing whatever was necessary. The days were punctuated by meals and Bible studies, and—gloriously—by moments when word would spread that someone had been healed.

One senses that the real life of Elim's past was to be found during that early time of relative chaos. State intervention and the leaders' efforts to comply with government regulations moved Elim from its original perspective. It was as though, in response to God, Dorothea Trudel challenged her society with

---

[49] Zeller, *Zweierlei Wunder,* 127

a profoundly loving, if untidy, response to the crying needs of the weakest people in it. Then slowly society diluted her vision and brought it under control. She created a place where the damaged and distraught could be healed. Society sterilized it and turned it into a retreat center. One of the more striking characteristics of Elim was patience. Trudel and Zeller were prepared to give people time to respond to God, and they were prepared to wait on God to move at his time. They struggled to forge a warm, supportive environment in which people could focus attention on God until such time as specific needs were met. Patience gave Elim its distinctive atmosphere. It appeared again in the following century in a residence in another Swiss town, Yverdon-les-Bains.

11

The Message of Morija
PERSEVERING PRAYER

Noise is often associated with healing. It might come from people crying in pain, begging for help, or shouting out their gratitude. There is often also a high energy level, as illustrated in Johann Christoph Blumhardt's early meetings where healing occurred and in the surge of people around Brother André at St. Joseph's Oratory. Morija is different.

Quiet prevails. Whether in an immaculately kept guest room, or in the lounge with its eclectic blend of modern and antique furniture, or in the carefully tended garden, one senses calmness. It is also present in the manner in which the energetic Josiane de Siebenthal guides a group through breakfast and devotions. It accompanied Marguerite Chapuis as she listened intently to a guest and then bowed with her to pray. I was not surprised to find Marguerite quoted as saying, "Healing . . . is rarely instantaneous. It is the fruit of persevering prayer."[1] That fits the unruffled, unrushed atmosphere of Morija perfectly. People really seem to believe that God is in control and that God can be trusted.

Morija (Moriah) is a complex of interconnected buildings, including a six-story residence, a large church, and a spacious, well-preserved three-story house dating to the last

---

[1] G. Mutzenberg, "La Fraternité chrétienne ou les chemins de la foi," in *Certitudes* (1975; reprint, Yverdon: Fraternité chrétienne, n. d.) 1.

century. It is located on a prominent corner in Yverdon-les-Bains, a small Swiss city north of Lausanne.

Morija has a very specific purpose. As one of its founders said: "The house of prayer and faith of the Christian Fraternity is open to all, without exception, for healing prayer, spiritual retreat, rest, the battle of faith, and exorcism. For everyone, it is called 'Morija,' that is, 'Chosen by the Eternal One.'"[2]

It functions as a center of spiritual, emotional, and physical help. This ministry is still the centerpiece of the Evangelical Church of the Christian Fraternity (La Fraternité chrétienne), a small Pentecostal denomination with congregations in the French-speaking sector of Switzerland. The relationship between the denomination and the residence is carefully defined in a number of legal documents.[3]

I am including Morija in this study because it is an excellent example of the incubational approach to healing. The ministries of Elim and Morija are both in Switzerland, and both share a basic approach to the issue of healing, along with other features, such as women in leadership. But they also differ in many respects. Morija presents a unique story.

The Story

Morija grew out of the ministry of Charles de Siebenthal. After a period of service in the Salvation Army, the mid-1930s found de Siebenthal pastoring an Evangelical Reformed Church of France congregation in south-central France.[4] In 1935–36, he encountered the ministry of British Pentecostal evangelist Douglas Scott. Scott had begun his ministry in France in 1930,

---

[2] Charles de Siebenthal, *25 ans de marche avec Dieu (1936–1961)* (Yverdon: Fraternité chrétienne, 1962) 19.

[3] See *Constitution de fondation, Morija; Fondation Morija avec siège à Yverdon: Règlement organique;* and *Statuts: Eglise évangélique de la Fraternité chrétienne,* Archives, Morija, Yverdon.

[4] De Siebenthal, *25 ans,* 9.

conducting services that were characterized not only by many conversions but also by miraculous healings.[5]

This contact opened de Siebenthal to the possibility of seeing the extraordinary power of God in his own ministry. Shortly thereafter, he began to experience that power. He was called to the home of a critically ill woman. Returning to her bedside after spending a night in fervent prayer, he found her completely healed.[6] This was the turning point of his life. He was ripe for what he called his "leap into space."

After an extended period of prayer and fasting, he resigned his church in France. His wife and he then moved their family to her home city, Yverdon, Switzerland, determined to live completely by faith without any regular source of income.[7] Their testimony was that God was faithful. Finances were tight, but there was always enough. Much later de Siebenthal commented that they always received money to pay their bills before the bills were due. This happened so consistently that whenever an unexpected cash gift arrived, Blanche, his wife, would prophesy, "There's a bill coming," and one always appeared.[8]

Despite the provision of the Lord, the next six years were difficult. De Siebenthal gradually moved into the leadership of a small group that began to hold meetings in the de Siebenthals' apartment. The little band devoted itself to prayer and fasting, and as it waited on God, it began to feel led toward what would become its ministry.[9] During this time Marguerite Chapuis joined the group.

In 1938 the de Siebenthals moved to a different apartment and welcomed a new child to their home. In the same year their fellowship started to show evidence of a greater sense of cohesion. A weekly newsletter appeared, outlining its beliefs

---

[5] P. D. Hocken, "Scott, Douglas R.," *DPCM*, 772.

[6] Marguerite Chapuis, interview by Pascal Chapuis, Yverdon-les-Bains, December 20, 1989.

[7] Marguerite Chapuis, *Lettre*, April 27, 1966.

[8] De Siebenthal, *25 ans*, 18.

[9] Chapuis, *Lettre*, April 27, 1966.

and practices. It was issued over the names of Charles de Siebenthal, Blanche de Siebenthal, and Marguerite Chapuis.[10]

Some of these changes meant that the group could no longer meet in Blanche and Charles's home, so it chose the out-of-doors. It met regularly in a nearby woods at 4 a.m.![11] During 1942 the group found a permanent home. Acting on faith, Marguerite Chapuis signed documents purchasing a very large house at 80, rue de la Plaine. She credited the Lord with providing the resources necessary to meet all financial obligations.[12]

Under the leadership of de Siebenthal, the ministry of the group developed strongly. The Christian Fraternity was organized, and a number of congregations were planted in Switzerland. People began to hear of Morija's ministry and came in hopes of finding healing or relief. While full guest lists are intentionally not kept at Morija, it is known that people came from all over Switzerland and Europe and from Asia, Africa, and North America.[13]

Charles de Siebenthal was kept very busy ministering to the sick who came, preaching in Christian Fraternity churches, and conducting outreach meetings. Until his death in 1966, he was the voice of Morija. Writing in elegant French, he composed weekly articles that were published in their newsletter. They provided teaching for the growing fellowship and, along the way, gave evidence that de Siebenthal was a well-read person.

In 1972 Morija took on the physical dimensions that one sees today. With plans in hand since 1967,[14] the group launched into a building program that gave it a new church and a residence complex complete with large dining room,

---

[10] Charles de Siebenthal, *Lettre*, November 24, 1938.

[11] Marguerite Chapuis, interview.

[12] Marguerite Chapuis, interview. The property was still in her name as late as 1967 (surveyor's plan, Yverdon, September 26, 1967, Archives, Morija, Yverdon).

[13] "A la veille d'une inauguration Yverdonnoise, qu'est au juste la Fraternité chrétienne?" *24 heures*, 1972, 18; and Marguerite Chapuis, interview.

[14] Surveyor's plan.

kitchen facilities, and a bright lounge to complement the very comfortable guest rooms.

When I spent a brief period there in the summer of 1991, approximately fifty people were in residence. The largest group was young families that were using Morija as a base for annual holidays. They spoke very appreciatively of the care and peace they found there.

There is a slight shift of focus in the promotional literature Morija produces. De Siebenthal customarily called Morija a "house of prayer and faith," but in 1948 he also referred to it as a "house of peace," or "house of rest" *(maison de repos)*. The use of this second name seems to have become more frequent.[15] This may signal a change in the leadership's understanding of Morija in light of the people who are now coming to it. Perhaps they are beginning to see it more as a retreat center than earlier. If that is the case, what are the long-term implications for its original aim of seeing the sick healed?

One other feature of Morija that begs discussion is the role women have played. While it is likely that during his life Charles de Siebenthal led the group, one official document refers to Marguerite Chapuis as cofounder[16] and another adds Blanche de Siebenthal.[17] Mutzenberg presents the Christian Fraternity as "the providential meeting of two callings," those of Charles and Marguerite.[18] In 1982 Marguerite was recognized as president and director of Morija,[19] and in 1987 she still occupied the position, signing a document as holder of that office.[20] In 1982 the nine-person board that she constitutionally designated was composed of five men and four women, among whom were Josiane de Siebenthal, daughter of Blanche and Charles, and Lucienne Golay, who was an early convert through Morija.

---

[15] See *Constitution de fondation* and *Fondation Morija*.

[16] *Constitution de fondation*.

[17] *Statuts*.

[18] Mutzenberg, "La Fraternité chrétienne," 1 and 2.

[19] *Constitution de fondation*.

[20] *Fondation Morija*.

Much of Morija's ministry is currently being carried out by nine or ten women, who to the outsider almost look like an unofficial order of sisters. They live in residence, willingly drawing very low salaries. They do not, however, regard this as particularly significant, explaining that they are simply carrying out the ministries to which they have been called. Their influence accounts for much of the quiet, orderly life that characterizes Morija. They also constitute a challenge. None of them is under fifty years of age. One wonders from where their replacements will come.

Ministry

Behind the story lie the ideas. From the very beginning, de Siebenthal attempted to locate the budding ministry in the center of traditional, historic Christianity.[21] Within that, he emphasized the importance of people's coming to know Christ as Savior.[22] This concern found expression in the efforts at evangelism he made throughout his ministry. In an interview in 1991, the current pastor of the Christian Fraternity in Yverdon, Jean-Pierre Chapuis, underlined the priority given to evangelistic outreach.[23]

It is difficult, however, to argue with the claim that healing through prayer has been the dominant feature of the ministry of Morija. De Siebenthal rooted this emphasis in Jesus. "He is the same yesterday, today, and forever," he would repeat,[24] and all healing flows from him.[25] He also believed that health is the human being's normal state.[26] The Christian Fraternity,

---

[21] De Siebenthal, *Lettre,* November 24, 1938.

[22] Charles de Siebenthal, *Lettre,* November 17, 1955, and November 23, 1965.

[23] Jean-Pierre Chapuis, interview by author, Yverdon-les-Bains, July 22, 1991.

[24] Charles de Siebenthal, *Lettre,* March 30, 1960.

[25] *Lettre,* November 23, 1965.

[26] *Lettre,* November 13, 1957.

and Morija in particular, was therefore committed to working toward the health of the people who came to it. There is frequent reference to prayer for the sick in its newsletter. Prayer was offered not only at the house of prayer and faith in Yverdon but during the Fraternity's services wherever they were held.[27] Healing was at the heart of its ministry.

At the center of its commitment to healing was the belief in persevering prayer. Lucienne Golay, a longtime staff member, said that the idea of determined, unrelenting prayer is the key to understanding Morija.[28] One author concludes that for the Christian Fraternity, "the way of faith is called perseverance."[29]

During the early, lean years between 1936 and 1938, the little group found itself moving toward a ministry of prevailing prayer. It was in this period that Charles de Siebenthal announced that it had been revealed to him that his ministry would be to fight for those who suffer, by means of persevering intercession.[30]

Shortly after moving into the house on rue de la Plaine, de Siebenthal called a week of special spiritual retreat, with prolonged prayer three times a day. The basic principle was simple: identify a need and then pray for it until God obviously responds.[31] This became characteristic of Morija's approach to healing. People who wanted help were welcome to come and stay at Morija. Once they arrived, they were encouraged to participate in the daily devotional periods, and they were prayed for repeatedly. The Christian Fraternity placed unrelenting emphasis upon prayer. The newsletter detailed times of prayer wherever there was a fraternity church, and there were also invitations to attend regular all-night prayer meetings.[32]

---

[27] *Lettre*, October 20, 1965.

[28] Lucienne Golay, interview by author, Yverdon-les-Bains, July 22, 1991.

[29] Mutzenberg, "La Fraternité chrétienne," 5.

[30] Marguerite Chapuis, interview.

[31] Ibid.

[32] Charles de Siebenthal, *Lettre*, November 2, 1965.

Chapuis and de Siebenthal found a model for their method of praying for the sick in Jas 5:13–16:

> Is any one of you in trouble? He should pray. Is anyone happy? Let him sing songs of praise. Is any one of you sick? He should call the elders of the church to pray over him and anoint him with oil in the name of the Lord. And the prayer offered in faith will make the sick person well; the Lord will raise him up. If he has sinned, he will be forgiven. Therefore confess your sins to each other and pray for each other so that you may be healed. The prayer of a righteous man is powerful and effective.

This passage appears over and over again in the literature produced by the Christian Fraternity. It is never exposed to careful analysis, at least in print, but instead serves as a kind of motto. It is on the cover of a pamphlet on Morija[33] and on the first page of a tract that provides testimonies of healings.[34] It is also listed in support of the passage on healing that appears in the official statement of faith. De Siebenthal cited it when stressing the importance of determined prayer and the laying on of hands in praying for the sick.[35]

The message found in Jas 5:13–16, the value of persevering prayer, worked its way out in a distinctive organizational feature of the Christian Fraternity: the Circle of Prayer. De Siebenthal thought the Circle of Prayer was of crucial importance to the life of the ministry,[36] and one of the pastors of the Yverdon church in the early 1970s called it the Christian Fraternity's backbone.[37] De Siebenthal was convinced that this special group had developed under the direct guidance of the Lord.[38]

The Circle of Prayer is a group of men and women who have bound themselves by a vow to be faithful in the ministry

---

[33] Charles de Siebenthal, *"Morija": La maison de repos de la "Fraternité chrétienne" pour convalescents, déprimés, et tourmentés* (Yverdon: Fraternité chrétienne [1948]).

[34] *Miracles au XXe siècle!* (Yverdon: Fraternité chrétienne, n. d.).

[35] Charles de Siebenthal, *Lettre,* March 15, 1962.

[36] *Lettre,* September 4, 1957.

[37] "A la veille d'une inauguration," 18.

[38] Charles de Siebenthal, *Lettre,* December 28, 1954.

of intercession.[39] They believe that they have been called to this work by God.[40] In addition to their vow to pray, they promise to guard the confidentiality of requests that they hear.

Originally, the Circle of Prayer met every day from 6 until 7 a.m. This was later cut back to five days a week and now stands at four. It meets in closed session twice a week, and twice nonmembers are welcome to be present. There were ten members in the circle at first, but this number rose to a high of approximately seventy. Membership now stands between twenty and twenty-five. Most of the present members are older, with no one under the age of fifty.[41]

This group takes prayer very seriously. On one occasion it prayed for forty hours without a break for a person who was experiencing episodes of insanity, resulting in a dramatic healing. In another case, members of the circle organized themselves so that they could maintain constant prayer for three months. De Siebenthal commented that these people prayed eagerly and vigorously until divine blessing was received.[42] Prayer is emphasized throughout the Christian Fraternity, but the shock troops are found in the Circle of Prayer; these are the "prayer warriors." And it appears that this prayer has brought results.

Testimonies

Many accounts of healings are associated with Morija, but they are all anecdotal. Documentation or medical certification to support them does not exist. There are simply the testimonies of people claiming to have been healed. As a result, we often do not have accurate diagnoses of illnesses, so that we are often not sure what illnesses were healed, if in fact they were. Furthermore, as I mentioned earlier, guest lists have not been

---

[39] Marguerite Chapuis, *Lettre,* April 27, 1966.
[40] Charles de Siebenthal, *Lettre,* December 12, 1954.
[41] Marguerite Chapuis, interview.
[42] De Siebenthal, *25 ans,* 13.

preserved, and so there is no permanent record of the illnesses with which people came to Morija. At this point, there does not seem to be a way of going beyond the testimonies. Nonetheless, in themselves they carry considerable weight.

Two of the cases illustrate well how the healing ministry was thought to work. One involved a woman who had a serious blood clot and was in danger of having one of her legs amputated. She came to Morija for a time, received prayer regularly, and was eventually able to return home completely well.[43] The people at Morija assumed that guests would be healed, but they also assumed that the healing would probably occur over a period of time.

The second case is reported by Lucienne Golay. A woman came to the house of prayer and faith, suffering from deep depression. Golay received a vision of her encased in a block of ice, and she realized that she was being shown that prayer would remove the depression, just as sun melts ice. Taking turns, those engaged in the ministry prayed continuously for the woman, and although it took a year, deliverance finally came.[44]

Commenting on the very early years of the Christian Fraternity's ministry, Marguerite Chapuis refers to the case of a young woman who came to Yverdon because she was dying from malnutrition. She was unable to keep any food in her stomach. Chapuis reports that "after many weeks of hard battle in prayer," she was totally healed.[45]

Chapuis herself almost died in 1946. We are not informed of the cause, but she said that for a time her temperature rose to approximately 106 degrees Fahrenheit and hovered there. She refused medical treatment, clinging to the message of James 5:13–16 while others prayed for her. Finally the Lord Jesus came to her in a vision, and when she awoke, she was completely healed. She said this taught her the importance of having a team of prayer warriors interceding constantly.[46]

---

[43] De Siebenthal, *Lettre*, October 20, 1965.

[44] Golay, interview.

[45] Marguerite Chapuis, interview.

[46] Ibid.

There are similarities among the accounts. The illnesses are usually described as serious, and the healings take time. There are, however, also many points on which they differ. Distinctions were obviously made between physical, emotional, and spiritual problems—"spiritual" here understood as arising from the activity of spiritual beings, demons. We hear of spinal injuries,[47] intestinal disorders,[48] and epilepsy[49] being healed, but we also find frequent accounts of exorcisms.[50] The people at Morija were responding to anything that came, and were reporting victories.

There may even be a story of a person's being raised from the dead. The account reads,

> It is simple, unshakable faith that permits a servant of God in our time to speak to his Master, in the presence of the dead body of a poor mother who had committed suicide in a "house of prayer and faith," saying, "No, Lord, you shall not permit the 'Prince of shadows' to do this in this house! I wait on you for the miracle of life to be performed on this matter, this flesh!" A few hours later he returned the woman to her children, fully alive. It is by faith, and the act of faith is always pleasing to God.[51]

This sounds like an event in which de Siebenthal was personally involved. The account contains details, and the phrase "house of prayer and faith" is often used to refer to Morija. Humility may have led him to substitute "a servant of God" for his own name. If it is a record of something that is supposed to have happened at Morija, then it is clearly intended to show that the power of God seen there had no limits.

Chapuis, de Siebenthal, and the others, however, suffered from neither naivete nor denial. They acknowledged that not everyone was healed. In one passage de Siebenthal advised that

---

[47] *Miracles au XXe siècle!* 3; and Charles de Siebenthal, *Lettre*, October 13, 1965.

[48] *Miracles au XXe siècle!* 10.

[49] Charles de Siebenthal, *Lettre*, December 8, 1965.

[50] *Lettre*, August 28, 1951, and November 23, 1965; and *25 ans*, 16.

[51] De Siebenthal, *"Morija."*

if healing does not occur, one should look for the obstacle pre-venting it and remove it.[52] Elsewhere he moved considerably beyond that. He seemed to be convinced that real life was to be found in the realm of the spiritual, not in material pleasure or riches or in the glory that accompanied them. It was not even to be found in perfect health.[53] Rather, one should focus on her or his relationship to God. De Siebenthal taught that prayer al-ways overcomes evil but it does not necessarily remove suffer-ing.[54] The goal of prayer is not to get things from God, not even healing. The goal is "to obtain God himself."[55] In these com-ments I do not see just a healer, but a healer whose approach was shaped by a thorough study of Reformed theology[56] with its profound respect for the majesty and sovereignty of God. De Siebenthal was convinced that we should pray for the allevia-tion of human suffering, but his ultimate focus was upon God and the importance of a human being's coming into relation-ship with him.

Conclusion

"Healing . . . is rarely instantaneous. It is the fruit of per-severing prayer."[57] This comment by Marguerite Chapuis en-capsulates the approach taken by the Christian Fraternity to healing. They look for healings, and the testimonies suggest that they have seen healings. But, for them, healing is a pro-cess. They pray for the sick in their services. But in working out their faith in a God who heals, they evolved a procedure that was basically incubational. They invite those in need to come and spend time with them. The staff will counsel with guests

---

[52] Charles de Siebenthal, *Lettre*, March 16, 1960.

[53] *Lettre*, August 15, 1957.

[54] *Lettre*, May 12, 1960.

[55] *Lettre*, June 9, 1960.

[56] This school of theology is associated primarily with John Calvin (1509–64).

[57] Mutzenberg, "La Fraternité chrétienne," 1.

and pray with them. The Circle of Prayer will take their cases before God during their times of prolonged intercession. Over time, they believe, God will move and people will be healed and delivered. They are convinced that fervent, earnest prayer is effective. It is an atmosphere of patience and peace.

Part 5

The Revelational Model

WILLIAM BRANHAM
KATHRYN KUHLMAN

Trusting God is a fundamental idea among those who have a healing ministry. Within the context of the Christian church, those who pray for the sick have recognized that they are dependent on God for the miraculous. They have, however, expressed this dependency in different ways.

For some, such as Dorothea Trudel, Charles de Siebenthal, and Marguerite Chapuis, it has meant persistence—praying until victory comes. By contrast, others came to expect that God would give them special knowledge, that God would show them what needs were present or who was being healed. This is another approach to healing, one I call *revelational*. God reveals information upon which the healer can act.

Once individuals received their revelation or special insight, they have responded in different ways. Some simply announced that God was healing, others issued a call to faith, and others laid hands on people and prayed. The actions differ, but the key element remains the same: God has shown them things they could not have known otherwise. William Branham and Kathryn Kuhlman, two different practitioners of this approach, will be studied.

12

William Branham
PROPHET OF THIS AGE?

> I'm not much of a preacher, because I'm not educated, and I don't know much of the Word and things. So I can't preach, but my work is to pray for sick people.[1]

> And so now, as you know, I did not get very much of a schooling, as I said, so, in my . . . in theology, I am the poorest there is, and I guess you know that. And as a preacher, I could hardly even call myself one, because of not getting schooling and knowing words, and so forth; but what little I have as my knowledge of knowing by His grace, the Lord Jesus, I try to share that with all my brothers everywhere—to share this.[2]

> In my own little fragile ministry that the Lord has given me, I have seen over a million souls come into the Kingdom of God.[3]

Who was this man who at one moment could express extreme humility and at the next claim to have won more than a million converts to Christ? William Marrion Branham (1909–65) was and is an enigma. He was born in poverty; he died in controversy, and his name is known around the world.

Branham's Life

Branham stands out in the print sources and the audio- and videotapes as a complex person. His birth in an impoverished home in rural Kentucky made him "of the people." He was, by his own account, not burdened by "high culture" or

---

[1] William Branham, "The Inner Veil," SW, January 1, 1956, 36.

[2] William Branham, "The Godhead Explained," SW, April 17, 1957, 1, 2.

[3] William Branham, "Christ's Second Coming," SW, April 17, 1957, 7.

much education. While his fractured grammar and very dis-
jointed speaking style expressed his humble origins in very
natural ways, Branham capitalized on his roots.

He comes across as a folksy, down-home person. He
sounds like a person who understood his audience very well.
He could make comments such as "Mr. [Banks] Wood quit
contracting and is loafing with me,"[4] knowing that his pre-
dominantly blue-collar audience would enjoy it. They all knew
Branham was not loafing, but he was well aware that people
from lower socioeconomic groups have a tendency to think
that way about the clergy. This simple attempt to maintain his
identity with the people who made up his support base was
typical of Branham's astute exploitation of his background.

Another incident points in the same direction. In a sermon preached on April 17, 1957, Branham said he had been so
busy the day before that he had not been able to get his shirt
on until 2 in the afternoon.[5] This would have brought smiles.
He was bridging the gap between the pulpit and the pew,
making clear that his roots were still firm.

Many times Branham vigorously attacked features of middle-class American religious life. He launched scathing dia-
tribes on education and denominational structures, and he
railed against various social values, particularly as they applied
to women. Women wearing pants or shorts were an abomina-
tion. He was "one of the people," representing the "old values"
of rural America, and he wanted to be seen that way. But this
is not the only way he presented himself.

On March 8, 1960, Branham addressed an interdenominational group of ministers. On that occasion, the tone of his
sermon was very different from what it usually was. The grammar was acceptable; the style was much less chatty and collo-
quial; there were no wild broadsides fired at middle-class
values; and he spoke in favor of organizations: "We all know
that any minister that is a preacher is a New Testament

---

[4] William Branham, "Visions and Prophecy," *SW,* April 8, 1956, 2.
[5] Branham, "Christ's Second Coming," 1.

prophet. If he is prophesying, (preaching) not to try to edify himself, to make a big name, or to edify his organization. . . . He should be in an organization. Here I am without one, but yet when you are preaching you should be in one that is right."[6] He also commended theological education.[7]

These contrasting styles suggest that Branham was not above trying to adapt to differing social contexts. Clearly, he could relate easily to those who were "just folks," but maybe he was less backwoodsy than he liked to let on. Branham was not a flat, two-dimensional character. At times he could be very confident[8] and at times remarkably bitter and angry: "Look at this country around us, with its hundreds and hundreds of Pentecostal people, and just because I am standing on the Truth, where are they this afternoon? It is because someone told them not to cooperate with the meeting. You poor illiterate person!"[9] "Illiterate" is not quite the appropriate word to use in this context. Earlier in the sermon he had flung it at anyone who might disagree with what he was saying and leave the meeting. It was as though he was extremely angry and "illiterate" was the worst thing he could think of to say about someone.

He could also feel profoundly alienated. At times he thought that everyone, even his own church, Branham Tabernacle, was turning against him.[10] He was convinced that he held a special relationship with God, but he could give indications that occasionally he was very insecure in it. A sermon he preached on August 12, 1959, is full of imploring questions: "Here is a showdown. Do you [congregation] believe I've told you the Truth? . . . You, sitting here in front. You believe me to be God's prophet? . . . You believe I have God's message? Do

---

[6] William Branham, "The Spirit Speaks through the Prophet," *SW,* March 8, 1960, 5.

[7] Branham, "The Spirit Speaks," 16, 17.

[8] William Branham, "Elijah and the Meal Offering, *SW,* March 11, 1960, 63.

[9] William Branham, "Jezebel Religion," *SW,* March 19, 1961, 15.

[10] William Branham, "Palmerworm, Locust, Cankerworm, Caterpillar," *SW,* August 23, 1959, 31, 32.

you believe that I'm telling you the Truth? Do you believe that Christ is giving witness of It?"[11]

In the same sermon, he did things to try to show that God really was with him. One of the abilities he claimed God had given him was to provide personal details about people whom he had never met. In this sermon, he twice turned his back on the audience to demonstrate that he could give this information even when he was not looking at the people. His receiving this material direct from God will require its own discussion, but what is striking here is his need to prove that it did indeed happen.

In 1946 Branham catapulted into the public eye when he developed a healing ministry. Critical to this was an experience he had on May 7, 1946. He claimed to have been visited by an angelic messenger. This visit turned out to be of great importance to his life.

> Then along in the night, at about the eleventh hour, I had quit praying and was sitting up when I noticed a light flickering in the room. Thinking someone was coming with a flash light, I looked out of the window, but there was no one, and when I looked back the light was spreading out on the floor, becoming wider. Now I know this seems very strange to you, as it did to me also. As the light was spreading, of course I became excited and started up from the chair, but as I looked up, there hung that great star. However, it did not have five points like a star, but looked more like a ball of fire or light shining down upon the floor. Just then I heard someone walking across the floor, which startled me again, as I knew of no one who would be coming there besides myself. Now, coming through the light, I saw the feet of a man coming toward me, as naturally as you would walk to me. He appeared to be a man who, in human weight, would weigh about two hundred pounds, clothed in a white robe. He had a smooth face, no beard, dark hair down to his shoulders, rather dark-complexioned, with a very pleasant countenance, and coming closer, his eyes caught with mine. Seeing how fearful I was, he began to speak. "Fear not. I am sent from the presence of Almighty God to tell you that your peculiar life and your misunderstood ways have been to indicate that God has sent you to take a gift of divine healing to the peoples of the world. IF YOU WILL BE SINCERE, AND CAN GET THE PEOPLE TO BELIEVE

---

[11] William Branham, "Discerning the Body of the Lord," *SW,* August 12, 1959, 18, 19, 21.

YOU, NOTHING SHALL STAND BEFORE YOUR PRAYER, NOT EVEN CANCER."[12]

Two months after this incident Branham got a call from a friend who was pastoring in St. Louis, asking him to come and pray for a daughter who was very ill. He agreed, and the girl soon showed improvement. Branham spent nine days there in June 1946, preaching and praying for the sick.[13] This event not only established him as a healing evangelist but propelled him to the head of a movement in which many imitated him.[14] Harrell observes that Branham's healing ministry had become a worldwide legend by the early 1950s.[15]

Stories of fabulous events associated with Branham began to circulate. People remembered a strange sense of awe that had filled the little shack in which he had been born.[16] Phenomena of light appeared near him several times as his ministry was beginning.[17] A halo of light appeared mysteriously above his head in a photograph taken of him in Houston in January 1950.[18] Branham himself said that the light was always present in his meetings.[19] He was also reputed to be able to check into correct hotels without prior information on where reservations had been made for him.[20] He had clearly made a strong impression on many people.

Unfortunately, controversy kept pace with legend. In 1947, one year after his initial foray into prayer for the sick, Branham held a series of meetings in Saskatoon, Saskatchewan. A pastor who had helped handle the logistics of the services later stated

---

[12] Gordon Lindsay, *William Branham: A Man Sent from God* (4th ed.; Jeffersonville, Ind.: William Branham, 1950) 77.

[13] David E. Harrell, Jr., *All Things Are Possible: The Healing and Charismatic Revivals in Modern America* (Bloomington and London: Indiana University Press, 1975) 30.

[14] D. J. Wilson, "Branham, William Marrion [1909–1965]," *DPCM*, 30.

[15] Harrell, *All Things Are Possible*, 36.

[16] Lindsay, *William Branham*, 139.

[17] Ibid., 41, 43.

[18] Ibid., 149, 150.

[19] Branham, "Inner Veil," 6.

[20] Lindsay, *William Branham*, 139.

that many whom Branham had pronounced healed in fact died.[21] The same charge was laid against the evangelist a year later by W. J. Taylor, a district superintendent with the Pentecostal Assemblies of Canada. He and his executive called for a thorough investigation.[22] While he expressed warm regard for Branham as a person, Taylor presented evidence to suggest that the claims on the numbers of people healed were vastly overdrawn, and he commented, "I firmly believe there is a possibility that this whole business is wrong."[23]

With the passing of time, the controversy surrounding Branham deepened. In his optimistic biography of Branham published in 1950, Gordon Lindsay stated approvingly that his subject scrupulously avoided doctrinal disputes, citing the verse that says, "Knowledge puffeth up but love edifieth."[24] Toward the end of the 1950s and into the 1960s, however, Branham laid aside his earlier caution and became increasingly radical in his teaching.[25]

The results of Branham's speculation were surprising. He developed a remarkably fanciful interpretation of church history,[26] denied an eternal hell,[27] and unleashed a withering attack on modern women with their "slacks" and "bobbed" hair.[28]

He also introduced the concept of the "Serpent's Seed." He used the expression to refer to that part of the human race descended from Cain, who, he believed, had been conceived

---

[21] Carl Dyck, *William Branham: The Man and His Message* (Saskatoon, Sask.: Western Tract Mission, 1984) 13.

[22] W. J. Taylor, letter to C. B. Smith, January 20, 1948, Archives, Pentecostal Assemblies of Canada, Mississauga, Ont., 1, 3.

[23] Taylor, letter, 3 and 4.

[24] Lindsay, *William Branham*, 11.

[25] C. Douglas Weaver, *The Healer-Prophet, William Marrion Branham: A Study on the Prophetic in American Pentecostalism* (Macon, Ga.: Mercer University Press, 1987) 96, 97.

[26] Branham, "Palmerworm," 19–22.

[27] William Marrion Branham, *An Exposition of the Seven Church Ages* (n.p.: William Marrion Branham, n.d.) 133, 134.

[28] Harrell, *All Things Are Possible*, 163. A profoundly disturbing misogyny runs throughout Branham's preaching.

through sexual intercourse between Eve and the serpent in the Garden of Eden.[29] These children of Cain were particularly susceptible to sin. Branham thought that this group included those who were educated, the doctors, lawyers, architects, and scientists. He also claimed that 80 percent of the criminals in the United States came from this class, not from among the poor and illiterate.[30]

Shortly after the election of John F. Kennedy to the presidency of the United States, he reminded a congregation of a vision he had in 1932, in which he saw that women who had been given the vote would elect the wrong man and pollute the United States.[31] This and other visions revealed to him that the country would be destroyed by a tremendous explosion, that the West Coast would slide into the ocean,[32] and that it would all happen by 1977, the year in which the millennium would begin.[33]

Throughout his ministry Branham insisted that people had to believe that he had a special relationship with God if they hoped to be healed.[34] It is certain that he thought he was the divinely appointed prophet for his generation, although he was remarkably coy about it.[35] People adopted a wide range of positions about Branham. Some thought he was divine. Julius Stadsklev, for example, stated that at Branham's birth a halo of light had appeared above the bed on which he and his mother lay.[36]

---

[29] William Branham, "Hybrid Religion," *SW,* November 13, 1960, 14, 15. According to Branham, the serpent was not a snake but, rather, a male representative of a species very close to humanity, but not human.

[30] Ibid., 27.

[31] Ibid., 5, 6.

[32] Weaver, *The Healer-Prophet,* 103.

[33] Branham, *Exposition,* 321, 322.

[34] See Lindsay, *William Branham,* 85; and Weaver, *The Healer-Prophet,* 81, 83.

[35] See Branham, "Jezebel," 17; "Works Is Faith Expressed," in *The Voice of The Prophet: Messages by William Marrion Branham* (Tucson: Tucson Tabernacle Books, n.d.) 50; and Weaver, *The Healer-Prophet,* 80.

[36] Julius Stadsklev, *William Branham: A Prophet Visits South Africa* (Minneapolis: Julius Stadsklev, 1952) 1.

In 1973 a 735-page computer-generated concordance to Branham's sermons appeared. The instructions for its use show the reverence in which Branham was held. Once the word to be studied has been chosen, one should consult the concordance to identify all the passages in Branham's works in which that word appears. The next step entails going to the printed texts to see how the word is used in context. The final step is a review of the audio tapes of the passages in which the word was used, in order to determine "phonetic emphasis or other sound expressions which reflect the actual delivery."[37] No effort could be spared in trying to understand exactly what the prophet had said.

The same profound respect can be detected in a comment of Lindsay's: "The story of the life of William Branham is so out of this world and beyond the ordinary that were there not available a host of infallible proofs which document and attest its authenticity, one might well be excused for considering it far-fetched and incredible."[38]

On the other hand, many others have had difficulty seeing the infallibility of the "proofs." Walter Hollenweger's assessment of Branham is, "However generously he is judged, it must be admitted that his sermons were not merely simple, but often naive as well, and that by contrast to what he claimed, only a small percentage of those who sought healing were in fact healed."[39] Carl Dyck[40] and Scott Moreau[41] are even less kind. They view Branham as a deluded mouthpiece of the devil.

Branham died on December 24, 1965, as the result of a car accident, but his influence persisted. Many people refused to accept his departure, leading to a delay of his funeral in hopes

---

[37] *Extensive Concordance: A Keyword Subject Arrangement of Sermons Delivered by Rev. William Marrion Branham* (Tucson: Tucson Tabernacle, 1973) iii. Apostolos David Mamalis held the copyright of this book.

[38] Lindsay, *William Branham*, 9.

[39] W. J. Hollenweger, *The Pentecostals* (trans. R. A. Wilson; 1972, reprint; Peabody: Hendrickson, 1988) 355.

[40] Dyck, *William Branham*, 9, 15, 16.

[41] A. Scott Moreau, "Branhamites," *East Africa Journal of Evangelical Theology* 7 (2, 1988) 13, 14.

that he would come back to life. His body was eventually buried, but he continues to have a large and devoted following. Some still expect him to rise from the dead.[42] All of them are convinced that his books and tapes must be circulated as widely as possible.[43] As a result, he is known in many parts of the world,[44] and he has influenced a number of younger healing evangelists. Douglas Weaver even suggests that "Branhamology" is a legitimate field of research, and briefly reviews the major positions people have developed regarding Branham's person.[45]

Branham's Ministry

Some features that were noticeable in earlier ministries reappear in his. For example, he drew on what is almost a standard collection of biblical passages on healing. Mark 16:17, 18; Heb 13:8; and Isa 53:4, 5 come up frequently. On the other hand, he was also an innovator. He developed the practice of having people who wanted to be prayed for approach him on the platform in a line, an arrangement that became widely known as the "healing line."

Other themes were unique to his ministry. In a sermon preached on April 8, 1956, he reported an occasion in which an angel revealed details about his future. Accommodating Branham's interest in the out-of-doors, the angel couched the revelation in ideas drawn from fishing. The angel spoke of three "pulls," as in pulls on a line when someone catches a fish.[46] Branham gave few details about the third pull,[47] but he spoke about the first two. We will first examine them and then turn attention to the angel. All three were important in setting

---

[42] Weaver, The Healer-Prophet, 153 and 154.

[43] Harrell, All Things Are Possible, 165.

[44] Weaver, The Healer-Prophet, 152.

[45] Ibid., 156, 157.

[46] Branham, "Visions," 14–16.

[47] Branham's followers close a web page with the promise of providing "a few brief quotes by Brother Branham to explain what the Third Pull is all about." See "The Three Pulls," http://www.biblebelievers.org/lcomm4.htm.

Branham's approach to healing. These were sources of information on which he relied heavily during healing services. This dependence on "divinely" imparted material is the basis for classifying Branham's ministry as revelational.

He was introduced to the first pull in the angelic visitation on May 7, 1946, in which he was commissioned to the healing ministry. At that time, the angel told him that he would be able to detect diseases by means of vibrations in his left hand.[48] F. F. Bosworth, who played a "godfather" role for many healers, describes this phenomenon as Branham explained it to him.[49] When a person wanting healing approached Branham, he would take her or his right hand in his left and begin to feel vibrations. These differed depending on the nature of the illness. Branham believed that evil spirits were behind all illness, accidents, and disease.[50]

During these moments of prayer evil spirits were being confronted. If the spirit was a strong one, the force of the encounter could be so great that it would stop Branham's watch. He would feel as though he was holding a live electrical wire, and his hand would swell and discolor. Once the healing was completed, Branham's hand would return to normal.[51] The letter written by a Canadian Pentecostal, W. J. Taylor, makes it clear that all this was well known to those who attended Branham's meetings.[52] Branham thought that the primary purpose of the vibrations was not the identification of illnesses. Rather, he saw them as a means of arousing faith in those who came for healing.[53]

The second pull was Branham's "gift of discernment": "You all know that this gift in my life is supernatural. It is a gift whereby the Holy Spirit is able to discern diseases, and thoughts of men's hearts, and other hidden things that only God

---

[48] Harrell, *All Things Are Possible*, 27.

[49] Ibid., 37.

[50] Weaver, *The Healer-Prophet*, 62.

[51] Lindsay, *William Branham*, 170.

[52] Taylor, letter, 2.

[53] Weaver, *The Healer-Prophet*, 75.

could know and then reveal to me."[54] This gift came in 1949. In spite of his comment on the gift and contrary to many of his followers, he did not think this was a gift of the Spirit such as other Christians might use. He identified it with Jesus' ability to know what was happening within people. He also thought that only one person in each generation could have the gift.[55]

He insisted that he had nothing to do with what happened when the gift was in operation. People would come before him one by one. Suddenly things relating to them would appear to him above them. He would simply tell them what he saw, unaware of what he was saying. Others would have to tell him later, or he would listen to what had been taped. He often referred to feeling a strain when the gift was in operation because the gift "pulled through" him. He gave no indication of what he meant by "pulled through." Indeed, he stated that it is the people who come for healing who actually operate the gift, even though they are entirely unconscious of doing so.[56]

Branham's claims to this gift left him open to much criticism. He knew that some thought "it was some kind of mental setup."[57] On one occasion, he went on the attack, saying, "Now what is this [gift]? It is not mind reading, it is not telepathy, nor is it witchcraft. It is a REVELATION by the Holy Ghost."[58] Those were the main objections being raised against the gift—mind reading, telepathy, witchcraft—and he flatly rejected them. Given the insecurity we have already seen in him, he had probably considered all these possibilities himself. Hollenweger, an expert on Pentecostal history, comments, "The author [Hollenweger], who knew Branham personally and interpreted for him in Zurich, is not aware of any case in which he was mistaken in the often detailed statements he made."[59]

---

[54] Branham, *Exposition*, 15.
[55] Weaver, *The Healer-Prophet*, 76.
[56] Branham, "Visions," 4–10.
[57] William Branham, "Tower of Babel," *SW,* January 28, 1958, 8.
[58] Branham, *Exposition*, 15.
[59] Hollenweger, *The Pentecostals*, 354.

Once again, as in the case of the vibrations, the point of the discernment was to build faith. Branham would ask people if they would believe that Jesus could heal them if he could reveal information about themselves he could not have known without divine help. He was convinced that this was the point of the gift. If they said yes, and those who came up onto the platform almost always did, then he would share what he saw and immediately pronounce them healed. This procedure appears repeatedly in the films that were made of his services.

One of the most striking features of Branham's healing ministry was his dependence upon an angel. There is no consistency in how he referred to this creature. He could call it an angel, a pillar of fire, a pillar of light, or even Jesus Christ.[60] Whatever he called it, "throughout the peak years of success, Branham manifested an extreme dependence upon the angel's presence," according to Weaver.[61] This was unsettling for many people. Taylor thinks Branham's praying to the angel was unacceptable.[62] Moreau goes further, accepting the suggestion that the angel was actually a demonic presence.[63]

Branham would not start to pray for the sick until he was sure the angel was present.[64] He filled in time with chatter until he knew the creature was there. On one occasion he delayed for thirty minutes before turning to the sick.[65] He was convinced he needed the angel to tell him about the people who came to him. The information was essential because it would help people to believe that God was responsible for their healings.

It is impossible to get even an approximate idea of how many people were healed through Branham's ministry. Some, such as Lindsay, thought there were multitudes, while others, such as Taylor and Hollenweger, placed the number much

---

[60] See William Branham, "God Called Man," *SW,* October 5, 1958, 30; Weaver, *The Healer-Prophet,* 75.

[61] Weaver, *The Healer-Prophet,* 72.

[62] Taylor, letter, 2.

[63] Moreau, "Branhamites," 13.

[64] Harrell, *All Things Are Possible,* 37.

[65] See Branham, "God Called Man," 20, 30.

lower. The procedure Branham followed worked against verifi-cation, but nothing suggests that he used the procedure for that reason. A number of people would be ushered onto the platform each night. He would talk to some, pray for some, lay hands on some, and send some on their way, telling them to go rejoicing because they were healed. There is no record of any consistent follow-up after people had been across the platform.

Watching films of the meetings and taking everything that happened at face value, the viewer would assume that almost everyone was healed. Eyewitness Taylor reports having that same impression "as one stands in the meetings."[66] After all, this man who pulled all that correct information about people out of the air said they were healed. Given his "gift," one might be inclined to believe him. When some sort of follow-up was done, however, the results were not nearly so encouraging.

Conclusion

William Marrion Branham played an important role in one part of mid-twentieth-century religious life. He was con-vinced that he was commissioned to be an agent of healing. People either loved him or hated him. Some thought he was God; others thought he was a dupe of the devil. Some thought he was the end-time messenger sent by God, and some still do.

However one assesses his work, it must be acknowledged that he did much to foster a very widespread expectation that God could be counted on to heal miraculously. This led to an international healing movement in which thousands of people were caught up. Weaver points to a consensus that the healing revival was over by 1958.[67] That observation may be more accurate for North America than for other parts of the world. In developing countries people such as Reinhold Bonnke con-tinue to conduct meetings that are very much like those of the earlier evangelists in their heydays. A major inspiration for the ongoing ministry of healing evangelism was William Branham.

---

[66] Taylor, letter, 3.
[67] Weaver, *The Healer-Prophet*, 93

13

Kathryn Kuhlman

A HANDMAIDEN OF THE LORD

At age 68, just months before her death, Kathryn Kuhlman exhibited a dominating personality as she ministered at a World Conference on the Holy Spirit in Israel. She conducted herself as one who demanded and received attention from those who listened to her. Her deliberate speech, characterized by theatrically elongated syllables, was punctuated by protracted silences during which she nodded her head as if tamping down into listeners' minds the points she was making. Here was a well-honed image cultivated over decades of public ministry. But here also was a person who longed to please God. Kuhlman was a study in contradiction.

Kuhlman was born near Concordia, Missouri, on May 9, 1907, and she died on February 20, 1976, in Tulsa, Oklahoma. With a preaching style to match her fiery red hair, Kuhlman plunged into evangelism in the western United States with Helen Gulliford in 1928.[1] Within five years she had established a very strong ministry in Denver, Colorado,[2] only to see it blow apart as a result of a tragic marriage to evangelist Burroughs A. Waltrip, Sr., who had deserted his wife and children for her.[3]

---

[1] Jamie Buckingham, *Daughter of Destiny: Kathryn Kuhlman—Her Story* (Plainfield, N.J.: Logos, 1976) 39.

[2] D. J. Wilson, "Kuhlman, Kathryn," *DPCM*, 529.

[3] See Buckingham, *Daughter of Destiny*, 70–77; and Wayne Warner, *Kathryn Kuhlman: The Woman behind the Miracles* (Ann Arbor: Servant, 1993)

With profound personal trauma, Kuhlman managed to leave Waltrip and pick up the thread of her life and ministry in Franklin, Pennsylvania, in 1946.[4] Four years of successful ministry led to a move to Pittsburgh,[5] and even though she opened another base of operations in Los Angeles in 1965, Pittsburgh remained home until her death.

Jamie Buckingham states that "Kathryn despised all purported faith healers,"[6] and she herself repeatedly insisted about her own healing ministry, "I had nothing to do with what was happening."[7] In spite of this and in spite of the consistent attempt she made to identify herself as an evangelist,[8] it was her ministry of healing that caught the public eye. Hundreds of thousands attended her meetings in search of cures, and many more tuned her in on radio and television.

Kathryn Kuhlman was clearly one of the dominant American religious personalities in the 1960s and 1970s. Buckingham, her longtime associate and ghost writer and then biographer, thought Kuhlman was "one of the greatest instruments of the miracle power of the Holy Spirit since the days of the apostles."[9] By contrast, Harrell devotes little space to Kuhlman in his study of American healing ministries, thinking she was "clearly only

---

81–99. Waltrip was close to being the prototype for the popular image of the southern evangelist. With the Great Depression raging around him, he was able to erect a remarkable building to house his ministry in Mason City, Iowa. It featured air-conditioning, a "star-lighted" choir loft, a forerunner to the ubiquitous overhead projector by means of which hymns were flashed on a remotely operated screen, and a retractable pulpit. In 1939, less than a year after the building's opening, Waltrip lost it through bankruptcy (Warner, *Kathryn Kuhlman*, 89).

[4] Buckingham, *Daughter of Destiny*, 82–86; and Warner, *Kathryn Kuhlman*, 101–13. Warner's research on the period of Kuhlman's life between 1939 and 1946 is particularly impressive.

[5] Buckingham, *Daughter of Destiny*, 105

[6] Ibid., 59.

[7] Kathryn Kuhlman, *I Believe in Miracles* (Englewood Cliffs, N.J.: Prentice-Hall, 1962) 199.

[8] See Wilson, "Kuhlman, Kathryn," 529; and "Kathryn Kuhlman: Dying to Self," *ChT*, March 12, 1976, 48.

[9] Buckingham, *Daughter of Destiny*, 47.

marginally related to the healing revival of the post–World War II period," although he also says, "No one typified the best hopes and aspirations of the movement better than Kathryn Kuhlman."[10]

Wayne Warner places her firmly among those mid-twentieth-century figures who had dramatic healing ministries. His general assessment is: "Some will argue that Kathryn Kuhlman can be listed behind Oral Roberts as having the greatest impact among healing evangelists. Others will put her in first place. I think Oral had the greater impact into the 1960s, but then Kathryn Kuhlman charged to the front and maintained that appeal until her death a decade later."[11]

She was a powerful character, driving relentlessly toward her goals, with controversy swirling in her wake.[12] Her practices related to healing and her thinking on the subject earn her a place in this study, but it will become clear that she defies easy categorization and simple analysis.

Healings?

Buckingham suggests that Kuhlman was introduced to the idea of divine healing in 1935 through the ministry of Phil

---

[10] Harrell, *All Things Are Possible*, 191. This book was important in the legitimization of twentieth-century Pentecostal and charismatic healers as subjects of serious study.

[11] Warner, *Kathryn Kuhlman*, 14.

[12] The controversy arose over a variety of issues. It began with her striking out into evangelism in 1928 as an attractive young woman, something that could arouse indignation in spite of remarkable predecessors, including Aimee Semple McPherson (see Edith L. Blumhofer, *Aimee Semple McPherson: Everybody's Sister* [Grand Rapids: Eerdmans, 1993]). It boiled over again as a result of her marriage to Burroughs A. Waltrip, Sr., and in Franklin, Pennsylvania, there was court action over facilities. Then in 1952 she was caught up in a very public debate over divine healing with Baptist pastor Dallas Billington in Akron, Ohio. Throughout her life she had a taste for the best in everything. This also attracted negative attention. In 1975 she found herself embroiled in a $430,000 lawsuit brought against her by a former business manager. It was eventually settled out of court. Finally, after her death the settlement of her estate resulted in considerable bitterness and ill will.

Kerr at her church in Denver.[13] But it seems that Kuhlman encountered prayer for the sick at least a decade earlier.

In the summer of 1924, Kuhlman traveled in evangelism with her sister and brother-in-law, Myrtle and Everett Parrott.[14] Everett had been drawn to Pentecostalism by Charles S. Price, and Warner states that during the summer she spent with them, Kuhlman was introduced to Price's ministry.[15] It is likely that she first became familiar with the practice of divine healing at that time.

Warner and others point out that prayer for the sick appeared in Kuhlman's ministry starting in the mid-1930s. She went on to evolve an approach to divine healing unlike that of most of the other practitioners of the day, even that of William Branham although their ministries had similarities.

The centerpiece of Kuhlman's ministry, the "miracle service," was freighted with drama, highlighting the revelational nature of her approach. She was the focal point of the service, insisting on absolute control.[16] Like Branham,[17] she delayed reaching toward the sick until she was confident that God was with her. An example is the last miracle service she ever held, in November 1975 in Los Angeles:

> "I'm not going to preach today," she assured the crowd. "I'm only going to speak ten minutes and then we're going to move right into the miracle service."

> But after making her announcement, Kathryn proceeded to speak for more than an hour. Of course no one present knew she was, even at that time, deathly sick. In fact, she was dying. But they did discern—many of them—that Kathryn dared not start the miracle service until there was an anointing from God. Until that anointing arrived

---

[13] Buckingham, *Daughter of Destiny*, 59.

[14] Buckingham, *Daughter of Destiny*, 59.

[15] Ibid., 25, 135. On Price, see R. M. Riss, "Price, Charles Sydney," DPCM, 726f.

[16] See Warner, *Kathryn Kuhlman*, 209ff.

[17] See pp. 178–79 above.

she had no choice but to keep on speaking, preaching to herself about the power of God and praying that power would soon manifest itself.[18]

Buckingham tells of seeing her pacing before services, praying desperately for the presence of the Holy Spirit,[19] and Warner recounts the experience of an Assemblies of God official, Charles Crabtree, after he arranged a meeting for Kuhlman in Des Moines, Iowa. He met with Kuhlman backstage before the service and watched as she waited on God.

> Time had slipped away and it was past time to start, but Kathryn kept pacing and praying. "I cannot go out there!" she finally blurted to the startled Crabtree.
>
> She was still waiting for the anointing.
>
> Crabtree will never forget the scene. "We had to hold up the meeting until she felt she had the anointing."[20]

She believed that through the anointing she would be given information about what God was doing among the people who were gathered. Her role was simply to announce that publicly: "There has been an ear opened somewhere toward the back"; "Some one in the balcony who came with a heart condition has just been healed!" Then she would encourage people who felt they were the ones whom God had healed to come to the platform to share it with the crowd. Kuhlman had been repulsed by the procedures she had seen used by healing evangelists.[21] In her meetings, by stark contrast, Warner writes, there were "no prayer cards. No long line of sick moving toward a ramp for a touch and prayer from Kathryn. No invalid tent. Everything was kept simple and in the open."[22] Questions could be raised about the simplicity, but the format was open,

---

[18] Buckingham, *Daughter of Destiny,* 124f.

[19] Ibid., 126.

[20] Warner, *Kathryn Kuhlman,* 235.

[21] See Harrell, *All Things Are Possible,* 191; and Buckingham, *Daughter of Destiny,* 61.

[22] Warner, *Kathryn Kuhlman,* 142.

and it appears to have been effective. Dwight J. Wilson comments in passing that there were "well-documented miracles."[23] But such claims have not gone unchallenged.

In 1974, William Nolen, a physician, decided to conduct an investigation into the reports that miracles were happening at Kuhlman's meetings. He served as a volunteer usher at one meeting in Minneapolis, interviewed Kuhlman, and did some follow-up. His approach was sympathetic and respectful, and the observations he made are important.

He reports how he was caught up in the excitement of the meeting: "You wanted to believe so badly you could hardly stand it. You didn't want to reason; you wanted to accept."[24] What struck Nolen was that all those people had assembled with all that suffering and someone was telling some of them that they had been healed. Then he saw those who thought they had been healed file to the platform to report on their healings.

At this point, and again in his follow-up work, Nolen began to see the kind of difficulties that one can observe on the videotapes of Kuhlman meetings. Kuhlman announced the healings. It was up to the people who had been healed to identify themselves. It is an open question which of these people could judge whether they had been healed. Did the absence of depression at that moment mean that the depression really was gone? Did the ability to run across the platform prove that a problem with a knee had been resolved?

After interviewing twenty-five people who claimed healings at the miracle service he attended, Nolen concluded that "none of the patients who had returned to Minneapolis to reaffirm the cures they had claimed at the miracle service had, in fact, been miraculously cured of anything, by either Kathryn Kuhlman or the Holy Spirit."[25] He decided that Kuhlman was

---

[23] Wilson, "Kuhlman, Kathryn," 529.

[24] William A. Nolen, *Healing: A Doctor in Search of a Miracle* (Greenwich, Conn.: Fawcett, 1974) 68.

[25] Ibid., 84.

completely sincere, but that she had trained herself to deny anything that would threaten the validity of her ministry. What had driven Nolen to his investigation and the follow-up was the tremendous pain he had seen on the faces of people who left the meetings with withered legs, dying children, or cancerous livers unhealed.[26]

In his very careful study of Kuhlman, Warner cites many cases in which healings did not occur.[27] But whether those who left the services unhealed were deeply damaged, as Nolen suggests, is an open question. Dr. Roberts Lamont, who was the pastor of First Presbyterian Church in Pittsburgh when Kathryn Kuhlman began to hold services there, told Warner that "when he talked to people leaving the building unhealed, the people spoke appreciatively of the singing, worship, the joy, and all that God was doing in their lives. It had brought a blessing to them."[28]

Buckingham does not let Nolen's comments pass uncontested. He points out that the physician attended only one service and interviewed only a handful of people. He also draws attention to the fact that Nolen was challenged publicly by another physician, Dr. H. Richard Casdorph of Long Beach, California, who had documentation supporting a claim to a healing.[29]

Kuhlman was open to having her work reviewed by the medical profession, having cooperated fully in Nolen's study.[30] In addition, Warner was able to list six physicians who had

---

[26] Ibid., 63, 94.

[27] Warner, *Kathryn Kuhlman*, 142ff.

[28] Ibid., 270 n. 25. Similar reactions were noted in those who had not been healed when they attended meetings conducted by John Wimber. See p. 58 above.

[29] Buckingham, *Daughter of Destiny*, 176. See also Warner, *Kathryn Kuhlman*, 182ff. H. Richard Casdorph details ten cases of what he regards to be healings, most of which occurred in association with Kuhlman's ministry. The meticulous documentation makes these accounts impressive (*The Miracles* [Plainfield, N.J.: Logos, 1976]).

[30] Nolen, *Healing*, 64ff.

either volunteered to help in her services or commended her ministry. Among these were Dr. Richard O'Wellen of Johns Hopkins Medical School and Dr. Robert Hoyt of Stanford University Medical School.[31] Hoyt says that after examining and interviewing people who had claimed healing through Kuhlman's ministry, "I came away absolutely convinced that God is still performing miracles."[32] Deborah McCauley correctly notes, "Kuhlman worked more closely with the medical profession than any other evangelist with a prominent healing ministry."[33]

The genuineness of the miracles associated with Kathryn Kuhlman is a topic to which Buckingham returns frequently in his biography. For example, he points to a stringent set of criteria an event had to meet before it could be published in one of Kuhlman's books as a miracle:

(1) The disease or injury should be organic or structural in nature—and should have been medically diagnosed.

(2) The healing should have occurred rapidly, or instantaneously. The changes would have to be abnormal, and not the kind that could result from suggestion.

(3) All healings would have to be medically verified—preferably by more than one doctor. At least one of the doctors must be the patient's private physician.

(4) The healing should be permanent, or at least of sufficient duration so as not to be diagnosed as a "remission."[34]

Meeting these criteria would go a long way toward demonstrating that there was something unusual about an event. If these criteria were in fact in place and applied consistently,

---

[31] Warner, *Kathryn Kuhlman*, 178.

[32] Robert S. Hoyt, "A Doctor's Quest," in *God Can Do It Again* (ed. Kathryn Kuhlman; Englewood Cliffs, N.J.: Prentice-Hall, 1969) 140.

[33] Deborah McCauley, "Kathryn Kuhlman," in *Twentieth Century Shapers of American Popular Religion* (ed. Charles H. Lippy; New York: Greenwood Press, 1989) 231.

[34] Buckingham, *Daughter of Destiny*, 152.

they would counteract the suggestion that Kuhlman was cavalier about the recognition of miracles.

Buckingham also cites many examples of healings, some complete with the names of doctors who could provide certification. Paul R. Gunn, who was diagnosed as having lung cancer on September 28, 1949, was healed in October and returned to work in January 1950. Charles C. Loesch, who had been injured in an accident in 1935 and had been left with one leg three and three-quarter inches shorter than the other, was healed in 1949 while listening to Kuhlman preach.[35] George Davis was healed of a heart condition, and, remarkably, both a pacemaker and the scar left from the operation during which it was inserted disappeared. Buckingham quotes a statement of confirmation made by Dr. George Johnston, of Philadelphia, who had been a consulting physician on the case.[36]

I found the story of Mary Pettigrew of Cobden, Ontario, particularly interesting, as I was able to discuss events with Mrs. Pettigrew herself.[37] Having experienced the debilitation of multiple sclerosis for six years, Mrs. Pettigrew with her husband attended a Kuhlman meeting in Pittsburgh in 1969. During the service she was instantly healed. Her physician later confirmed that she had made a 90 percent recovery. She and her physiotherapist subsequently appeared on Kuhlman's telecast to report on the healing. When I interviewed her on the telephone, Mrs. Pettigrew was able to relate that there had been no recurrence of the multiple sclerosis in the twenty-six years since her healing.[38]

---

[35] Ibid., 103–4.

[36] Ibid., 153.

[37] Kuhlman gives an account of Pettigrew's experience in *God Can Do It Again*, 231–50.

[38] Mary Pettigrew, telephone interview by author, Cobden, Ont., May 23, 1995. In his discussion of this healing based on an earlier interview, Warner says that Mrs. Pettigrew told him that her doctor would have been willing to certify a 100 percent cure if she had been willing to expose herself to another battery of tests in the hospital. At the time, Mrs. Pettigrew was not prepared to go through that again (Warner, *Kathryn Kuhlman*, 224).

Her Theology

Kuhlman's contribution to the practice of divine healing was much greater than to the theory. This is not to say, however, that no theology lay behind the practice. Warner was able to extract an early theology of healing from a booklet, published by Kuhlman probably during World War II, entitled *The Lord's Healing Touch*. Warner identifies three main ideas: healing is in the atonement,[39] healing did not end with the apostles, and faith is crucial to all healing.[40] When she first began to pray for the sick regularly in 1946, Kuhlman was distressed that not everyone was healed through the ministries of the healing evangelists.[41] She devoted herself to a search for an explanation.

As she studied the ministry of Jesus, she became impressed with the diversity of his healing methods, pointing to John 9 and Luke 18:35–43 to illustrate the point.[42] She also came to realize that since the day of Pentecost the ministry of Jesus was being carried on by the Holy Spirit. This meant that the Holy Spirit could be relied upon to perform the healings—and that was what Kuhlman believed took place in one of her meetings on Sunday, April 27, 1947.

On April 28 a woman testified that while Kuhlman was preaching the previous night, emphasizing the Spirit's work in continuing Jesus' ministry, she had suddenly become aware that a tumor that she had had was gone. She went to her doctor for verification and then returned to tell her story.[43] Kuhlman's understanding of Scripture was confirmed by this miraculous cure. The event set a pattern for her ministry for the next thirty years. April 27–28, 1947, was a pivotal point in her

---

[39] See pp. 7–8 above, and 199–201, 205–7, and 208–9 below.

[40] Warner, *Kathryn Kuhlman*, 136f.

[41] Kuhlman, *I Believe in Miracles*, 195–97.

[42] Ibid., 17.

[43] See Warner, *Kathryn Kuhlman*, 131f.; and Buckingham, *Daughter of Destiny*, 92ff.

career. From that point on, she would rely exclusively upon the Holy Spirit. She said, "I understood that night why there was no need for a healing line; no healing virtue in a card or a personality; no necessity for wild exhortations 'to have faith.' "[44]

This reliance on the Holy Spirit was central to Kuhlman's ministry. She waited impatiently to sense what she thought was the Spirit's anointing before she would launch into her miracle services, and she highlighted the Spirit's role in healing:[45] "The Presence of the Holy Spirit has been in such abundance that by His Presence alone, sick bodies are healed, even as people wait on the outside of the building for the doors to open."[46]

Warner comments that as part of a tribute to Kuhlman, "Oral Roberts characterized her affinity with the Holy Spirit as being wrapped up in each other. 'It was like they were talking back and forth to each other and you couldn't tell where Kathryn started and the Holy Spirit left off. It was a oneness.' "[47]

Another important feature of Kuhlman's healing theology was faith. She assumed that faith was essential to healing—there could be no healing without it—but also that it was something that had to be given: "Faith comes from God and it a gift of God."[48] She carried the definition further, insisting that "faith is not a condition of the mind. It is a divinely imparted grace to the heart."[49] Kuhlman feared that people had missed the essential givenness of faith: "We have made faith a product of a finite mind when all of the other gifts of the Spirit we have attributed to God. To many people, faith still is their own ability to believe a truth, and is often based on their struggles and their ability to drive away doubt and unbelief through a process of continued affirmations."[50] She was convinced that this

---

[44] Kuhlman, *I Believe in Miracles*, 198.

[45] Warner, *Kathryn Kuhlman*, 21.

[46] Kuhlman, *I Believe in Miracles*, 198.

[47] Warner, *Kathryn Kuhlman*, 234.

[48] Kuhlman, *I Believe in Miracles*, 253.

[49] Kuhlman, *God Can Do It Again*, 252.

[50] Ibid., 253.

placed faith in precisely the wrong light, making it something a human being could generate. In fact, it was something entirely dependent upon the grace and mercy of God.

From this point, it was a short step to what may be the most fundamental point in her thinking on healing. She insisted that the responsibility for healing rests firmly with God: "Healing is the sovereign act of God."[51] If God controlled the dispensing of the faith without which there could be no healing, then obviously God determined if and when healing would occur. This, in turn, made Kuhlman's place in the process abundantly clear: "From the beginning, as now, I was wholly sure of two things: first, that I had nothing to do with what was happening, and second, I knew that it was the supernatural power of Almighty God."[52] Buckingham quotes her stating, "I have no healing virtue. . . . I cannot heal a single person. All I do is preach faith. God does the healing. Whom He heals and whom He chooses not to heal is His business. I am but His handmaiden."[53]

Buckingham came to know Kuhlman through long contact with her, collaborating with her on a number of her books. He watched her in action in many services, and in the light of it all, he accepted this understanding she had of herself: "All she had was faith to believe and a word of knowledge concerning where that gift had been bestowed."[54]

One final practical issue with immense theological implications haunted Kuhlman throughout her ministry: not all were healed. She faced this question repeatedly from reporters and investigators, and she struggled with it herself. The answer to which she came fitted well with the rest of her thinking on healing: "'Why are not all healed?' the only honest answer I can give is: I do not know. And I am afraid of those who claim they do know. For only God knows, and who can fathom the

---

[51] Ibid., 254.
[52] Kuhlman, *I Believe in Miracles*, 199.
[53] Buckingham, *Daughter of Destiny*, 47.
[54] Ibid., 197.

mind of God? Who can understand His reasoning? I think there are some simple matters we can look into, but the ultimate answer as to who is healed and who is not healed lies with God alone."[55]

Considerable mystery surrounds the origins of Kuhlman's theology. In one revealing passage, Buckingham says,

> In one of her rare moments of nostalgia, Kathryn did talk about her theology. "When word got back to Myrtle that we were having services in Idaho [1928], she sent me a telegram from Spokane, Washington. It was terse but profound: 'Be sure you have your theology straight.'
>
> "I didn't even know what theology was," Kathryn chuckled. "I'm glad I was stupid, stupid enough to believe that all I had to do was preach the Word and God would take care of my theology."[56]

Kuhlman consistently distanced herself from formal theological training. The information that she gave to those who wrote about her emphasized that whatever she had learned she had learned from her study of the Bible and from the Holy Spirit.[57] But this appears to have been misinformation.

Before the publication of Warner's biography of Kuhlman, it was unknown publicly that she had been enrolled at Simpson Bible Institute in Seattle from 1924 to 1926 and that she had sat in on classes at L.I.F.E. Bible school in Los Angeles shortly after.[58] The former was operated by the Christian and Missionary Alliance, and the latter founded by the famous Aimee Semple McPherson. Attendance at these two institutions would certainly have introduced her to theology.

Why Kuhlman suppressed these facts is unclear. In the first instance, she was probably not particularly proud of her time at Simpson Bible Institute. Warner's research suggests that she had trouble with the restrictive rules of the Bible

---

[55] Kuhlman, *God Can Do It Again*, 250.

[56] Buckingham, *Daughter of Destiny*, 48.

[57] Warner, *Kathryn Kuhlman*, 33f.

[58] Ibid., 31–36. Warner builds a strong case for his conclusions on the basis of archival research and interviews with contemporaries of Kuhlman.

school, leading to her expulsion in 1926.[59] A second explanation for her secretiveness, Warner proposes, might have been a desire not to be associated with McPherson, who was fighting off a scandal of her own in 1926, and a third possibility was that "Kathryn wanted to make it on her own. She and the Holy Spirit and self-study made her what she was. Not Everett and Myrtle Parrot. Not Simpson Bible Institute. Not L.I.F.E. Not Aimee Semple McPherson."[60] All three proposals are useful, but the third is especially important, given that the whole of Kuhlman's public life was characterized by a fierce independence.

Buckingham refers to her as a loner and as one who refused advice: "If Kathryn had any one great weakness in her long and fruitful career, it was her refusal to submit herself to the godly people around her. Moses submitted himself to elders. And the Apostle Paul taught Christians to 'submit one to another.' But, for some strange reason, the whole idea threatened her."[61] She seems to have been predisposed not to acknowledge theological indebtedness.

In terms of specific theological ideas, it appears that the explicit and repeated emphasis on the Holy Spirit in healing was unique to her. Of course, other Christians with healing ministries believed in the Holy Spirit. But before Kuhlman no one had located that member of the Trinity so centrally in the healing process. It is an idea that has had some influence and is worthy of further analysis. Other theological concepts do not seem to have come to her quite so unmediated.

As part of the foundation of her ministry to the sick, Kuhlman believed that healing was made available through the death of Christ, that "healing is in the atonement." It is likely that this was an idea she had been taught.

Kuhlman had spent almost two years at the Bible school of the Christian and Missionary Alliance, a denomination founded in 1887 by A. B. Simpson. Along with other emphases,

---

[59] Ibid., 34.
[60] Ibid., 35.
[61] Buckingham, *Daughter of Destiny*, 75.

Simpson made prayer for the sick a central part of his work; some thought it was the most influential part of his ministry.[62] Crucial to Simpson's teaching on the subject was the idea that healing is in the atonement. It is improbable that Simpson's emphasis on healing and the atonement was absent from Simpson Bible Institute when Kuhlman was there, just five years after Simpson's death. It is also improbable that Kuhlman would have missed it.

Another concept that was important to Kuhlman's healing ministry was faith. Indeed, it assumed a central place in her teaching. Strong evidence suggests that here, too, she owed an unacknowledged debt. There are several remarkable verbal similarities between Kuhlman's teaching on faith and Charles S. Price's discussion of the same subject. Kuhlman's comments are found in books she published in the 1960s, while Price published his in 1940.[63]

First, in *God Can Do It Again,* Kuhlman wrote, "The faith that Jesus talked about can no more manifest itself without result than the sun can shine without light and heat";[64] Price had said, "Genuine faith can no more manifest itself without result than the sun can shine without light and heat."[65] Kuhlman also stated, "Faith is not a condition of the mind. It is a divinely imparted grace to the heart";[66] this is very close to an echo of Price's teaching: "We have made faith a condition of mind when it is a divinely imparted grace of the heart."[67] Both Kuhlman and Price said that faith cannot be manufactured[68] and that it is "a gift of God or a fruit of the Spirit."[69] Verbal similarity becomes identity in the following

---

[62] See P. G. Chappell, "Healing Movements," *DPCM,* 863.

[63] Charles S. Price, *The "Real" Faith* (Pasadena: C. S. Price, 1940).

[64] Kuhlman, *God Can Do It Again,* 252.

[65] Price, *The "Real" Faith,* 9.

[66] Kuhlman, *God Can Do It Again,* 252.

[67] Price, *The "Real" Faith,* 9.

[68] Kuhlman, *God Can Do It Again,* 252; Price, *The "Real" Faith,* 12.

[69] Kuhlman, *I Believe in Miracles,* 202; Price, *The "Real" Faith,* 36, 82.

statement, which appears in the writings of both: "You are nearest your possession of this imparted grace when you realize your own helplessness and your complete and entire dependence upon the Lord."[70]

It seems impossible to deny influence, and given the fact that Price published twenty years before Kuhlman, the influence probably ran from him to her. Furthermore, although Kuhlman first encountered Price in 1924,[71] she would not have drawn this particular view of faith from him then, because at that time he did not hold it. According to Price himself, only later in his ministry did he come to understand faith as radically dependent on God's imparting it.[72] Insofar as there is no indication of direct contact between Price and Kuhlman during that time, the late 1930s and early 1940s, she may have taken these ideas over from his book.

It seems clear that Price was the source of these ideas rather than others active in the North American healing movement, who taught a different understanding of faith and saw it as the responsibility of those who wished to be healed. For them, the sick had to discipline their minds and spirits to force out any doubt about God's willingness to heal. The sick had to cling to the "promises of God," which were understood as God's commitment to heal those who came to him with perfect faith, regardless of pain or other symptoms.

It was this perception of faith from which Price had recoiled and that Kuhlman found so offensive. They held a unique position on faith among those in North America who prayed for the sick. And it is likely that Kuhlman obtained her doctrine of faith from Price, for some reason choosing not to acknowledge it.

---

[70] Kuhlman, God Can Do It Again, 253; Price, The "Real" Faith, 105.

[71] Warner, Kathryn Kuhlman, 135. Buckingham dates this to 1923 (Daughter of Destiny, 47).

[72] Price, The "Real" Faith, 7.

Conclusion

Kathryn Kuhlman is one of the major names in healing in the mid–twentieth century. But there is tension between her theology of healing and her practice. She was convinced that healing flowed from God and that people were absolutely dependent upon him for this, as for everything else. She emphasized his sovereignty, and she called herself his handmaiden. She would pace agitatedly, waiting to hear from him before she would dare to speak on his behalf.

This humility did not, however, correspond well to her conduct. Her performance was ostentatious; her speech and movement, overdrawn. Her clothing was flashy. What she said directed attention to God; the way in which she acted pulled attention to herself. There are contradictions about all of us, but in Kuhlman they were particularly striking.

PART 6

THE SOTERIOLOGICAL MODEL

ORAL ROBERTS

Unlike the revelational model found in Kuhlman or Branham, proponents of the next approach to healing have been very theologically self-conscious, careful to provide an intellectual context for the ministry they have extended to the sick. Briefly, the *soteriological* perspective on healing has taught that people can be miraculously cured through the same means by which they become Christians, through the atoning work of Christ. The slogan one hears from those who subscribe to this model is, "Healing is in the atonement." Here the attack upon illness is located within soteriology, that is, the doctrine of salvation.

This concern for theological integration should not be surprising given the surroundings out of which the approach arose. Its roots are found in the mainstream of American religious life in the second half of the nineteenth century, which was a relatively sophisticated theological environment. People were comparatively well informed theologically and were interested in clarity and consistency. For the most part, they were also "evangelical," placing emphasis on the authority of Scripture and on personal faith in Jesus Christ.

As the nineteenth century drew to a close, some of the proponents of this thinking stood further from the center of the stream, but the people who were originally involved thought of themselves as just Episcopalians, Presbyterians, or Baptists.

Discussing the question of beginnings, Donald Dayton points to the "radicalization of Holiness doctrine,"[1] finding support in Paul Chappell.[2] Dayton then traces the concept of healing in the atonement through people such as Carrie Judd Montgomery, R. L. Stanton, A. B. Simpson, A. J. Gordon, and R. Kelso Carter.[3] The last of these luminaries stated, "The Atonement provided for the body all that it provided for the soul."[4] Edith Blumhofer adds Alexander Dowie to the list.[5]

---

[1] Donald W. Dayton, "The Rise of the Evangelical Healing Movement in Nineteenth Century America" (paper read at the conference of the Society for Pentecostal Studies, Tulsa, Oklahoma, 1980).

[2] Paul Chappell, "The Divine Healing Movement in America" (Ph.D. diss., Drew University, 1983) vi.

[3] Donald W. Dayton, *Theological Roots of Pentecostalism* (Grand Rapids: Francis Asbury, 1987) 125–29.

[4] R. Kelso Carter, *The Atonement for Sin and Sickness; or, A Full Salvation for Soul and Body* (Philadelphia: Willard Tract Repository, 1884); reprinted in *"The Higher Christian Life": Sources for the Study of the Holiness, Pentecostal, and Keswick Movements* (ed. D. W. Dayton; New York and London: Garland, 1985) 12. Carter wanted to underline the instantaneous nature of salvation, sanctification, and healing (*The Atonement*, 12). Dayton's comments make it clear that many others shared this thinking ("Rise," 16).

By contrast, nineteenth-century Protestant healing ministries in Europe were much more patient. Blumhardt and Trudel were content to establish residences to which people could come and stay in order to be prayed for as long as necessary (see pp. 44 and 144–46 above). They assumed that healing would be gradual. This thinking appeared in the twentieth century at Morija in Yverdon-les-Bains (see pp. 161–64 above).

Blumhardt and Trudel, along with Otto Stockmayer, provided a model for American healers. Carter reported that there were over thirty "faith homes" in America in 1897 (*"Faith Healing" Reviewed after Twenty Years* [Boston and Chicago: Christian Witness Company, 1897; reprinted in Dayton, *"The Higher Christian Life"*] 35). The connection came directly through Dr. Charles Cullis (W. H. Daniels, *Dr. Cullis and His Work* [1885; reprint, New York and London: Garland, 1985] 126, 340; and Dayton, *Theological Roots*, 122). The American faith homes seem, however, to have disappeared early in the twentieth century. It appears that something in the Yankee spirit has insisted that satisfaction, even healing, should be achieved immediately.

[5] Edith L. Blumhofer, "The Christian Catholic Church and the Apostolic Faith: A Study in the 1906 Pentecostal Revival" (paper read at the conference of the Society for Pentecostal Studies, Pasadena, California, 1982) 18.

The idea that healing has a soteriological base is examined here through the twentieth-century tradition that has emphasized it most strongly—Pentecostalism. This religious grouping erupted out of events occurring at Topeka, Kansas, and Los Angeles, California, in the first decade of this century. It has been characterized by the expectation that God will routinely and frequently break into people's lives in dramatic, powerful ways.

It is popularly assumed that Pentecostalism's most identifiable hallmark has been the speaking in tongues, but Wacker makes a strong case in support of the idea that healing was an equally important emphasis from the beginning of the movement.[6]

In the last two decades Pentecostalism has gained recognition as a phenomenon of global importance, and, as such, it has come under scrutiny from nearly every direction imaginable. This meticulous examination has made it clear, on the one hand, that Pentecostalism is deeply indebted to nineteenth-century religious currents, particularly the Holiness Movement in the United States, and, on the other, that healing is part of its idea of salvation.[7] Our window through which to view Pentecostal healing is Oral Roberts.

---

[6] Grant Wacker, "The Pentecostal Tradition," in *Caring and Curing: Health and Medicine in the Western Religious Traditions* (ed. R. L. Numbers and D. W. Amundsen; New York: Macmillan, 1986) 521.

[7] Miroslav Volf, "Materiality of Salvation: An Investigation in the Soteriologies of Liberation and Pentecostal Theologies," *Journal of Ecumenical Studies* 26 (1989) 457.

14

Oral Roberts
QUINTESSENTIAL PENTECOSTAL

Although a native of Oklahoma, Roberts is no "Okie from Muskogee." Here is a figure much larger than life. I find it difficult to use him as an illustration, even of something as important as an approach to healing, since the bulk of his personality eclipses the larger study. But I chose Roberts to illustrate the "healing in the atonement" model because he is the most widely known proponent of the approach.

Born in 1918 and miraculously cured of tuberculosis and stuttering in 1935,[1] Roberts struck out into a healing ministry on May 25, 1947.[2] Massive crowds flocked to his campaigns, which featured both a healing line, which once brought 9,300 people under Oral's hands in a single evening, and an "invalid section," where he prayed for desperately ill people in a less public setting.[3]

His career as a campaigner ended in December 1968, the year he transferred his ordination to the United Methodist Church. By that time, however, he had already established a

---

[1] P. G. Chappell, "Roberts, Granville Oral," *DPCM*, 759.

[2] Harrell, *Oral Roberts*, 68. This biography enjoyed a warm response and is the most comprehensive study of Roberts to date. Examples of the very positive reviews it received are those by Richard Quebedeaux, *The Christian Century* 102 (1985) 1008f.; and Nancy A. Hardesty, *Church History* 57 (1988) 122f.

[3] Harrell, *Oral Roberts*, 100, 105.

television ministry and an institution of postsecondary education, Oral Roberts University (ORU). Characterized by Star Wars architecture and the latest in educational technology, ORU gained accreditation in just six years.[4]

Pursuing his visions, Roberts opened a huge, state-of-the-art medical facility, the City of Faith, on November 1, 1981, expecting it to become the "Mayo Clinic of the Southwest" and the place where the cure for cancer would be found.[5] Unfortunately, a totally undreamed of patient shortage plunged the City of Faith into financial difficulty[6] and bludgeoned Roberts into closing it in late 1989 in order to save the rest of his ministry.[7] The Oral Roberts Evangelistic Association was still struggling with financial difficulties in 1992.[8] In October of that year, Roberts experienced a major heart attack and received a coronary angioplasty. He has recovered fully with no residual damage.[9] In January 1993 he retired as president of ORU, turning the chair over to his son, Richard.[10]

Oral Roberts has been a spell-binding character. One eyewitness account of a campaign Roberts held in Durham, North Carolina, in June 1948 sketched a remarkable picture. Wrung out first by preaching and then by praying over the prayer line for hours, Roberts was sagging on his chair as the last of the suppliants filed by beneath his hands. Suddenly a rejuvenating divine power surge struck him and brought him leaping off the platform among the crippled and the ill who crushed toward him. Touching and being touched, he scattered healing left and right.[11] Almost half a century later, he can still hold a crowd.

---

[4] Chappell, "Roberts," 760.

[5] Peggy Wehmeyer, "Oral Roberts Opens His Tulsa Hospital," *ChT*, December 11, 1981, 41.

[6] "Financial Crisis Grips Oral Roberts's Medical Complex," *ChT*, August 10, 1984, 46.

[7] Samuel Autman, "City of Faith Gets Tenant," *Charisma*, April 1990, 18.

[8] *Charisma*, October 1992, 76.

[9] *Charisma*, December 1992, 50.

[10] *Charisma*, March 1993, 67.

[11] Harrell, *Oral Roberts*, 86.

Stephen Pullum made him one of the subjects of a doctoral dissertation on the mass appeal of Pentecostal televangelists.[12]

It is difficult to disassociate Roberts from an emphasis upon the miraculous.[13] His reputation as a source of solutions to irresolvable problems has given him much of his hold on people. The validity of his claims to the miraculous has been disputed.[14] Nonetheless, some of the miracle accounts are compelling, for example, that of Fred O'Dell of Jacksonville, Florida, who returned a year after he had claimed a healing to show a crusade audience X rays demonstrating that his cancer really had left.[15] In addition, Roberts's comments about Gladys Hanson of San Francisco, who seems to have been healed from a kind of paralysis, also carry considerable credibility.[16]

In spite of the many obvious features of Roberts's life that set him apart from most other Pentecostals, he offers a strikingly suitable example of their healing theology. This is especially so of the early Roberts, the Roberts of the pre-ORU, pre–City of Faith era, with whom Pentecostals have felt the most comfortable. How closely the healing theology of the early Roberts conforms to that found in Pentecostalism generally becomes apparent as one reads him. One finds an oscillation between poles that characterizes Pentecostal teaching on healing on a wide scale.

First Pole: Certainty

As Chappell puts it, "The whole thesis of his [Oral's] ministry has been that God is a good God and that he wills to

---

[12] Stephen Pullum, "A Rhetorical Profile of Pentecostal Televangelists: Accounting for the Mass Appeal of Oral Roberts, Jimmy Swaggart, Kenneth Copeland, and Ernest Angley" (Ph.D. diss., Indiana University, 1988) 66–109.

[13] See ibid., 67.

[14] Harrell, *Oral Roberts*, 161–65.

[15] Ibid., 167.

[16] This in spite of the medical naiveté they show: "Her heart had collapsed. Her spinal cord was blocked." This is not a technical diagnosis (Oral Roberts, *Deliverance from Fear and from Sickness* [Tulsa: Oral Roberts, 1954] 61).

heal and prosper his people (3 John 2)."[17] This is an optimistic theology, and central to it is an emphasis on healing, understood as "wholeness." Harrell suggests this view of healing appeared in the late 1950s,[18] but, in fact, it can be found in Roberts's writing as early as 1952: "The healing that Jesus brings is more than spiritual, more than mental, more than physical—it is that and more; His healing is to make us 'whole.' Health in soul, mind and body. Healthy relations, healthy attitudes, healthy habits."[19] Roberts has in mind a comprehensive improvement of one's life.

In league with Pentecostalism as a whole, Roberts rooted this healing in the atonement, the act by which Jesus opened the way to reconciliation between God and humanity. This idea surfaces in Roberts's writing and preaching over and over again: "Healing is in the atonement therefore it includes all";[20] "Each one of us has a perfect right to God and just as He will forgive all our sins, He will heal our diseases";[21] "KNOW THAT GOD'S WILL IS TO HEAL YOU."[22] That expresses a very high level of certainty. And what will make it happen?

"How are you healed? . . . —by faith alone," Roberts answers. "It is faith that heals the sick."[23] As step four on the road to healing, Roberts exhorts, "Turn your faith loose—now!" and then he develops that, saying, "God wants to heal you now. The best time is when God is ready; He is ready now!"[24] It is difficult to misunderstand this. Roberts states very concretely that on the basis of the atonement, a person can experience healing at precisely the moment when it is needed.

---

[17] Chappell, "Roberts," 760.

[18] Harrell, *Oral Roberts*, 456.

[19] Oral Roberts, *If You Need Healing, Do These Things* (New York: Country Life Press, 1952) 16.

[20] Ibid., 42.

[21] Ibid., 60.

[22] Ibid., 20, 23. Emphasis his.

[23] Oral Roberts, *Oral Roberts' Best Sermons and Stories* (Tulsa: Oral Roberts, 1956) 109.

[24] Roberts, *If You Need Healing*, 39.

Roberts also insists that a "point of contact" is very important: "The point of contact is any point where your faith makes contact with God's power. Any point whether it is the spoken word, the hem of Jesus' garment, the laying on of hands, or anything else. The point of contact is important because it sets the time and is the point of expectation for your healing."[25] Rather than let your faith float, by selecting a point of contact you "set the time" when your faith will be released. This, he says, makes healing much more likely.

The idea of a point of contact is a "Roberts original," but the certainty based on the atonement is not. That is vintage Pentecostalism, and the idea has appeared throughout the movement's history. Some Pentecostals have held this position with an absolutely rigid consistency, for example, Smith Wigglesworth (1859–1947):

> There is healing through the blood of Christ and deliverance for every captive. God never intended His children to live in misery because of some affliction that comes directly from the devil. A perfect atonement was made at Calvary. I believe that Jesus bore my sins, and I am free from them all. I am justified from all things if I dare to believe. He Himself took our infirmities and bore our sicknesses; and if I dare believe, I can be healed.[26]

And Wigglesworth's son-in-law, Stanley Frodsham, quotes him as saying, "God has blessed me in so many ways. I have seen sight restored to persons born blind. I have seen three persons come to life after being dead. All these things that I have passed through only make me to know that Christ's promises concerning the greater works are true, and we must give Him all the glory for them."[27] Frodsham admits that his father-in-law was tortured with kidney stones for six years, eventually

---

[25] Roberts, *Deliverance*, 59.

[26] Smith Wigglesworth, *Ever Increasing Faith* (1924; reprint; Springfield, Mo.: Gospel Publishing House, 1971) 43.

[27] Stanley Frodsham, *Smith Wigglesworth: Apostle of Faith* (London: Elim, 1949) 49.

passing several hundred of them, and that on other occasions he suffered from sciatica, a rupture, and sunstroke.[28]

Kenneth Hagin demonstrates the level of denial Pentecostals have been prepared to entertain in order to maintain a consistent belief in the concept of healing in the atonement:

> Through natural human truth a person realizes that he is sick, that he has pain or disease. But God's Word reveals that "Himself took our infirmities, and bare our sicknesses" (Matt. 8:17), and that by His stripes we are healed (1 Pet. 2:24). Isn't God's Word just as true when you have sickness and are suffering as it is when you are well? By believing what your physical senses tell you, you would say, "I don't have healing. I am sick." But by believing the truth of God's Word you can say, "I am healed. By His stripes I have healing."[29]

The first pole in Roberts's thought on divine healing is certainty. Healing is in the atonement, and that settles it. Everyone can be healed instantly. People such as Wigglesworth and Hagin have held that position without qualification. Like most Pentecostals, however, Roberts does not. There is another pole in his thinking, as in that of Pentecostals at large: sovereignty. In his teaching on healing, Roberts does not embrace either pole. Rather, he oscillates between them. He repeatedly presses the case for certainty, but he intersperses asides on sovereignty. It is as though Roberts would much rather sound like Wigglesworth but his conscience does not permit it.

Second Pole: Sovereignty

As Roberts carried on his ministry, he made observations that he could not ignore. In the light of his clear-cut endorsement

---

[28] Ibid., 91, 94.

[29] Kenneth E. Hagin, *The Real Faith* (Tulsa: Kenneth E. Hagin Evangelistic Association, 1977) 9. One of the strongest nineteenth-century proponents of this doctrine, R. L. Stanton, died in 1885 of malaria on board ship sailing for London—while refusing treatment. See R. J. Cunningham, "From Holiness to Healing: The Faith Cure in America, 1872–1892," *Church History* 43 (1974) 506.

of certainty through the atonement, it is remarkable to find him raising the question "What to do when God says, 'No.' "[30] He knows that frequently people are not healed. The answer he gives to his question is that when God says "No," one simply has to recognize that it means that God has a better way.

He can even talk about sickness that glorifies God: "The sickness that glorifies God is the one He does not feel best to heal but that gives way to a greater miracle and to serve a larger purpose." Roberts applies the same thinking to a situation in which healing is delayed. He explains this by proposing that God occasionally makes someone wait when he is attempting to achieve something more important than the healing.[31]

Harrell suggests that there has always been more room in Roberts's thought for what defies explanation than in that of most faith healers. Roberts most certainly does not like what can be seen as ambiguity. Indeed, he is deeply troubled that many are not healed, and he deals with it by attributing it to the sovereignty of God. "He could only accept the mystery and keep trying."[32] There is the oscillation. He acknowledged the sovereignty and preached the certainty.

Toward the end of the last century, R. Kelso Carter[33] had come to a position that much more closely embraced the second pole. Dayton correctly argues that by 1897 Carter had abandoned the idea that healing was definitely and mechanically in the atonement in such a way that continuing disease was a sign of continuing sin or lack of faith.[34] Already in an earlier book Carter had to acknowledge that sometimes healing is not instantaneous.[35] In 1897 he said, "That the Atonement of Christ covers sickness and disease as well as sin, is but to say that the effects are necessarily embraced in the root cause.

---

[30] Roberts, *If You Need Healing*, 51.

[31] Ibid., 55–56.

[32] Harrell, *Oral Roberts*, 426, 456.

[33] See p. 200, n. 4 above.

[34] Dayton, *Theological Roots*, 130.

[35] Carter, *The Atonement*, 211.

There was and could be no error there. But to claim that ALL the results of that Atonement are NOW open to the present living Christian is a grave mistake."[36]

The last sentence marks Carter's departure from the rigid position he had held earlier. He also argued that all the great faith healers of his time—Dowie, A. B. Simpson, and Montgomery, who were all friends of his—in practice had arrived at the same position. Carter had come to see healing not as a right that could be demanded but as a special favor from God.[37] This was also the opinion to which the great twentieth-century healing evangelist Charles S. Price ultimately came. He argued that the faith to be healed had to be given immediately and directly by God. It cannot be worked up:

> The truth I want to emphasize is this: you cannot mix the ingredients of your own mental manufacture in a spiritual apothecaries' crucible, and produce faith. You cannot get a little more confidence and an extra pinch of trust and add a little stronger belief plus a few other things, and produce faith that moves mountains. You are nearest your possession of this imparted grace when you realize your own helplessness and your complete an´ entire dependence upon the Lord.[38]

I mention Carter and Price to indicate that while some Pentecostals, Wigglesworth and Hagin, assumed unshakable positions emphasizing the certainty of healing through the atonement, others settled upon the sovereignty of God. The more typical Pentecostal position, however, is characterized by oscillation between the two poles, such as one sees in Roberts.

For example, Canadian Pentecostal Gordon F. Atter argues that disease entered the world through the fall. He also asserts that the only adequate response to the fall was the substitutionary death of Christ on the cross. From this he concludes, "The cause of sickness clearly implies that the cure is through the atonement." But he goes on to take the position

---

[36] Carter, *"Faith Healing,"* 167.

[37] Ibid., 117, 123.

[38] Price, *The "Real" Faith*, 105.

that healing rests on God's sovereign will.[39] He recognizes this sovereign will in cases in which people are not healed. On the one hand, Atter acknowledges that Jesus always healed the sick who came to him, but, on the other, he adds, "To say that He will still always heal, provided conditions are met, is not entirely borne out in either Scripture or experience. Age, God's sovereignty, and other unknown factors affect the case."[40] Atter, too, thus oscillates, trying, on the one hand, to maintain loyalty to the idea of healing in the atonement and the ready accessibility of healing and, on the other, to deal honestly with experience and Scripture.

In an interesting paper comparing views of salvation held by Pentecostals and liberation theologians, Miroslav Volf offers an explanation of the Pentecostals' view of healing. He presents it in its complexity, commenting, "The majority of Pentecostalists claim that divine healing is provided in the atonement, yet they caution that the Bible does not teach 'that every sickness will flee in the face of faith in the same way sin is overcome in every instance where the sinner repents and believes.' "[41] This is tacit recognition of the oscillation to which I have pointed.

Finally, in her study of Pentecostal thought and experience on divine healing, involving 1,275 people from sixteen congregations of the Assemblies of God (USA) in five states, sociologist Margaret Poloma offers important observations. Among other things, she discovered that 48.9 percent of the respondents disagreed with the statement "Divine healing will always occur if faith is strong enough," while 32.6 percent agreed with it.[42] The Pentecostals she studied grouped around

---

[39] Gordon F. Atter, *The Student's Handbook on Divine Healing* (Peterborough, Ont.: G. F. Atter, 1960) 54, 92.

[40] Ibid., 72.

[41] Volf, "Materiality of Salvation," 458. His quotation is from Raymond M. Pruitt, *Fundamentals of the Faith* (Cleveland: White Wing Publishing House and Press, 1981) 316.

[42] Margaret M. Poloma, "An Empirical Study of Perceptions of Healing among Assemblies of God Members," *Pneuma* 7 (1985) 68.

the two poles I have identified, with the larger group gravitating toward an emphasis on God's sovereignty. This study of one of the largest Pentecostal denominations in North America thus provides statistical evidence in support of my suggestion that in Pentecostalism thinking and practice regarding healing tend to polarize around the concepts of certainty and sovereignty.

Conclusion

Before his recent difficulties, Oral Roberts served as a kind of model to many Pentecostals. He showed just how good it could be if one "turned loose" that spiritual entrepreneurship that Pentecostals have so long admired. A huge television audience, communications with presidents of the United States and entertainment stars such as the late ex-Beatle, John Lennon, recognition as a major figure in the charismatic renewal—that is the stuff of dreams. And it was all tied to a very Pentecostal canvas cathedral, to expectant lines of suffering people, and to hours of sitting on a chair absorbing pain.

The old maxim promising business success says, "Find a need and meet it." The need Roberts felt himself propelled toward was bottomless human suffering, and thousands upon thousands were convinced that he could meet it. His success carried him to remarkable heights.

But a theology took him to that chair in that tent before those people. It was a theology he had absorbed by listening to the preaching of his father and other older Pentecostals. He did not refine that theology by consulting theologians. Any modifications he made were results of "hands-on" experience gained through an endless succession of nights under canvas.

Typically, he was bold and confident, full of promise and certainty. But the reality of disappointing failures to heal humbled him and forced him to acknowledge God's sovereignty. When it came to healing, the early Roberts was the quintessential Pentecostal.

Conclusion

Helmut Thielicke notes:

> What we hear in the Bible again and again is that the powers of sin and
> suffering and death are *hostile* powers, enemies of God. God did *not* will
> that they should exist. They are disorderly and unnatural powers which
> broke into God's plan of creation. They are the dark henchmen of
> original sin, our *own* sin. . . . In the healing of the paralytic, Jesus again
> makes it very plain that the sickness which he healed is only the other
> side of the same derangement and disorder which sin brought into the
> world. All these things are signs of the disorder, the rift that runs
> through the midst of creation.[1]

These are passionate words from Thielicke, a German
pastor-theologian who died in 1986. The passion comes from
the evidence he saw around him. He was delivering a series of
sermons on the Lord's Prayer in Stuttgart between bombing
raids during World War II. The signs of the hostile, disorderly,
unnatural powers were everywhere. In this passage, Thielicke
casts the healing ministry of Jesus as part of the divine response
to that hostile world.

This is the light in which I have presented Jesus' ministry.[2] The Bible shows him as having come in order to bring
about a profound change in the human condition. I have argued that what I have called divine healing, the restoration of

---

[1] Helmut Thielicke, *The Prayer That Spans the World: Sermons on the
Lord's Prayer* (trans. J. W. Doberstein; Cambridge: James Clarke, 1965) 25.

[2] See pp. 3–9 above.

health through the direct intervention of God, is part of the biblical portrayal of Jesus' mission. Indeed, it is a very important component. This aspect of Jesus' incarnational life set the expectations of the community that grew out of his work. This study has been an attempt to trace the appearance of the healing impulse throughout the experience of the Christian church.

At many times, starting quite early, this impulse has been expressed through the practice of medicine. The church played an important role in the development of this discipline. But a thread running throughout the life of the church has been the belief that God may intervene in human suffering directly, often in response to prayer.

The Bible leads us to believe that some of these interventions are to improve social, cultural, and economic circumstances. This is what I have called the wide view of healing, and the Scriptures suggest that God wants to use human agents in carrying out these improvements. On the other hand, some of these interventions result in physical or emotional cures that are quite inexplicable and often more or less instantaneous. These constitute the narrow view of healing. It is this type of healing that is most common in Jesus' ministry and in the work of the agents of healing whom I have studied. I call these interventions miracles. That people continue to be very interested in them is demonstrated by a recent cover article of *Time* magazine dealing with the miraculous.[3]

The verification of claims to miracles is clearly a very important issue. During various periods in history, sloppy thinking has characterized many Christians. The faithful may be encouraged by unexamined claims, but Christians have a responsibility toward those both inside and outside the communities of faith. Attempts should be made to authenticate miracle claims, and in that exercise, the criteria outlined by Latourelle deserve consideration.[4]

---

[3] Nancy Gibbs, "The Message of Miracles," *Time*, April 10, 1995, 39–45.
[4] See p. xxxi above.

In the attempt to understand how belief in the ongoing healing ministry of Jesus has been carried into action, the concept of diversity is of great importance. People who are presented by the historical record as having had healing ministries differ from each other dramatically, and they have carried out their work in an astonishing variety of circumstances: Oral Roberts under a canvas tent and Marguerite Chapuis in a quiet garden, or St. Augustine attesting to miracles at shrines and Johann Christoph Blumhardt praying for people privately in his stately *Kurhaus*. There is nothing stereotypical about healing.

Finally, another key to approaching healing with some level of comfort is the acceptance of the idea of mystery. At times cures that are beyond the best knowledge and effort of medical practitioners seem to occur in Christian settings. The best way of accounting for them appears to be by making reference to the good pleasure of God, and who can penetrate that? To the believer, God is beyond final comprehension, and so is the healing that comes directly from God. There are no formulas to assure that a miraculous cure will take place; there are no foolproof rituals or infallible places. In the end, one must acknowledge that healing arises out of one's relationship with God. And that is enough.

Select Bibliography

General

Dawe, Victor. "The Attitude of the Ancient Church toward Sickness and Healing." Th.D. diss., Boston University, 1955.

Finucane, R. C. "The Use and Abuse of Medieval Miracles." *History* 60 (1975) 1–10.

Harnack, Adolf von. *The Mission and Expansion of Christianity in the First Three Centuries*. Edited and translated by James Moffatt. Theological Translation Library 19. 2d ed. London: Williams & Norgate, 1908.

Harrell, David E., Jr. *All Things Are Possible: The Healing & Charismatic Revivals in Modern America*. Bloomington: Indiana University Press, 1975.

Kelsey, Morton. *Psychology, Medicine, and Christian Healing*. San Francisco: Harper & Row, 1989.

Latourelle, René. *Miracles of Jesus and the Theology of Miracles*. Translated by M. J. O'Connell. New York: Paulist, 1988.

Lewis, David C. *Healing: Fiction, Fantasy, or Fact?* London: Hodder & Stoughton, 1989.

Nolen, William A. *Healing: A Doctor in Search of a Miracle*. Greenwich, Conn.: Fawcett, 1974.

Wagner, C. Peter. *How to Have a Healing Ministry without Making Your Church Sick!* Ventura, Calif.: Regal, 1988.

Introduction

Fung, Raymond. "A Monthly Letter on Evangelism, World Council of Churches, Commission on World Mission and Evangelism." March/April, 1989, 1–7.

Mangiapan, Theodore. "Le contrôle médical et la reconnaissance des guérisons de Lourdes." L'Osservatore romano 34, August 22, 1989, 5.

Richardson, Cyril. "Spiritual Healing in the Light of History." Pastoral Psychology 5 (1954) 16–20.

Chapter 1. Jesus the Healer

Baxter, J. Sidlow. Divine Healing of the Body. Grand Rapids: Zondervan, 1979.

Beyer, H. W. "θεραπεία, θεραπεύω, θεράπων." 3.128–32. In Theological Dictionary of the New Testament. Edited by G. Kittel. Translated by G. Bromiley. 10 vols. Grand Rapids: Eerdmans, 1964–76.

Borgen, Peder. "Miracles of Healing in the New Testament: Some Observations." Studia theologica 35 (1981) 91–106.

Bornkamm, Günther. Jesus of Nazareth. Translated by Irene and Fraser McLuskey with J. M. Robinson. New York: Harper & Row, 1960.

Boyd, David P. "Mini-Exegesis: Isaiah 53:4–5." Eastern Journal of Practical Theology 2 (1988) 24.

Carter, P. H. "Use of the Bible by Protestant Healing Groups." Southwestern Journal of Theology 5 (1963) 43–53.

Cranfield, C. E. B. "St. Mark 9:14–29." Scottish Journal of Theology 3 (1950) 57–67.

Dunn, James D. G. Jesus and the Spirit. London: SCM, 1975.

Flusser, David. "Healing through the Laying-on of Hands in a Dead Sea Scroll." Israel Exploration Journal 7 (2, 1957) 107–8.

Oepke, Albrecht. "ἰάομαι, ἴασις, ἴαμα, ἰατρός." 3.194–215. In Theological Dictionary of the New Testament. Edited by G. Kittel. Translated by G. Bromiley. 10 vols. Grand Rapids: Eerdmans, 1964–76.

Ikin, A. G. "New Testament and Healing." *Pastoral Psychology* 7 (1956) 33–44.

Shogren, Gary S. "Will God Heal Us?—A Re-examination of James 5:1–16a." *Evangelical Quarterly* 61 (1989) 99–108.

Wilkinson, J. "Study of Healing in the Gospel According to John." *Scottish Journal of Theology* 20 (1967) 442–61.

Chapter 2. The Early Years: A Church Triumphant

Cyprian. *That Idols Are Not Gods.* Translated by R. J. Deferrari. Fathers of the Church 36. New York: Catholic University of America Press, 1958.

_____. *Letters (1–81).* Translated by Rose B. Donna. Fathers of the Church 51. New York: Catholic University of America Press, 1964.

_____. *Mortality.* Translated by R. J. Deferrari. Fathers of the Church 36. New York: Catholic University of America Press, 1958.

Eusebius. *Ecclesiastical History.* Translated by Kirsopp Lake and J. E. L. Oulton. Loeb Classical Library. London: Heinemann, 1965.

Hippolytus. *The Treatise on the Apostolic Tradition of St. Hippolytus of Rome.* Translated by Gregory Dix. London: S.P.C.K., 1937.

Irenaeus. *Against Heresies.* Translated by A. Roberts and J. Donaldson. In vol. 1 of *The Ante-Nicene Fathers.* Peabody: Hendrickson, 1994.

Justin Martyr. *Dialogue with Trypho. The Writings of Saint Justin Martyr.* Translated by T. B. Falls. Fathers of the Church 6. New York: Catholic University of America Press, 1948.

Lactantius. *The Divine Institutes, Books I–VII.* Translated by Mary Francis McDonald. Fathers of the Church 49. New York: Catholic University of America Press, 1964.

Minucius Felix. *Octavius.* Translated by G. H. Rendall. Loeb Classical Library. London: Heinemann, 1960.

Novatian. *The Treatise of Novatian on the Trinity.* Translated by H. Moore. London: S.P.C.K., 1919.

Origen. *Contra Celsum.* Translated by Henry Chadwick. Cambridge: Cambridge University Press, 1953.

Tertullian. *Apology*. Translated by T. R. Glover. Loeb Classical Library. London: Heinemann, 1960.

_____. *Prayer*. Translated by Emily J. Daly. Fathers of the Church 4. New York: Catholic University of America Press, 1959.

_____. *To Scapula*. Translated by Rudolph Arbesmann. Fathers of the Church 10. New York: Catholic University of America Press, 1950.

_____. *De spectaculis* [*The Shows*]. Translated by T. R. Glover. Loeb Classical Library. London: Heinemann, 1960.

Chapter 3. J. C. Blumhardt: "Jesus Is Victor!"

Blumhardt, Johann Christoph (1805–1880). A27, 267. Related material in Archiv, Überkirchenrat, Württemburgischen Landeskirche. Stuttgart.

_____. *Besprechung wichtiger Glaubensfragen aus der Seelsorge hervorgegangen*. Edited by Christoph Blumhardt. Karlsruhe: Evangelischer Schriftenverein für Baden, 1888.

_____. *Blätter aus Bad Boll*. Vols. 1 and 4. Göttingen: Vandenhoeck & Ruprecht, 1968 and 1970.

Blumhardt, Johann Christoph, with Paul Ernst. *Der Kampf in Möttlingen*. Vol. 1, *Texte*. Edited by Gerhard Schäfer. Vol. 2, *Anmerkungen*. Edited by Dieter Ising and Gerhard Schäfer. Göttingen: Vandenhoeck & Ruprecht, 1979.

_____. "Krankheitsgeschichte der G[ottlieben] D[ittus] in Möttlingen." In Vol. 1, *Texte*, of *Der Kampf in Möttlingen*. Edited by Gerhard Schäfer. Göttingen: Vandenhoeck & Ruprecht, 1979.

Blumhofer, E. L. "Jesus Is Victor: A Study in the Life of Johann Christoph Blumhardt." *Paraclete* 19 (2, 1985) 1–5.

Eller, Vernard. *Thy Kingdom Come: A Blumhardt Reader*. Grand Rapids: Eerdmans, 1980.

Guest, W., ed. *Pastor Blumhardt and His Work*. With introduction by Rev. C. H. Blumhardt [Johann Christoph Blumhardt's brother]. London: Morgan and Scott [1881].

Ising, Dieter, ed. *Johann Christoph Blumhardt: Ein Brevier*. Göttingen: Vandenhoeck & Ruprecht, 1991.

Lejeune, Robert. *Christoph Blumhardt and His Message.* Translated by Hela Ehrlich and Nicolin Maas. Riften, N.Y.: Plough, 1963.

Macchia, Frank D. *Spirituality and Social Liberation: The Message of the Blumhardts in the Light of Wuerttemberg Pietism.* Pietist and Wesleyan Studies 4. Edited by David Bundy and J. Steven O'Malley. Metuchen, N.J.: Scarecrow Press, 1993.

The New International Dictionary of the Christian Church. Edited by J. D. Douglas, E. E. Cairns, and J. E. Ruark. Grand Rapids: Zondervan, 1974.

Nigg, Walter. "Johann Christoph Blumhardt: Ein Heiliger der Neuzeit." In *Wie heilig ist der Mensch?* Edited by Wolfgang Böhme. Herrenalber Texte 69. Baden: Evangelische Akademie, 1986.

Rüsch, E. G. "Bemerkungen zum theologischen Studiengang J. C. Blumhardts." *Theologische Zeitschrift* 13 (1957) 102–8.

_____. "Dämonenaustreibung in der Gallus-Vita und bei Blumhardt dem Älteren." *Theologische Zeitschrift* 34 (1978) 86–94.

Sauter, Gerhard. "Zur Blumhardt-Forschung." *Evangelische Theologie* 43 (1983) 380–82.

_____. *Die Theologie des Reich Gottes beim älteren und jüngeren Blumhardt.* Studien zur Dogmengeschichte und systematischen Theologie 14. Zurich-Stuttgart: Zwingli Verlag, 1962.

_____. "Johann Christoph Blumhardt: Bausteine zu einer Biographie." *Johann Christoph Blumhardt: Leuchtende Liebe zu den Menschen: Beiträge zu Leben und Werk.* Stuttgart: J. F. Steinkopf, 1981.

Scherding, Pierre. *Christoph Blumhardt et son père: Essai sur un mouvement de réalisme chrétien.* Etudes d'histoire et de philosophie religieuses 34. Paris: F. Alcan, 1937.

Schulz, M. T. *Johann Christoph Blumhardt: Leben—Theologie—Verkündigung.* Arbeiten zur Pastoraltheologie 19. Edited by Martin Fischer and Robert Frick. Göttingen: Vandenhoeck & Ruprecht, 1984.

Theologische Realenzyklopädie. Edited by Gerhard Krause and Gerhard Müller. Berlin: Walter de Gruyter, 1980.

Zündel, Friedrich. *Pfarrer Johann Christoph Blumhardt: Ein Lebensbild.* 5th. ed. Zurich: S. Höhr, 1887.

Chapter 4. John Wimber: The Keeper of the Vineyard

Armstrong, John H. "In Search of Spiritual Power." Pages 61–88. In *Power Religion: The Selling Out of the Evangelical Church*. Edited by Michael S. Horton. Chicago: Moody, 1992.

Benn, Wallace, and Mark Burkill. "A Theological and Pastoral Critique of the Teachings of John Wimber." *Churchman: Journal of Anglican Theology* 101 (2, 1987) 101–13.

Beverley, James A. "John Wimber, the Vineyard, and the Prophets: Listening for a Word from God." *The Canadian Baptist*, March/April, 1992, 32–38.

Boice, James M. "A Better Way: The Power of the Word and Spirit." Pages 119–36. In *Power Religion: The Selling Out of the Evangelical Church*. Edited by Michael S. Horton. Chicago: Moody, 1992.

Carson, D. A. "The Purpose of Signs and Wonders in the New Testament." Pages 89–118. In *Power Religion: The Selling Out of the Evangelical Church*. Edited by Michael S. Horton. Chicago: Moody, 1992.

Deere, Jack. *The Vineyard's Response to "The Briefing."* Vineyard Position Paper 2. Anaheim: Association of Vineyard Churches, 1992.

Friesen, Abraham. "Wimber, Word and Spirit." Pages 35–42. In *Wonders and the Word: An Examination of the Issues Raised by John Wimber and the Vineyard Movement*. Edited by J. R. Coggins and P. G. Hiebert. Winnipeg, Man.: Kindred Press, 1989.

Grudem, Wayne. *The Vineyard's Response to "The Standard."* Vineyard Position Paper 3. Anaheim: Association of Vineyard Churches, 1992.

Lewis, Donald M. "An Historian's Assessment." Pages 53–62. In *Wonders and the Word: An Examination of the Issues Raised by John Wimber and the Vineyard Movement*. Edited by J. R. Coggins and P. G. Hiebert. Winnipeg, Man.: Kindred Press, 1989.

Maudlin, Michael G. "Seers in the Heartland: Hot on the Trail of the Kansas City Prophets." *Christianity Today*, January 14, 1991, 18–22.

Parrott, Les, III, and R. D. Perrin. "The New Denominations." *Christianity Today*, March 11, 1991, 29–32.

Sarles, Ken L. "An Appraisal of the Signs and Wonders Movement." *Bibliotheca Sacra* 145 (1988) 57–82.

Springer, Kevin. "KCF Renamed the Metro Vineyard." *Equipping the Saints* 4 (4, 1990) 14.

_____. *Power Encounters among Christians in the Western World*. San Francisco: Harper & Row, 1988.

Stafford, Tim. "The Fruit of the Vineyard." *Christianity Today*, November 17, 1989, 35–36.

_____. "Testing the Wine from John Wimber's Vineyard." *Christianity Today*, August 8, 1986, 17–22.

Vooys, John. "Church Renewal for the 1980s?" Pages 65–68. In *Wonders and the Word: An Examination of the Issues Raised by John Wimber and the Vineyard Movement*. Edited by J. R. Coggins and P. G. Hiebert. Winnipeg, Man.: Kindred Press, 1989.

Wacker, Grant. "Wimber and Wonders—What about Miracles Today?" *The Reformed Journal* 37 (1987) 16–19.

White, John. *When the Spirit Comes with Power: Signs & Wonders among God's People*. Downers Grove: IVP, 1988.

Williams, Don. *Signs, Wonders, and the Kingdom of God*. Ann Arbor: Vine Books, 1989.

Wimber, John. "A Response to Pastor Ernie Gruen's Controversy with Kansas City Fellowship." *Equipping the Saints* 4 (4, 1990) 4–7, 14.

_____. "Were We Healed at the Cross?" *Charisma*, May, 1991, 75–82.

_____. *Why I Respond to Criticism*. Vineyard Position Paper 1. Anaheim: Association of Vineyard Churches, 1992.

_____. *Power Healing*. San Francisco: Harper & Row, 1987.

_____. *Power Points*. San Francisco: Harper, 1991.

_____. *Study Guide to Power Healing*. San Francisco: Harper & Row, 1987.

Wimber, John, and Kevin Springer. *Power Evangelism*. San Francisco: Harper & Row, 1986.

Zuck, Roy. Review of *Power Healing*, by John Wimber and Kevin Springer. *Bibliotheca sacra* 145 (1988) 102–4.

Chapter 5. Saints on High: Help from Beyond

Ambrose. *Letters*. Translated by M. M. Beyenka. Fathers of the Church 26. New York: Catholic University of America Press, 1954.

Augustine. *City of God, Books VIII–XVI*. Translated by G. G. Walsh and Grace Monahan. Fathers of the Church 14. New York: Catholic University of America Press, 1952.

_____. *City of God, Books XVII–XXII*. Translated by G. G. Walsh and D. J. Honan. Fathers of the Church 24. New York: Catholic University of America Press, 1954.

_____. *Confessions*. Translated by J. G. Pilkington. In vol. 1 of *The Nicene and Post-Nicene Fathers, First Series*. Peabody: Hendrickson, 1994.

_____. *Answers to Letters of Petilian, Bishop of Cirta*. Edited by M. Petschenig. Corpus scriptorum ecclesiasticorum latinorum 52. Vienna: F. Tempsky, 1909.

_____. *Letters*. Vol. 1. Translated by Sister Wilfrid Parsons. Fathers of the Church 12. New York: Catholic University of America Press, 1951.

_____. *Sermons on New Testament Lessons*. Translated by R. G. MacMullen. In vol. 6 of *The Nicene and Post-Nicene Fathers, First Series*. Peabody: Hendrickson, 1994.

Basil. *Letters*. Vol. 1. Translated by A. C. Way. Fathers of the Church 13. New York: Catholic University of America Press, 1951.

Elliott, J. K. "The Apocryphal Acts." *Expository Times* 105 (1993) 71–77.

_____. *The Apocryphal New Testament: A Collection of Apocryphal Christian Literature in an English Translation*. Oxford, Clarendon Press, 1993.

Foster, John. "Healing in the Early Church." *London Quarterly and Holborn Review* 182 (1957) 217–22, 299–304.

Gregory the Great. *Epistles*. Translated by James Barmby. In vol. 12 of *The Nicene and Post-Nicene Fathers, Second Series*. Peabody: Hendrickson, 1956.

Gregory Nazianzus. *On His Sister, St. Gorgonia.* Translated by Leo P. McCauley. Fathers of the Church 22. New York: Catholic University of America Press, 1953.

———. *Oration 43.* Translated by C. G. Browne and J. E. Swallow. In vol. 7 of *The Nicene and Post-Nicene Fathers, Second Series.* Peabody: Hendrickson, 1994.

Hennecke, E., and W. Schneemelcher. *New Testament Apocrypha.* Revised edition. Translated by R. McL. Wilson. 2 vols. Philadelphia: Westminster Press, 1991–92.

John Cassian. *Second Conference of Abbott Nesteros.* Translated by E. C. S. Gibson. In vol. 11 of *The Nicene and Post-Nicene Fathers, Second Series.* Peabody: Hendrickson, 1994.

John of Damascus. *An Exact Exposition of the Orthodox Faith.* Translated by F. H. Chase, Jr. Fathers of the Church 37. New York: Catholic University of America Press, 1958.

James, Montague R. *The Apocryphal New Testament.* Oxford: Clarendon Press, 1924.

Keenan, Mary E. "St. Gregory of Nazianzus and Early Byzantine Medicine." *Bulletin of the History of Medicine* 9 (1941) 8–30.

Metzger, B. M. *An Introduction to the Apocrypha.* New York: Oxford University Press, 1957.

Rordorf, Willy. "*Terra incognita*: Recent Research on the Christian Apocryphal Literature, Especially on Some Acts of Apostles." Pages 142–58. In *Studia patristica* 25. Edited by E. A. Livingstone. Louvain: Peeters, 1993.

Rousselle, Aline. "From Sanctuary to Miracle-Worker: Healing in Fourth-Century Gaul." In *Ritual, Religion, and the Sacred: Selections from "Annales: Economies, sociétés, civilisations," Volume 7.* Edited by Robert Forster and Orest Ranum. Translated by Elborg Forester and P. M. Ranum. Baltimore and London: Johns Hopkins University Press, 1982.

Sulpicius Severus. *First Dialogue; Second Dialogue; Third Dialogue; Life of Saint Martin, Bishop and Confessor.* Translated by B. M. Peebles. Fathers of the Church 7. New York: Catholic University of America Press, 1949.

Wilson, R. McL. "New Testament Apocrypha." Pages 429–55. In *The New Testament and Its Modern Interpreters*. Edited by E. J. Epp and G. W. MacRae. Philadelphia: Fortress, 1989.

Chapter 6. Brother André: Miracles on the Mountain

Bergeron, Henri-Paul, C.S.C. *Brother André, C.S.C.: The Wonder Man of Mount Royal*. Translated by Réal Boudreau, C.S.C. Montreal: Saint Joseph's Oratory, 1988.

Bernard, Henri. "Le problématique de l'Oratoire Saint-Joseph." *Les Pèlerinages au Québec*. Quebec: Les Presses de l'Université Laval, 1981.

Brault, Marie-Marthe. "L'Oratoire Saint-Joseph-du-Mont-Royal: Etude d'un sanctuaire de pèlerinage catholique." M.A. thesis, Université de Montréal, 1969.

Catta, Etienne. *Le frère André (1845–1937) et l'Oratoire Saint-Joseph du Mont-Royal*. Montreal and Paris: Fides, 1965.

Garigue, Philip. "Saint Joseph Oratory: A New Look at Its Meaning." *La nouvelle revue canadienne*, March/April, 1956, 241–54.

Gauthier, Roland. *L'Oratoire Saint-Joseph du Mont-Royal: A l'occasion de 75e anniversaire de sa fondation*. Montreal: Oratoire Saint-Joseph, 1979.

Hanley, Boniface, O.F.M. *Brother André: All He Could Do Was Pray*. Montreal: St. Anthony's Guild, 1979. Reprint. Montreal: St. Joseph's Oratory, 1981.

Lafrenière, Bernard, C.S.C. *Brother André: According to Witnesses*. Montreal: St. Joseph's Oratory, 1990.

Sinclair-Faulkner, Tom. "Sacramental Suffering: Brother André's Spirituality." *Canadian Catholic Historical Association: Study Sessions* 49 (1982) 111–34.

Chapter 7. Mary of Medjugorje: Apparitions and Healing

Bartulica, Nicholas. *Medjugorje: Are the Seers Telling the Truth? A Psychiatrist's Viewpoint*. Chicago: By the author, 1991.

Bax, Mart. "The Madonna of Medjugorje: Religious Rivalry and the Formation of a Devotional Movement in Yugoslavia." *Anthropological Quarterly* 63 (1990) 63–75.

Bedard, Bob. *Prophecy for Our Time?* Ottawa: n.p., 1984.

Janz, Denis R. "Medjugorje's Miracles: Faith and Profit." *Christian Century* 104 (1987) 724–25.

Kraljevic, Svetozar. *The Apparitions of Our Lady at Medjugorje 1981–1983: An Historical Account with Interviews.* Edited by Michael Scanlan. Chicago: Franciscan Herald Press, 1984.

Laurentin, René. *La prolongation des apparitions de Medjugorje: Délai de miséricorde pour un monde en danger?* Paris. O.E.I.L., 1986.

Laurentin, René, and Ljudevit Rupcic. *Is the Virgin Mary Appearing at Medjugorje?* Translated by Francis Martin. Washington: The Word among Us Press, 1984.

Laurentin, René, and Henri Joyeux. *Scientific and Medical Studies on the Apparitions at Medjugorje.* Translated by Luke Griffin. Dublin: Veritas, 1987.

Miravalle, Mark I. *The Message of Medjugorje: The Marian Message to the Modern World.* Lanham, Md.: University Press of America, 1986.

Weible, Wayne. *Medjugorje: The Message.* Orleans, Mass.: Paraclete Press, 1989.

Chapter 8. Relics and Healing: Bones of Blessing

Ambrose. *Letters.* Translated by M. M. Beyenka. Fathers of the Church 26. New York: Catholic University of America Press, 1954.

Boussel, Patrice. *Des reliques et de leur bon usage.* Paris: Balland, 1971.

Brown, Peter. *The Cult of the Saints: Its Rise and Function in Latin Christianity.* Haskell Lectures on History of Religions 2. New Series. Chicago: University of Chicago Press, 1981.

Cruz, Joan C. *Relics: The Shroud of Turin, the True Cross.* Huntington, Ind.: Our Sunday Visitor, 1984.

Finucane, Ronald C. *Miracles and Pilgrims: Popular Belief in Medieval England.* Totowa, N.J.: Rowman & Littlefield, 1977.

Geary, Patrick J. *Furta sacra: Thefts of Relics in the Central Middle Ages.* Princeton: Princeton University Press, 1978.

Komonchak, J., M. Collins, D. A. Lane, editors. *The New Dictionary of Theology.* Wilmington, Del.: Michael Glazier, 1987.

Rousselle, Aline. *Croire et guérir: La foi en Gaule dans l'antiquité tardive.* Paris: Fayard, 1990.

Sacramentum mundi: An Encyclopedia of Theology. Montreal: Herder & Herder, 1970.

Dictionnaire de théologie catholique. Paris: Letouzey & Ané, 1939.

Ward, Benedicta. "Miracles and Miracle Collections, 1015–215." D.Phil. thesis, Oxford University, 1978.

Chapter 9. The Miracles at St. Médard: The Convulsionaries

Adhemar d'Alès, Alphonse. "La théologie du diacre Pâris." *Recherches de science religieuse* 10 (1920) 373–87.

Cognet, Louis. "Jansenism in Eighteenth-Century France." *The Church in the Age of Absolutism and Enlightenment.* Translated by G. J. Holst. History of the Church 36. Edited by Hubert Jedin and John Dolan. New York: Crossroad, 1981.

Knox, Ronald. *Enthusiasm: A Chapter in the History of Religion.* Oxford: Clarendon, 1950.

Kreiser, B. Robert. *Miracles, Convulsions, and Ecclesiastical Politics in Early Eighteenth-Century Paris.* Princeton: Princeton University Press, 1978.

Pâris, François de. Related material in Bibliothèque nationale, Fr. 22, 245. Paris, France.

Requeste présentée au Parlement par vingt-trois curés de la ville, fauxbourgs & banlieue de Paris, contre l'instruction pastorale de M. Languet, archevêque de Sens, imprimée en 1734, au sujet des miracles opérés par l'intercession de M. de Paris. Paris: n.p., 1735.

Vidal, Janiel. *Miracles et convulsions jansénistes au XVIIIe siècle: Le mal et sa connaissance.* Sociologie d'aujourd'hui. Paris: Presses universitaires de France, 1987.

Chapter 10. Männedorf: Place of Mercy

Aus dem Protokoll des Regierungsrates, 1901. 656 Privatkrankenanstalten. Kantonal Archiv, Zurich.

Erster Bericht über das Krankenasyl Männedorf an die Gemeindseinwohner. July, 1882. Kantonal Archiv, Zurich.

Bibel- und Erholungsheim Männedorf: Entstehung—Weg—Auftrag. Männedorf: Bibel und Erholungsheim, [1979].

Hausordnung für die Patienten des Krankenasyls Männedorf. Kantonal Archiv, Zurich.

Provisorische Statuten für das Krankenasyl Männedorf. July 5, 1883. Kantonal Archiv, Zurich.

Zeller, Alfred. *Samuel Zeller: Züge aus Seinem Leben.* TELOS. Lahr-Dinglingen: St.-Johannis C. Schweickhardt, 1979.

———. *Was er dir Gutes getan: 28. November 1860–28. November 1910; Rückblicke beim 50jahrigen Arbeitsjubiläum unseres lieben Hausvaters Samuel Zeller in Männedorf.* Männedorf: self-published [1910].

———. *Zweierlei Wunder.* Basel: Heinrich Maier, 1944.

Zeller, Konrad. *Dorothea Trudel von Männedorf: Ihr Leben und Wirken.* TELOS. Lahr-Dinglingen: St.-Johannis C. Schweickhardt, 1971.

Zeller, Samuel. "Liebe Gottes in Vergangenheit, Gegenwart und Zukunft." In *Gerne will ich Sie lieben.* 2d. ed. Männedorf: n.p. [1904].

———. "To the Board of Governors of Medical Affairs of the Canton of Zurich" [May 28, 1869]. In *Besick Meilen, 1857–1889.* Translated by Jerry Hoorman. Kantonal Archiv, Zurich.

Chapter 11. The Message of Morija: Persevering Prayer

Chapius, Marguerite. *Lettre hebdomadaire et convocation.* April 27, 1966. Archives, Morija, Yverdon-Les-Bains, Switzerland.

Constitution de fondation, Morija. Feb. 17, 1982. Archives, Morija, Yverdon-Les-Bains, Switzerland.

De Siebenthal, Charles. *25 ans de marche avec Dieu (1936–1961).* Yverdon: Fraternité chrétienne, 1962.

_____. *Lettre hebdomadaire et convocation.* November 24, 1938.

_____. *"Morija": La maison de repos de la "Fraternité chrétienne" pour convalescents, déprimés et tourmentés.* Yverdon: n.p. [1948].

Fondation Morija avec siège à Yverdon: Règlement organique. Jan. 13, 1987. Archives, Morija, Yverdon-Les-Bains, Switzerland.

Miracles au XXe siècle! Yverdon: Fraternité Chrétienne, n.d.

Mutzenberg, G. "La Fraternité chrétienne ou les chemins de la foi." In *Certitudes,* 1975. Reprint. Yverdon: Fraternité chrétienne, n.d.

Statuts: Eglise Evangélique de la Fraternité chrétienne. April 19, 1980. Archives, Morija, Yverdon-Les-Bains, Switzerland.

Chapter 12. William Branham: Prophet of This Age?

Branham, William. "Christ's Second Coming." *The Spoken Word,* April 17, 1957.

_____. "Discerning the Body of the Lord." *The Spoken Word,* August 12, 1959.

_____. *An Exposition of the Seven Church Ages.* William Marrion Branham: n.p., n.d.

_____. "Visions and Prophecy." *The Spoken Word,* April 8, 1956.

_____. "Works Is Faith Expressed." In *The Voice of the Prophet: Messages by William Marrion Branham.* Tucson: Tucson Tabernacle Books, n.d.

Dyck, Carl. *William Branham: The Man and His Message.* Saskatoon, Sask.: Western Tract Mission, 1984.

Extensive Concordance: A Keyword Subject Arrangement of Sermons Delivered by Rev. William Marrion Branham. Tucson: Tucson Tabernacle, 1973.

Hollenweger, W. J. *The Pentecostals.* Translated by R. A. Wilson. 1972. Reprint. Peabody: Hendrickson, 1988.

Lindsay, Gordon. *William Branham: A Man Sent from God.* 4th. ed. Jeffersonville, Indiana: William Branham, 1950.

Moreau, A. Scott. "Branhamites." *East Africa Journal of Evangelical Theology.* 7 (2, 1988) 1–18.

Stadsklev, Julius. *William Branham: A Prophet Visits South Africa.* Minneapolis: By the author, 1952.

Weaver, C. Douglas. *The Healer-Prophet, William Marrion Branham: A Study of the Prophetic in American Pentecostalism.* Macon, Ga.: Mercer University Press, 1987.

Chapter 13. Kathryn Kuhlman: A Handmaiden of the Lord

Buckingham, Jamie. *Daughter of Destiny: Kathryn Kuhlman—Her Story.* Plainfield, N.J.: Logos, 1976.

"Kathryn Kuhlman: Dying to Self." *Christianity Today*, March 12, 1976, 47–48.

Kuhlman, Kathryn, ed. *God Can Do It Again.* 1969. Reprint, Spire, n.p., 1974.

_____. *I Believe in Miracles.* Englewood Cliffs, N.J.: Prentice-Hall, 1962.

McCauley, Deborah Vansau. "Kathryn Kuhlman." Pages 225–33. In *Twentieth Century Shapers of American Popular Religion.* Edited by Charles H. Lippy. New York: Greenwood Press, 1989.

Warner, Wayne. *Kathryn Kuhlman: The Woman behind the Miracles.* Ann Arbor: Servant, 1993.

Chapter 14. Oral Roberts: Quintessential Pentecostal

Chappell, Paul G. "The Divine Healing Movement in America." Ph.D. diss. Drew University, 1983.

Cunningham, R. J. "From Holiness to Healing: The Faith Cure in America 1872–1892." *Church History* 43 (1974) 499–513.

Dayton, Donald W. *Theological Roots of Pentecostalism.* Reprint. Peabody: Hendrickson, 1987.

Harrell, David Edwin, Jr. *Oral Roberts: An American Life.* San Francisco: Harper & Row, 1985.

Poloma, Margaret M. "An Empirical Study of Perceptions of Healing among Assemblies of God Members." *Pneuma* 7 (1, 1985) 61–78.

Roberts, Oral. *Oral Roberts' Best Sermons and Stories.* Tulsa: Oral Roberts, 1956.

_____. *Deliverance from Fear and from Sickness*. Tulsa: Oral Roberts, 1954.

_____. *If You Need Healing Do These Things*. 2d. ed. New York: Country Life Press, 1952.

Wacker, Grant. "The Pentecostal Tradition." Pages 514–38. In *Caring and Curing: Health and Medicine in the Western Religious Traditions*. Edited by R. L. Numbers and D. W. Amundsen. New York: Macmillan, 1986.

Subject Index

apocryphal literature, 64; historical value of, 66; miracles and sexual purity in, 68; position of apostles in, 68, 70

Asclepius, Greek god of healing, 3; temple at Epidaurus, 3; demanded belief, 16

Atter, Gordon F., Canadian Pentecostal, 209–10. *See also* healing in the atonement

Blumhardt, Christoph, succeeded his father, 36

Blumhardt, Johann Christoph: ministerial career and education, 34–35; mentor to Karl Barth, 34; incubational aspect of ministry, 44. *See also* models of healing, incubational

Branham, William Marrion: populist, xxii, 168–69; complex personality, 170–71; beginning of healing ministry, 171–72; fabulous stories, 172; controversy over claims to healing, 172–73; radical theological positions, 173–74; claimed to be the prophet for the generation, 170, 174; the "three pulls," 176–78

Brother André: life, xxiii, 82–85; process towards canonization, 83 n.1, 84; devotional life, 86–87; revelation in his ministry, 97–98.

See also models of healing, revelational

Chapuis, Marguerite (cofounder of Morija), 157–58

circle of prayer (ministry of Morija), 161–62

convulsionaries, 136. *See also* Pâris, François de; Saint Médard

demonic, 5, 22–27; John Wimber's teaching, 52–54. *See also* exorcism

divine healing: definition, xv; scope of study, xvii, xix–xx; and medicine, xv n.1, 146–47, 187–88

Elim Institution: diagnosis and treatment of mental illness, 144; biblical foundation, 144–45; conflict with Canton of Zurich, 148–51

eschatology, J. C. Blumhardt's belief in, 37–38

European approach to healing, compared to North American, xxi–xxii, 53 n.35, 200 n.4

evidence of healing: girl in Britain, xxv; early church, 20–22, 28–29, 66–70, 124–25, 126–27; at Medjugorje, 108–11; associated with relics, 125–27; at St. Médard, 133; attributed to

François de Pâris, 138–39; David
Hume regarding St. Médard,
139; at the Elim Institution, 143,
147–48; testimonies at Morija,
162–63; examples from Kathryn
Kuhlman, 189; cases from Oral
Roberts's ministry, 204
exorcism: early church, 23–26;
through sign of the cross, 26
n.16; of Gottliebin Dittus,
40–41; at Morija, 164

faith: related to Jesus's healing
ministry, 12–16; emphasized by
Kathryn Kuhlman, 191, 195–96;
importance to Oral Roberts, 205

healing in the atonement, 7–8; in
John Wimber's teaching, 52;
Kathryn Kuhlman's early
teaching, 190; nineteenth
century American healing
movement, 199–200; central to
Oral Roberts, 205–7

illness: categories, xxvi n.18; causes,
5–6

Jesus, healing ministry of, xvi–xvii,
1–12
John of Damascus, teaching of,
regarding saints, 75–76

Kuhlman, Kathryn: life, 181–84;
early healing theology, 190;
emphasis on the Holy Spirit,
190, 194; indebtedness of later
theology to A. B Simpson and
Charles S. Price, 193–96

Latourelle, René (theologian dealing with the miraculous),
xxviii–xxix, xxxi, 1–2, 10–11.
See also verification of claims of
healing
laying on of hands: among the
Essenes, 3 n.6; at the Elim

Institution; en masse by Oral
Roberts, 203
Leo the Great (Pope), 69

Medjugorje: the apparitions, 101–5;
analysis of Virgin Mary's
message, 103; visionary, Vicka
Ivankovic, 107; Fr. Philip Pavic,
107; prayer for the sick, 111–12;
position of Christ, 113
miracles as proof of doctrinal
correctness: denied, xxiii–xxiv,
79; contrary position of
Jansenists, 134. See also Pascal,
Blaise
models of healing, xx–xxi; confrontational, 19; intercessory, 61;
reliquarial, 115; incubational,
141 (see also Blumhardt, Johann
Christoph); revelational, 167
(see also Brother André); soteriological, 199
Morija: atmosphere, 154; prominent
role of women, 158–59
mysterious nature of healing, xxiii,
80, 215

Noailles, Cardinal Louis Antoine de
(Archbishop of Paris), 132–33
Nolen, William (physician who
investigated Kathryn Kuhlman),
186–87
not healed, people who were: in
John Wimber's meetings, 58;
received Brother André's
counsel, 98; advised by Charles
de Siebenthal, 164–65; from
Kathryn Kuhlman's services, 187;
considered in Kathryn Kuhlman's
teaching, 192

"official" positions on health and
healing in the early church,
76–78

Pâris, François de, 130–32, 139. See
also Saint Médard

Pascal, Blaise, opinion of, on Jansenist miracles, 134 n.13

Peterman, Marylyn (woman healed of viral encephalitis), xxiv–xxv

Pettigrew, Mary (woman healed of multiple sclerosis), 189

physical material associated with healing, 88, 113–14, 138–39. *See also* Pâris, François de

relics: definition, 115; their use and popularity, 118–23; abuses, 123; decline in interest, 124

resurrections: in Jesus's ministry, 11; evidence from early church, 29–30; discussion, 30; possible claim at Morija, 164

Roberts, Oral, 202–3. *See also* faith; healing in the atonement

Saint Joseph (patron saint of Roman Catholic Church and of Canada), 85

Saint Joseph's Oratory, role and significance of, in Quebec society, 90, 92–93

Saint Médard (site of cemetery in Paris in which François de Pâris was buried), 130; onset of convulsions, 134–35; closure of the cemetery, 135. *See also* convulsionaries; Pâris, François de

Siebenthal, Blanche de (cofounder of Morija), 156–58

Siebenthal, Charles de: early career, xxiii, 155–56; voice of Morija, 157

Thomassin, Achilles (investigator at St. Médard), 137

Trudel, Dorothea (founder of the Elim Institution), xxii, 142–45, 148–49, 152–53

verification of claims of healing: estimated percentages of healings, xxii, 58; Lambertini's criteria, xxvi; medical science as a means of validating the miraculous, xxvi–xxxi; the importance of verification, xxix; patient reports, xxx, xxx n.29; Latourelle's criteria, xxxi, 136; in J. C. Blumhardt's ministry; at St. Joseph's Oratory, 95; at Medjugorje, 109–11; at St. Médard, 139; related to the Elim Institution, 147–48; authenticity in William Branham's ministry, 179–80; associated with Kathryn Kuhlman, 187–88

Vineyard Christian Fellowship, 46–47

Wigglesworth, Smith, teaching of, on healing, 206

Wimber, John: concept of healing, 51–52; possible influence from Christian Growth Ministries, 52; democratization of healing, 55; study of the results of a conference, 57–58

xenodochia, opened by Basil, 77

Zeller, Samuel (successor to Dorothea Trudel), 143, 149–51

Scripture Index

Gen
1–3 7

Exod
3:14 12

Isaiah
53:4–5 176

Matt
4:1–11   6
4:23–24   10
8:1–4   15
8:5–13   1, 15
8:14   14
8:16–17   7
9:27–31   14
9:20–22   117
9:35–36   11
10:1   17
10:8   145
11:4   11
12:1–5   1
12:28   38, 39

Mark
1:23–26   5, 9
1:29–31   1
1:39   11
2:1–12   6, 13

3:11–12   9
5:21–24   12
5:24–34   15
5:35–43   12
9:14–29   13, 16, 41
10:51–52   13
16:18   145, 176

Luke
6:17–19   9
7:11–17   11
8:2   9
10:9   17
10:20   79
11:14–20   7
13:10–13   5
17:11–19   13
18:35–43   190

John
5:1–9   13
6:35   12
9:1–12   4, 6, 190
11:1–44   4
12:31   7, 12
14:6   12
14:12   17, 75
14:30   7, 12
18:5   12

Acts
3:1–11   17
8:14–24   67
16:16–18   17
19:11f.   117

Rom
8:18–22   7
15:19   17

1 Cor
12:8–9   17

2 Cor
12:12   17

Heb
2:4   17
11:4   11
13:8   176

James
5:13–16   17, 145,
     161, 163

1 John
3:8   12

3 John
2   205